Henry Ford

LIVES AND LEGACIES

———

Larzer Ziff
MARK TWAIN

David S. Reynolds
WALT WHITMAN

Edwin S. Gaustad
ROGER WILLIAMS
BENJAMIN FRANKLIN

Gale E. Christianson
ISAAC NEWTON

Paul Addison
CHURCHILL: THE UNEXPECTED HERO

G. Edward White
OLIVER WENDELL HOLMES JR.

Craig Raine
T. S. ELIOT

Carolyn Porter
WILLIAM FAULKNER

Donald E. Pease
THEODORE SEUSS GIESEL

Vincent Curcio
HENRY FORD

HENRY FORD

———

VINCENT CURCIO

OXFORD
UNIVERSITY PRESS

Oxford University Press is a department of the University of Oxford.
It furthers the University's objective of excellence in research, scholarship,
and education by publishing worldwide.

Oxford   New York

Auckland   Cape Town   Dar es Salaam   Hong Kong   Karachi
Kuala Lumpur   Madrid   Melbourne   Mexico City   Nairobi
New Delhi   Shanghai   Taipei   Toronto

With offices in

Argentina   Austria   Brazil   Chile   Czech Republic   France   Greece
Guatemala   Hungary   Italy   Japan   Poland   Portugal   Singapore
South Korea   Switzerland   Thailand   Turkey   Ukraine   Vietnam

Oxford is a registered trade mark of Oxford University Press
in the UK and certain other countries.

Published in the United States of America by
Oxford University Press
198 Madison Avenue, New York, NY 10016

Library of Congress Cataloging-in-Publication Data
Curcio, Vincent.
Henry Ford / Vincent Curcio.
pages cm. — (Lives and legacies series)
Includes bibliographical references and index.
ISBN 978-0-19-531692-6 (hardback)
1. Ford, Henry, 1863-1947.   2. Industrialists—United States—Biography.
3. Automobile industry and trade—United States—History.
4. United States—Biography.   I. Title.
CT275.F68C87 2013
338.7'6292092—dc23
[B]
2012043539

1 3 5 7 9 8 6 4 2
Printed in the United States of America
on acid-free paper

For Steven Englund,
without whose help and encouragement
I never would have had a writing career.

We must go ahead without the facts. We will learn as we go along.

—Henry Ford

CONTENTS

Introduction

Make your program so long and so hard that the people who praise you will always seem to be talking about something very trivial in comparison to what you are really trying to do.... Get a good start on it.... Then you will be free to work. And, being free to work, you will have achieved the truest success and satisfaction.

—Henry Ford

Success is not the result of spontaneous combustion. First you have to set yourself on fire.

—Fred Shero

THERE ARE A FEW INDIVIDUALS, A VERY FEW, WHOSE WORK and influence are so profound that over time they fundamentally change the ways in which people live. Because of Johann Guttenberg, for instance, people came to know and understand the world around them in a radically different manner. Because of Martin Luther, people learned to think for themselves in ways they had not done before about a range of issues that began with choices in religion and later extended to the basic social orientations of human lives and destinies. The French Revolution, and the American one, would not have been possible without the consequences of Luther's independent cast of mind.

Henry Ford was one of these few individuals. It wasn't because of the assembly line or the Model T, but for something much more significant: the democratization of prosperity. His method was mass production, which took raw materials and processed them by rational means into sophisticated industrial products that vastly improved the material conditions of existence for everyone, because these items could be bought and enjoyed by everyone, including the workers who made them, for the very first time. He mobilized ordinary people to do his bidding, and in the process made them upwardly mobile. This was a revolutionary idea and a revolutionary fact. Ford's system had an immediate impact far beyond his own industry because of his generosity, for he did not try to safeguard, patent, trademark, or sell it. He gave it away freely to anyone who wanted to learn and use it, causing its influence to spread quickly throughout the world.

He didn't do it alone, of course. A group of extremely talented men worked on mass production for him, and without them it might never have come together. Ford was lucky too in his timing, for the way had been prepared for him by earlier pioneers, whose multiplicity of ideas and practices he could build on in such areas as mechanization, organization, and business. It helps to arrive at the end of a long, complicated process rather than at the beginning, as Swiss historian Sigfried Giedion pointed out, and that was what happened to Ford. But in the end it was his particular vision, initiative, and responsibility that made the whole system solidify. "We did the work and he took the bows, yet none of us would have gone very far without him," Charles Sorensen said in 1956.

The underlying principle of Ford's system, distilled into a single word, is "movement": continuous, uninterrupted, compressed, rational, efficient, economical, repeatable movement. Ford's ability to mobilize all aspects of the production chain brought stasis, interruption, and waste in the workplace to an end. This caused enormous leaps in the quality, scope, and reach of the products that were generally available. People were gradually freed from servitude to items and processes that ate up their time and energy in the course of daily life, as such things as mass-produced refrigerators, washing machines, and radios became commonplace in their homes. They could now live, think, aspire, and attain in ways that were previously unavailable, except to the rich and the fortunate.

In the wake of the announcement of the five-dollar, eight-hour day at the Ford Motor Company at the beginning of 1914, Ford was lionized, and sometimes mobbed, by a grateful populace. They considered him a public benefactor of the highest quality, a force for good far beyond that found in the souls of ordinary men. He rode a long way on the attendant social benefits of the Model T. Waves of approbation continued for him after the introduction of the Model A in 1927 (as chic and classy as the Model T had been utilitarian) and the low-priced V-8 in 1932. And his work in agriculture, a field in which he was enormously influential during his lifetime, would have assured him greatness all by itself.

But as early as the end of 1915, cracks began to appear in the edifice of Ford's reputation. That year he inaugurated a "Peace Ship" mission to end the Great War, a fiasco that held him up to public ridicule. Then he "rewarded" some of his oldest and most gifted associates with dismissal in the 1920s and alienated his labor force with a speed-up on the assembly line and inhumane working conditions in his factories at that time too. This was succeeded by the police-state atmosphere that he created in his plants in the 1930s.

And then there was the matter of the Jews. Until 1915, Henry Ford seems to have held garden variety Midwestern Judeophobic views, drawn from such sources as the series of *McGuffey Readers* used to educate tens of millions of Americans in grammar schools throughout most of the 19th century. His contact with actual Jews was quite limited. But somewhat inexplicably, beginning at that time, something changed—a virulent prejudice against Jews sank pylons deep into his mind, becoming the support for a vast edifice of lifelong and enormously influential hatred against them. Indeed, Ford's reputation for Antisemitism has long outlasted him, and it remains the worst part of his legacy.

Yet he employed and worked with many Jews. Albert Kahn, for instance, the foremost industrial architect of his time, designed Ford's revolutionary Highland Park factory and remained his principal architect thereafter, continuing to design hundreds of buildings for him. At no time after his factories were working at full tilt did fewer than 3,000 Jews work for Ford.

Additionally, he had highly enlightened employment policies concerning the handicapped, blacks, ethnic groups, women, and even ex-criminals. At Ford, anyone who wanted to work could find a job; it wasn't your past that mattered, but your future.

How could such malignancy, and greatness too, coexist in one person? On the one hand, Ford was an uneducated, simple farmer with a wide streak of meanness and a nearly mindless, almost atavistic, hatred toward a whole category of humanity. He seemed blind to the consequences of that. On the other hand, he was a millennial visionary who worked for the betterment of humankind. Though in some ways he was the most modern of men, he was also the product of a pre-modern, far less enlightened era. Ultimately, he was an enigma: maddening, querulous, sometimes repulsive, yet also astonishing and inspiring. Little wonder that there are shelves of books on him, not to mention articles by the thousands. And yet there is always more to say. Ford is one of those touchstone figures like Columbus, traditionally celebrated as the man who opened up the Americas to European civilization, and later reviled as the ignominious villain who visited the depredations of civilization on the native peoples whom he and his successors found there. In the sharp, and not unjustified, criticisms of him, the great achievement got lost.

Ask anyone today about Henry Ford; the first, and often the only, thing that pops out of their mouths is, "Oh, he was a terrible Antisemite." Press them further, and "Model T," "assembly line," or "mass production" may come up, often somewhat vaguely.

Well, he *was* a terrible Antisemite, and such works as Neil Baldwin's *Henry Ford and the Jews* and Albert Lee's book of the same title have done a great service by investigating the full extent of that side of his character. Ford was perhaps more influential than any other Antisemite outside of Nazi Germany, and he needs to take full blame for the repercussions of this fact. Yet he was still, despite this, a man of monumental accomplishment. If you're going to look at him, you have to look at all of him, and keep the whole picture in sight.

This book is an attempt to consider, at brief length, all of the important elements that make up his life. I will try to give you both the cathedral of his achievements, as well as the gargoyles that can be seen glowering from its heights.

HENRY FORD

ONE

How It All Began

The Fords were a very old family, English in origin. They might have immigrated to Ireland as early as the beginning of the 17th century, as the result of Elizabethan land grants there. Or they might have arrived there as late as the early 19th century to seek a more prosperous life. No one knows for sure. But we do know that the first Fords in Henry Ford's line to immigrate to the United States were three brothers, his grand-uncles, Samuel, Henry, and George. Two of them arrived at what is now Dearborn, Michigan, in 1832, along with many others seeking cheap land, social freedoms, and the opportunity for economic advancement. If your family had been tenant farmers in Ireland, chances were that they would remain so forever; in America, that status could change overnight.

Dearborn, though located only a few miles from the old French trading port of Detroit, was then an area of dense hardwood forests in a frontier territory rich in minerals and game, filled with the abundance, and dangers, of nature (and Native Americans too.) Within five years Michigan would become a state with a burgeoning population made possible by water transportation on Lake Erie and the Erie Canal, and the construction of the Detroit-Chicago road. Henry's grandfather John, his son William, and the rest of his family (16 in all), decided to join their American family in 1847, having been evicted from their tenant farm during the worst of the famine caused by the potato blight, which killed a million people and caused more than another million to immigrate to America in the next few years. Probably by route of Quebec, the John Ford family arrived at Dearborn in late 1847, joining those who had preceded them, and buying their own 80 acres on January 15, 1848. Like their elders and neighbors before them, these Michigan pioneers cleared their land, took their wood to the sawmill, and built their own house. Forty years later, in a time far removed from those frontier days, in a far less rustic Dearborn, a 25-year-old Henry Ford would do almost the same thing after his marriage. And 27 years after that, he carved on a mantel at his mansion, Fair Lane: "Chop Your Own Wood and It Will Warm You Twice." The roots of the farm, and the pioneer, ran deep in his spirit.

Henry's father William, a sturdily handsome man with a piercing gaze, worked on the farm and also as a carpenter for the rapidly growing Michigan Central Railroad, which then employed some 2,500 men in constructing buildings to support an operational force of only 276. William used his extra money to pay off his father's mortgage, which was retired in 1850. By 1858 he had done well enough to buy 40 acres from his father for $600, and three years later, he felt financially confident enough to marry and start his own family.

He married Mary Litogot O'Hern, a small, vivacious and earnest brunette whom he had known for 10 years, since she was 12. Of Flemish or Dutch (Henry preferred to say the latter) extraction, she had been orphaned when her carpenter father fell off a roof. Patrick and Margaret O'Hern, a moderately prosperous but childless couple, took her in and raised her lovingly as their own. William, who began helping out on the O'Hern farm in the early 1850s, watched her grow and came to love her as she matured. They were married by an Episcopal clergyman in Detroit on April 25, 1861, coincidentally just two weeks after the start of the Civil War.

The Fords and the O'Herns, who had come from the same part of Ireland, formed very close familial bonds. Of course William built, and then expanded, a new house for himself and his bride, in which the aging O'Herns eventually joined them. In return for running the farm and a lifetime tenancy, the O'Herns sold William their 91 acres, which he paid for in part by selling for $2,500 the 40 acres he had bought from his father.

Henry Ford was to say that the idea that his family came from poor farming stock was a myth. They weren't rich, but they were solidly prosperous, in a prosperous place. (The value of the timber cut from the Michigan forests alone between 1840 and the turn of the 20th century exceeded the value of all the gold extracted from California—by $1 billion.) And the notion that even the common man could become prosperous seems to have been instilled in him early on. His father thought the miracle of America was that a man could own the land on which he lived and worked; in a far distant time Henry would create a new kind of American miracle: that the common man could own, in a new industrial setting, not the means of production, but wondrous new things that he produced by those means, vastly improving his lot in life.

Henry Ford came into the world on July 30, 1863, when the smoke had barely cleared from the Battle of Gettysburg, when Queen Victoria and Napoleon III were in the middle of their reigns, and before the electric lightbulb, the telephone, or the phonograph had been invented.

The first of four boys and two girls, he lived the life of a typical farm boy of his time and place, but from early on it was apparent that he didn't fit in with the others. His siblings were content with the farmer's life, which he found hard and tedious—and inefficient. "I have followed many a weary mile behind a plow and I know all the drudgery of it. What a waste...when in the same time a tractor could do six times as much work," he would say in his autobiography. His displeasure with farm work in fact gave him a lifelong incentive to improve and alleviate the burdens of a farmer's toil.

William Ford taught his son to understand and love nature, an inclination that remained with him all his life. But that was in the wild. On the farm, nature was something to be subjugated, transformed, and conquered. Henry was drawn to machines, and with those he would transform the world into which he was born. It was not for nothing that he felt (and probably somewhat imagined) a conflict between himself and his father over the way in which he would live his life, for William had little taste for anything but farm life, believing in a sort of Jeffersonian ideal of the self-sufficient farmer. However much in theory Henry might have subscribed to such a view himself, he did more than any other man in history to undermine it.

He may have felt ambivalence about his father, but in his youth, the heart of the matter was his mother. "I never had any particular love for the farm," he said later. "It was the mother on the farm I loved." Mary Ford was a hard-working farm wife, who gave her children a sense of duty and self discipline, but who also had a light-hearted spirit that led to a happy home life. "More than once I've heard her say...that if we couldn't be happy here in this house we'd never be happy anywhere else," Henry would remember.

She guided her children by example and exhortation, laced with many a wise maxim: "The best fun follows a duty done," "You may have pity on others, but you must not pity yourself," and "Do what you find to do, and what you know you must, do to the best of your ability," were some of the ideas that were taught, appreciated, and followed in the bosom of the family.

Unlike her husband, she understood Henry's inherent mechanical bent when he was very young, and she encouraged him by giving him old knitting needles and corset stays to use to fashion his tools. And she taught him to read before he started school.

School for Henry began at the nearby Scotch Settlement School on January 11, 1871, when he was seven and a half years old (typical for the time). In addition to mathematics and spelling, students were instructed in reading through the series of *McGuffey Readers* turned out by the tens of millions in the 19th and early 20th centuries.

While teaching the essential skills of reading by having the child identify with the learning process through stories close to their own lives, these books, devised by William Holmes McGuffey, an Ohio pedagogue, also provided moral, historical, and political lessons through prose, poetry, and oratorical selections from the great writers of the past. Much has been made of the effects of the Antisemitic slant contained in McGuffey selections about Shylock and Fagin on the future life of the young Henry Ford, but it is interesting to note that the selection *Things By Their Right Name*, which called soldiers murderers, may have also had a long-lasting effect, as Henry was publicly expressing and acting on its pacifist sentiments 45 years later. (As a side note, it seems quite clear from all of this that he read perfectly well—spelling was another matter—despite the opposite impression he was willing to give in his *Chicago Tribune* lawsuit in 1919, which turned in part on whether or not he was an ignorant man.)

Meanwhile, at home, aided and abetted by his mother, the boy tinkered and tinkered. No toy, no clock was safe from his investigations into their workings. He flooded a potato field in a milling experiment, blew up a boiler in another experiment involving a steam turbine (he supervised while the other fellows happily did the work, a lifelong modus operandi), and invented and repaired things on the farm.

In 1876, several major events occurred in Henry's life. First, in March, his beloved mother died from the effects of childbirth; it was a terrible shock. Henry became withdrawn and guarded, speaking little, and confiding in no one. "It is not necessary to expose your inner self to anyone," he told a friend. Without his mother, the family homestead to him had become "like a watch without a mainspring."

A few months later in the summer, Henry and his father, while driving a hay wagon, encountered a large, bulky, unwieldy steam engine moving about for the purpose of threshing or sawing wood. It had one remarkable feature: It moved under its own power, rather than being pulled by horses. Henry fairly flew off the wagon, peppering the steam engine driver with questions about the mechanism. It was the first time he had ever encountered such a machine. Over the next year he would be allowed to fire it up and run it many times, and he began to think of himself as an engineer. He also began to think of the possibilities of a self-propelled vehicle, ideas that he would expand beyond limits he couldn't have guessed at on that first, fateful day.

Almost simultaneously, Henry was given a watch as a present, probably for his 13th birthday. He immediately took it apart and reassembled it, and before long he understood its workings perfectly, a far more important issue to him than its beauty or utility. Within two years he began repairing watches, teaching himself, and soon everyone in the neighborhood brought him their broken ones for fixing, until his father pointed out that he should be paid for his services; though he never asked for money—he did it for sheer pleasure. "Machines are to a mechanic what books are to a writer," he said later. "He gets ideas from them and if he has any brains he will apply them."

Lastly in 1876, Henry's father traveled to Philadelphia for the Centennial Exhibition, where he saw, and later related to his son, all the mechanical wonders on display. There was the famous Bell Telephone of course, wonderful new machine tools, and demonstrations devoted to the production of everything from watches to pins. Many exhibits had to do with new applications for the use of steam, which fired the imagination of 13-year-old Henry, who was already filled with enthusiasm for all things to do with steam, especially when related to transportation. Henry, like countless others, was enthralled by the possibilities of the new, ever-growing mechanical age, and this was a great spur for him to pursue those possibilities.

He was 13 now, and everything was on the boil. The year 1876 reflected the larger struggle of Henry's early life, one that was symbolically divided in two. The death of his mother marked the close of his rural childhood and the past. The discovery of steam engines, watches, and other mechanical marvels that clanked and whirred propelled him into the future. It would take another 13 years and a false start before he would firmly begin living in that future, and nearly another lifetime for him to master it. But once he did, neither his world, nor the greater world, would ever be the same.

For the next three years he remained on the farm, assuming more of the chores as his body strengthened and grew. Though only 5' 8" tall, and never more than a lean 148 pounds, he was tough, strong, and quick, as he would be for the rest of his life. His ever-increasing load of farm drudgery constantly spurred his desire to escape from it. By late 1879, when he was 16 and had finished his schooling, he began to discuss with his father more and more frequently his desire to leave the farm and go to work with machinery in Detroit. William was opposed, of course, but gradually he accepted that there was nothing to be done about it. It was just a question of when it would happen. The day arrived soon enough, and the event happened in a way that would be typical of the manner in which Henry Ford would conduct himself at crucial moments for the rest of his life.

Two

Walking into the Future

On december 1, 1879, henry went to live and work in Detroit. When he made the trip, it was not on a train, a wagon, or a buggy, and God knows, it was not on a horse. He simply packed up and, without a word to anyone, left home and walked the six miles to the city. It was a headstrong gesture, but it was not unexpected or strange. Everyone knew he was going there, and why.

Detroit, a fast-growing city of 115,000, was perfectly situated as a transportation hub on the Great Lakes, and was a center for manufacturing all kinds of things, from wagons and railroad cars, to stoves, ships, and cigars. And every one of those businesses needed hardworking, quick-witted young men to apprentice in their shops. It was the place to be to learn about what mattered most to Henry: machinery.

He went to stay with his Aunt Rebecca Flaherty at first. And in fact his father, despite general opposition to his son's plans, may have used his influence to arrange a job for him at the James Flower & Brothers Machine Shop, though this was not where he went first for employment. He got his own job at the Michigan Car Company; it lasted only six days. His employment ended when he quickly solved a problem that senior hands had worked on for hours. "I learned then not to tell all you know," he said of the experience. He also learned something else. In this shop (said to be the country's largest railroad car manufacturer by 1885), the cars were made according to a crude form of progressive assembly. Starting with a pile of parts at one end of the works, "everything goes in one direction," said a contemporary account of working methods at Michigan Car, where successive groups of workmen were directed from one location to another working on parts and finally assembling them into complete units on chassis set on rails in a 200' by 80' setup room; from there, they were pushed into a paint room, from which they emerged as finished products.

After he was let go, Henry did indeed go to work at James Flower & Brothers, a foundry and machine shop highly respected for its English tradition of thorough workmanship. Its apprentices were trained to very exacting standards, and some turned into fine mechanics, among them a future car manufacturer named David Buick. Henry learned a great deal here, including the ability to make and use blueprints, a fact that undermines the claims of future commentators who maintained that Ford always insisted on seeing models of new units because he couldn't read the blueprints. He could; he just didn't like to, probably because when he looked at an actual *machine*, he could figure it out immediately. As Ford biographer and journalist Roger Burlingame wrote, "From a glance at any machine he could understand the interdependence of its parts—follow a line of reasoning, however long, through gears, ratchets, cams and levels." Ford simply wanted to play to his strengths.

His weekly pay of $2.50 at Flower was not enough to cover his room and board, which cost $3.50 at Mrs. Payton's establishment on Baker Street, where he had moved after leaving his aunt's house. So the enterprising youth walked into the McGill Jewelry Store a few doors down the block and got a second job immediately, at first cleaning clocks, and then repairing watches. Although his work was first-rate, he looked so young that McGill hid him at a bench in the backroom, lest his customers become frightened at the sight of a mere boy working on their expensive timepieces. Henry got two dollars a week for his labors, enough to put him ahead of his expenses by one dollar. (In 1940, he found the first watch he had ever worked on and repaired it in just a few minutes.)

By the summer of 1880, Henry thought it was time to move on once again. Flower's mechanics had taught him all that they knew, but there were many areas in which they were not experts. So he went to the Detroit Drydock Company, the city's largest shipbuilding firm, which built and repaired vessels of all sorts, whether made of wood, iron, or steel. He stayed there much longer than he had at Flower, and easily completed his three-year apprenticeship long before the term had ended. He labored there in the engine works, learning a great deal about various sorts and sizes of power plants.

While at Detroit Drydock, Henry encountered the famous consulting and construction marine engineer Frank E. Kirby. One day Kirby saw the youth struggling with a heavily loaded wheelbarrow on a steep incline, about to lose his footing. "Stick in your toenails, boy, and you will make it!" he yelled. Ford admired Kirby greatly, and when he summoned him to construct his Eagle boats decades later during World War I, he mentioned the incident to him and remarked, "I have been sticking in my toenails ever since."

Though Ford was probably making decent wages as he went along (he originally accepted a pay cut of 50¢ to get the job), he was still repairing watches at night. But now there was something else going on with his sideline, nascent and as yet inchoate. He decided he wanted to manufacture watches in quantity at low cost, reasoning that if he could make them for 30¢ each and sell them for 50¢, a decent profit could be made, provided he could manufacture 2,000 per day. Ford even found a partner and worked on designing the requisite machinery at Mrs. Payton's. But then he realized he was up against a major challenge that he couldn't come close to figuring out. How do you get people to buy something they don't consider a universal necessity, especially if you have to sell 600,000 of them a year to make good? At this point Ford was still decades away from mastering the exigencies of mass production, including one of the most important factors pertaining to it: How do you create a mass market for a product for the masses? But at least he was beginning to see his ultimate goal for the first time, albeit through a glass, darkly. Over the next 25 years the gloom would lift, and his vision would become crystal clear.

One of the great puzzlements of Henry Ford's life occurred in 1882. Having completed his apprenticeship and learned a great deal about his beloved machinery, Ford turned around and went back to Dearborn. Why ever in the world would he do that? Had his father's importunings finally convinced him? Was he tired of machines and the city as his father had hoped he would be? Well, for one thing, this was a return with a difference. His labor as a farmhand was no longer needed, as his younger brothers were now old enough to manage without him; so he did no farm work for a long time, and then only a little, with reluctance. Mostly he repaired things and operated machinery at the homestead. In the summer, he earned his living operating and repairing about 20 steam engines on local farms for the Westinghouse Company; he made that connection after he began operating one of them for a prominent Dearborn farmer named John Gleason. These machines were self propelled, like the one he saw in 1876, and did much the same work. In the winter, he probably took whatever machine shop jobs he could rustle up in Detroit, which perhaps is the key to his return to Dearborn. Jobs in engineering at that place and time were not so easy to get, and he did what he had to in order to live.

In addition to working, Ford also took business courses at night at the Goldsmith, Bryant and Stratton Business University in Detroit, where he studied typewriting, bookkeeping, and mechanical drawing to improve himself.

Through it all he kept on tinkering, now in a workshop in the backyard of his father's house, fitted out with all sorts of tools he had fashioned. Notably, he designed and built a single piston motor and attached it to an old broken-down mower, in a crude and primitive attempt to create a tractor. The thing ran for 40 feet and died, but it marked the beginning of a lifelong pursuit to alleviate the weariness, strain, and boredom of hard manual farm labor. Ford had labored under its heavy yoke himself and wanted to lift this burden from others in his own time and after. He didn't know how yet, but at least he was beginning to get a very loose grip on how to learn to know how.

Perhaps this intense discipline makes Ford sound like a stick-in-the-mud, joyless and solitary. One might think he had no social graces and youthful high spirits, or even much ordinary humanity. But he did. There were friends he palled around with, notably his old school mate Edsel Ruddiman, whose brother eventually married Ford's sister Margaret, and for whom he named his only child, and fellow apprentice Frederick Strauss, with whom he was to work on several projects over the years. He was enormously fond of practical jokes, went to church socials and barn dances as other young folks did, and attended circuses and fairs. Ice skating was a lifelong pleasure, as were long, solitary walks in the beauties of nature.

He claimed (and as far as anyone knows) he never touched alcohol or tobacco, either then or at any time in his life. He considered them to be poisons that were physically and mentally deleterious, capable of ruining the potential of a person who partook of them, as well as the lives of those close by.

With regard to religion, there was a certain lightness he had learned from his family. William Ford was an Anglican, the O'Herns were Catholic, and the family attended the Christ Episcopal Church of Dearborn every Sunday. Despite this mix, there was never much debate over religion in the household. His sister said, "We felt that one church wasn't the real answer. It was the way you lived and used your training." Ford had as much Sunday go-to-meeting religion as anybody else, but his attitude toward it did not differ in any way from that of anyone else in his family. As with other things in his life, it wasn't the theory, but the practice that counted.

Dynamic and attractive, Ford exuded a self confidence that made him a presence whenever he walked into a room. This made him a magnet for girls, just as it made him a natural leader among men. But though he enjoyed the company of young women, he was too wrapped up in other things to ever be serious about any one girl until, at the age of 22, he met *the* one girl, Clara Bryant. Ford claimed that he knew she was the right girl for him within 30 seconds of meeting her. Actually, it took a little longer than that.

Clara Bryant was a petite, pleasingly plump girl of 18 when she and Ford met. Her sweet round face was supported by a strong jaw and crowned by abundant dark-chestnut hair that more than anything else defined her as a local belle. The eldest girl among ten children of a prosperous local farm family, she was bright and popular, but also thoughtful and sober, qualities guaranteed to appeal to the son of Mary Litogot Ford. They were introduced by Ford's sister Margaret, probably on New Year's Eve of 1885, but things really began in earnest between them at a dance (Ford had enthusiastically learned the latest dance steps at parties to augment his social graces) a few months later. That night he showed her a double-dialed watch (one for railroad standard time and the other for local sun time) he had made; this really impressed her. "He's a thinking, sensible person—a serious-minded person," she told her family when she returned home that night. "He's worked out something different."

That admiring view of Ford was to last for the rest of her life, and meant more than anything else to him. His lifelong nickname for her was "The Believer."

Soon they were courting. He bowled her over with a sleek little forest-green, low-slung sleigh called a cutter that he bought for her, just as a beau of today might impress his girlfriend with a snazzy new convertible; they were often seen riding about the countryside in it. In addition to picnics, dances, and buggy rides, they also joined the Bayview Reading Circle, a local Chatauqua-inspired cultural group. (Again surprising for someone who was later alleged to be unable to read.) And of course, they joined in a mutual enthusiasm for music and dancing (she was quite a good dancer too.) By 1886, they were engaged—but only after a certain transaction had taken place.

Henry had been back from Detroit for four years now, and William Ford began to think that he would stay in Dearborn for keeps. To help things along, he offered his son the chance to make some good money. There were 40 acres of uncut timber on an 80-acre property that William owned, and if Henry would clear it, he could keep the money he made from the wood—provided, that is, he would give up being a machinist. Henry only agreed provisionally, as that money would give him the chance to get married. There was already a small house on the property, and he built a little mill there and acquired an engine to operate a saw, so he was in business and making money in short order. Of course, he also built himself a machine shop for his tinkering, which he wasn't about to give up. With all this in place, Henry and Clara at last felt secure enough to announce their engagement.

The wedding took place two years later, on April 11, 1888, on Clara's 22nd birthday, at the Bryant family home. The bride made her own wedding dress, and Henry wore a blue suit. The Rev. Samuel W. Frisbie, of St. James Episcopal Church in Detroit, conducted the ceremony. Clara's brothers served the wedding supper, and Henry's sister prepared his little house to receive the newlyweds for their honeymoon.

For the Fords, marriage was a partnership, each of them contributing to and responsible for the happiness and well-being of the other. They worked hard and saved (she was in charge of the money) to build a bigger, much better house that Clara designed for them. It was a 31-foot, four-square, one-and-a-half-story American Colonial building, simple on the inside but festooned on the outside with fancy balustrades that gave it a certain imbalanced opulence. It didn't cost them a nickel. Henry sawed, milled, and seasoned the wood for it himself. Every board that went into it had been cut on the farm; the sawmill had paid for the cost of building; and they had traded lumber for furniture. As a grace note, an organ was purchased for it some time after they moved into it in the spring of 1889.

So it seemed that the Fords were to be a settled farm couple after all—at least on the surface. Yet Henry never did the obvious thing, that is, to start farming once the timber was cut and the land cleared. What he did do, aside from his sawmill work, was to build and repair machines in what he called the "first class" shop he attached to the house. Although Ford later claimed he put together some experimental steam and gas engines there, neither his wife nor his sister corroborated that. On more than one occasion Ford's penchant was to rewrite history at a future date, to make aspects of it seem more prescient or dramatic. He did, however, continue to complain about the wastefulness and inefficiency of horses, and startled his wife with talk of a desire to build horseless carriages.

As he had over a decade earlier, Ford was once again thinking about leaving Dearborn. The man who came back to the town in 1882 was much different from the boy who had left it in 1879, more knowledgeable and more experienced. In the intervening years, remarkable things were happening in the world of science, technology, and the field that interested him most, transportation. An electrically powered traction system was introduced in Virginia. The two-cycle Brayton internal combustion engine, named for the New England engineer George Brayton, had become known and been demonstrated. More important, the far more sophisticated four-stroke Otto internal combustion engine—named for the German inventor Nikolaus Otto, who developed it in the 1860s—had come into use and was the basis for the first functional gasoline cars, invented almost simultaneously in the mid 1880s by Gottlieb Daimler and Karl Benz in Germany. Westinghouse had sent Ford to see a demonstration of this type of engine in 1890, and shortly he knew enough about it to be called to Detroit to repair one. He wanted to work with all the new mechanical wonders to get to know more about them, and just as he had left Flower Brothers to go to Detroit Drydock, for similar reasons, he now needed to leave Dearborn to advance himself into the world of technological progress, which he knew he would find in Detroit. In fact he became more and more unsettled by the thought that he was not part of what was taking place just a short distance from where he lived. By the middle of 1891, Ford was actively looking for opportunities there.

By 1891, he was 28 years old, not exactly the first blush of youth in those days. Why did it take him so long to leave Dearborn and pursue opportunities in Detroit? Did he lack knowledge or the confidence he needed to kick over the traces of his rural life? Did he lack organization or a systematized approach to this new world? He had self- confidence surely, and he was certainly an extraordinarily gifted mechanic. But Ford knew that a lot of other men were too. Besides, individual motorized transportation was considered a curiosity the widespread use of which would not begin to be revealed for several more years. It was not considered a serious occupation for a family man then.

But even when the incredible potential for motorized transportation became clear, and Ford began to see the automobile and an industry to build it coalesce into a kind of primitive but definite shape, and even when he became a part of the great American automobile enterprise himself, it still took him years of trial and error before his own place in it became secure. He would be 40 years old, and on his third company, when he found success.

That this success would be exponential and total is almost completely unpredictable from any one individual thing, or all of them taken together, in his past life. At 45, he was rich, but no richer than many other prominent businessmen, and still barely known in the big world beyond Detroit. It was only at 50, an age when Alexander the Great was long in his grave and Shakespeare was retired, that he emerged as a world-class, millenial figure, a man whose revolution, according to R. L. Bruckelberger, was more important for the 20th century than Lenin's.

This revolution, which would quite properly come to be called Fordism, was composed of the work of many other people, which Ford did his best to hide or ignore when praise was given for his accomplishments. But still, as Galileo said about the earth in the heavens, nevertheless it moved, and when it did, the effects on humanity were unprecedented. The world got the Henry Ford it needed just when it needed him.

Early or late, or just on time, one night in September of 1891, after returning from repairing an Otto engine in Detroit and finally realizing its innate superiority to steam as a means of locomotion, Henry reiterated to Clara his desire to build a horseless carriage. He even sketched out a possible engine for her on the back of a piece of sheet music. She had complete confidence in what he showed and explained to her. Then he dropped the bombshell that, in order to build his machine, he would have to learn more about electricity, and to do that, he needed to go to Detroit to find a job where he could accomplish that. In fact, he said, he had been offered just such a position at the Edison Illuminating Company there.

Clara was heartbroken at the prospect of leaving their home, family, and security for a veiled, uncertain, and completely unknown new life. But she told him he had better do it. It was not for nothing that Henry called her The Believer.

It was a good thing that she responded the way she did, because Ford had already taken the job. So on September 25, 1891, they packed their belongings and moved to a new apartment on John R. Street in Detroit. This meant that the long days of Henry's farm life were now over forever. It was the city and the machine age that would claim his attention in one way or another from then on.

At that time Detroit Edison Illuminating served 1,200 of the 1,650 households that were electrified, as well as 5,000 of the municipal streetlights, thus making it the leading provider of power in the city. Given that Detroit was then a city of some 205,000, it was clear that electric power, though rapidly growing, was still in its nascent stages both as a business and as a service. Ford began by working as a mechanical engineer on a 12-hour shift, beginning at 6 p.m., at a substation for $45 a month. His abilities were quickly recognized (he could keep a generator going all by himself), and soon he was earning $75 a month; not long after that he rose to become chief engineer at the plant at a pay rate of $1,000 a month. Part of his responsibilities entailed being on call 24 hours a day to deal with any emergency equipment breakdowns, so he slept ready to jump into his clothes and shoes at a moment's notice. This new responsibility also gave him the chance to use company equipment for his own personal projects. In addition, he taught night classes in mechanics at the Detroit YMCA, which also gave him access to their shop facilities, something that probably meant more to him than the $2.50 he earned for each session.

Edsel, the Fords' only child, came into the world on November 6, 1893. A beautiful, amiable boy, he later was to work closely with his father, and he maintained intimate bonds with both his parents throughout his life. The Fords were a happy little band.

When Henry got another raise a few days after Edsel's birth, along with a promotion to chief engineer at the main Edison plant downtown, they had to move, for the new shop was over a mile from where they lived. (By this point they had already moved several times). Thus they came to a little two-family house at 58 Bagley Street, which providentially came with a fair-sized brick storage building in the back that Henry was to put to excellent use. For it was here that he would assemble his first automobile.

THREE

COOKING WITH GAS

Henry Ford was always fond of neat explanations for how and why something came about long after it happened, so the story of his simultaneous realization of the superiority of the gas engine and the necessity of moving to Detroit fall into a familiar pattern. It is unclear exactly when he decided to work with gas, or how he arrived at this conclusion. After all, he had known about gasoline motors and their properties, and had seen them demonstrated, for a number of years. Furthermore, steam, which he knew a great deal about, seemed at the time to be another good candidate for providing automotive self- propulsion, as did electricity a short time later.

Steam had a long history as a self-propelling force, going back to Hero of Alexandria's aeolipile, which he described in his *Pneumatica* in 130 B.C.E. The Italians, and later the English, improved upon Hero's ideas in the 17th century, and in the 18th, the English lay Baptist minister and ironmonger

Thomas Newcomen went further by creating a successful piston engine (separating it from the boiler). James Watt went further still, developing the separate condenser and the crank, which allowed rotary motion to replace the up-and-down motion of the piston.

The problem that they all faced, and nobody since Hero except for a Jesuit named Father Verbiest at the court of the Chinese emperor in 1665 had solved, was how to make the steam engine mobile—make it "portable, gear it to wheels, and get it on the road," as automobile historian Arthur Pound put it. That was up to Captain Nicolas-Joseph Cugnot, who created an enormous three-wheeled artillery gun tractor in 1769, at the behest of the French government. Oliver Evans in America and Richard Trevithick in England demonstrated steam-propelled carriages, and in 1805 the latter was credited with the invention of the steam locomotive. Train technology spread rapidly by the 1830s, and by 1860, Amédée Bollée operated a fleet of steam-driven carriages in Paris. But it was Leon Serpollet's 1889 invention of the flash boiler, which was much lighter and used minimal amounts of water, that made steam a more practical application for individualized transportation.

Though such vehicles as the White and Stanley steamers (the latter without the flash boiler) were to have considerable success, Ford was right to turn away from this type of power. Steamers were fast, great hill climbers, had no transmissions or cranks, and thus were easy to keep in repair. But it could take a long time to boil enough water to move; they could get clogged with lime from hard water; their open flames frightened people; and most important, they were not nearly as thermally efficient as internal combustion engines.

The other option was electricity. Electric cars became the vogue in the late 1890s. They were clean, quiet, had few moving parts, and were considered the perfect vehicles for women to operate. Colonel Albert A. Pope, with his Columbia Electric, produced over 50 percent of the cars in the United States in 1899, marketing them to the elite and also for urban commercial applications. But electric cars couldn't do more than 12 miles per hour, and their enormous storage batteries were cumbersome and required constant recharging. (It is interesting to note that more than 100 years later, after we have split the atom and found the means to propel spaceships beyond the edges of the solar system, we have only now begun to manage to invent an efficient, easy-to-recharge storage battery for automobiles; it makes one wonder about possible industrial obstructions regarding improved technology.) Colonel Pope thought the electric car was the wave of the future, "because you can't get people to sit over an explosion," he said of the combustion engine to his employee Hiram Percy Maxim.

But he was wrong; you could. Maxim turned out to be a seminal figure in developing the internal combustion engine for use in automobiles as early as 1892. The gas car triumphed because it was small, light, cheap to run, and most importantly, it did not require an external power source.

The first internal combustion engine used gunpowder as its explosive force and was invented by a Dutchman, Christiaan Huygens, in 1665; he also invented the pendulum clock and discovered Saturn's rings. Many experimented with the engine, and the first American patent for one was given in 1829 to Samuel Morey of Philadelphia, who put it in a vehicle, which he fell out of, and caused it to crash, thus creating America's first auto accident. In France, Etienne Lenoir patented a two-cycle engine in 1862, and Nikolaus Otto and Eugen Langen in Germany patented a four-cycle one in 1867 (apparently developed from one that Alphonse Beau de Rochas patented in France in 1862). It took another 18 years for Daimler and Benz in Germany to make one of these engines work in a vehicle.

By 1891, the horseless carriage was transformed into the modern automobile through "Le Système Panhard," developed by Émile Constant Levassor of the French firm Panhard et Levassor. This was the modern arrangement with the engine in front, passengers seated behind it in rows (instead of above it), and the "drive taken through a clutch to a set of reduction gears and thence to a differential gear on a countershaft on which the road wheels were driven by chains" (*Encyclopedia Britannica*).

None of this would have been possible without the craze for the bicycle that grew in the 1880s and 1890s. The modernization of this semi-mechanized form of transportation contributed much to the development of the automobile. Chain drive, ball and roller bearings, differential gearing, and steel tube framing all came from the bicycle. These advancements inspired French engineers to think about the car mechanism, instead of the carriage or buggy body that obsessed English and American inventors. Leaders in the early automotive movement, the French even contributed to it many of the terms still in use today—chassis, garage, chauffeur, and even the word "automobile" itself. But a lack of cheap labor, market, and physical space for the automobile caused them to fall behind; the French were permanently overtaken as automobile manufacturers by the Americans in 1906.

Though there were plenty of experiments beforehand, for all intents and purposes, the founding of the American automobile industry occurred in Springfield, Massachusetts, when two former bicycle mechanics, brothers J. Frank and Charles E. Duryea, ran their gasoline vehicle for the first time on the streets of that city on September 21, 1893. Two years later, their Duryea Motor Wagon Company became the first American firm founded for the express purpose of manufacturing automobiles. Hot on the Duryeas' heels were Elwood G. Haynes and another set of brothers, Edgar and Elmer Apperson. Haynes designed and the Appersons built (along with Jonathan Dixon Maxwell, another important pioneer) an 820-pound vehicle that they ran on the streets of Kokomo, Indiana, on July 4, 1894. By 1895, they too had formed a company to manufacture automobiles.

Haynes was one of the few formally trained early auto engineers; he also invented the vapor thermostat and the process for making carbon steel. He read German and probably knew about Daimler and Benz's pioneering efforts from reading German-language publications. Of some 300 or so mechanics working to attach some sort of engine to some sort of chassis before 1900, many, if not most, like Walter Chrysler, were inspired by a series of articles on the subject in *Scientific American*, a major force in turning the idea of the automobile into a movement in America. Everyone knew that the time of the automobile was coming, and this magazine provided a venue for distribution of the available information that could be used to create the longed-for reality.

In the same month, September 1896, both Alexander Winton in Cleveland and Ransom E. Olds, in Lansing, Michigan, drove experimental gasoline vehicles on the streets of their respective cities. Henry Ford in Detroit bested them by a couple of months. He drove one on June 6 of that year.

Though he read about the Duryeas' work, as well as Haynes's and the Appersons', Ford was most influenced by Charles B.

King, who beat him to the punch by three months when he became the first person to drive a gasoline vehicle on the streets of Detroit in March of 1896.

Ford and a few colleagues at Detroit Edison rented a space near the plant to use as a workshop for developing gasoline engines. They created such items as cylinders made from scrap pieces, and came up with the notion of a gravity gasoline feed, with Ford as usual supervising and everybody else doing the work. He claimed that on Christmas Eve of 1893, he was far enough along to clamp a small engine to his sink, let Clara pour gas into it from above, and watch it sputter to life. That success was a great spur for him.

A short time before, while on Detroit Edison business, Ford had met King, a Cornell- trained engineer, who had invented a highly regarded pneumatic hammer in 1890. Both men were interested in designing and building motor vehicles, and they developed a friendship. King employed a highly competent 17-year-old shop assistant named Oliver Barthel, who was to be very important to both him and Ford. The three of them developed both two- and four-cycle engines, the latter of which King was to use in his vehicle.

Barthel claimed, and another Ford assistant from Detroit Edison backed him up, that an article in *American Machinist* from November 7, 1895, explaining how to build a gas engine from odd bits of material, inspired Ford to build his gasoline vehicle. King later claimed that the kitchen sink/engine episode occurred at the end of 1895, not 1893, and that he saw it. That doesn't mean that Ford hadn't done it before, on another engine. But what matters is that none of his experimental motors was developed enough to be practicable, and that he asked King for help.

King finally gave a demonstration ride of his four-cycle, 1,300-pound motor wagon on the streets of Detroit on March 6, 1896. The press was invited and remarked upon the appearance of this "most unique machine." But despite King's abilities and his success, he didn't bring his accomplishment to fruition. He had intended to enter vehicles in two important races for the publicity, but he was never able to raise the cash for this and had to halt work.

However, that was not the case for the wiry man on a bicycle who followed the vehicle during its test run, intently studying its movements. Along with Barthel and fellow Edison employees Jim Bishop, George Cato, and Spider Huff, Ford continued to work intently on his own vehicle. (It is interesting to note that all the pioneers adapted their motors from already-existing commercial ones, in Ford's case the Kane-Pennington, which was described in a second automotive article in the January 9, 1896, edition of *American Machinist.*)

Ford learned a great deal from King's vehicle and also from a Duryea he saw at the Detroit Horse Show in April, 1896. Ford called his a quadricycle; it had four bicycle wheels and pneumatic tires and a body that could be used with either a bicycle seat or a wagon seat. Definitely of the horseless carriage rather than the true automobile type, it weighed only 500 pounds, and was far, far lighter than anything that had been made before. King gave Ford advice that helped with the transmission.

Finally, in the early morning hours of June 4, 1896, the car was ready to be tested. One difficulty remained, however. The men had built it inside the shed on Bagley Avenue as one might build a ship in a bottle. Ford had to grab an axe and smash the front of the building to create an opening for the car to emerge. It was raining, and Clara came out and held an umbrella over his head. Finally, after he made the hole large enough, he started up the quadricycle, maneuvered it out of the shed, and began to drive it down the street. Jim Bishop went ahead to warn people that the vehicle was coming. After a short breakdown, the two men drove it back home, completing the round trip.

Ford's landlord was so impressed with what had happened that he repaired the shed opening to make it wider and even allowed Ford to install a swinging door on it, thus creating the world's first garage door.

Ford got no publicity for his drive, and that was fine by him, for he knew he wasn't ready for a public demonstration yet. But the thing ran, and Ford knew that he was off and running too. "I cannot say that it was hard work," he said. "No work with interest is ever hard."

As for money, that came out of his own pocket. Others, like the Duryeas, Haynes, the Appersons, and King, were in a constant search for cash to support their projects, but Ford paid for his out of his not inconsiderable earnings from Detroit Edison. This put a strain on Clara, because all the family's extra cash went into the work, and many times she had to stretch their credit to the limit. Ford had willing and able associates who contributed their effort and time too. Ford was proud to have underwritten the creation of the quadricycle himself, and though he was to work with the support of other peoples' money for almost a quarter of a century after this, he was never again content until he owned and supported 100 percent of his company himself, after the buyout of his shareholders in 1919.

The original car was worked over many times after that initial ride, and once Ford had learned from it all that he could, he sold it for $200 to Charles Ainsley of Detroit, in what was America's first used-car sale. (The Duryeas had made the first new-car sale earlier in 1896.) The original car was later resold to bicycle dealer A. W. Hall, and it gave several more years of sterling service.

Ford's greatest piece of encouragement during this time came from his idol, Thomas Edison. Ford's boss, Alexander Dow, took him to the annual convention of the Association of Edison Illuminating Companies in New York that August. There he met the great man, and after hearing that he had actually built and operated a horseless carriage, Edison peppered him with questions. Leaning into his good ear, Ford sketched for him as he explained, and when he was finished, Edison banged his fist on the table, exclaiming, "Young man, that's the thing! You have it—the self contained unit carrying its own fuel with it! Keep at it!" With this approbation from the world's greatest inventor (who had been saying for some time that the horse was doomed), Ford was now bursting with self-confidence. Shortly thereafter he sold his first car to Ainsley and started work on his second.

But now Ford knew he needed more backing for his work than he was able to supply by himself. It showed up in the person of William C. Maybury, a longtime family friend who was also the mayor of Detroit. With Maybury footing some bills, and obtaining important items on loan, Ford was able to create his own machine shop in a new location; this allowed him to do more sophisticated work. The mayor also issued him a driver's license, the first in the United States, for the purpose of preventing complaints from the populace as he tooled around city streets in his noisy new machine. By 1898, Ford had produced a second, sleeker and improved car.

When that same year he received a carburetor patent, Maybury was able to secure more backers, who would receive interests in any patents Ford received and any cars sold; if a corporation were to be formed, they would own some of that too.

Canny as ever, Ford had scads of people working in his new machine shop, though they were never sure exactly what their goals were. Ford never did any of the actual work himself; he would just lay it out and supervise. That, to him, was his job. He would look up a patent attorney whenever he thought something innovative might pan out. The workers didn't share in any of this; they just got their wages. Why didn't they complain about this? As Fred Strauss put it, "He had a dream...a kind of magnet.... He had something over me."

The year 1899 was a watershed one for the burgeoning automobile industry. Both Olds and Packard began manufacturing cars; auto clubs were forming in both Europe and the United States; and the first auto show was held at Madison Square Garden in New York. It was a significant year of achievement for Ford too. By August, he had put together a third car, in every way a vast improvement over the first two models. Maybury was now able to attract a dozen Detroit high rollers into backing Ford's first company, the Detroit Automobile Company, capitalized at $150,000, with 10 percent paid in cash; it was the first firm in Detroit organized to manufacture cars. Ford was asked to be the "mechanical superintendent"—to put together a line of cars and organize a plant to build them—for $150 a month. Ten days after the firm began, Dow offered him a position as general superintendent of Detroit Edison if he would give up his experiments with gas cars; Ford quit his job instead, to devote himself to automobile manufacturing fulltime.

The firm was full of promise, but it was beset by problems. On January 12, 1900, the first machine, a two-seat delivery wagon, was rolled out, months behind schedule. Many other types of vehicles were promised by the spring, at first on a ten-per-month basis, then a on a two-per-day basis. The reality was much different. Every one of the 12 or so vehicles produced through late 1900 had its own unique set of problems, causing rip ups, tear downs, and redos that resulted in extensive, and expensive, delays. Motor vehicles retailed to the public for $1,000 were in fact costing about $1,250 to build. True, they were better than the early Benz and Duryea cars of just a few years earlier, but they were still not reliable. It was therefore not surprising that they did not sell. The Detroit Automobile Company was finished before the end of 1900, with its assets sold off in the new year.

For the Fords this was a period of retrenchment. At first they moved into smaller quarters and later shared a home with William Ford, who was now too old to farm and had moved to Detroit. He seems to have taken every opportunity to cast aspersions on his son's efforts with the new company. "You'll never make a go of it," he would say. The constant love and support of Clara, and their mutual joy in Edsel, now seven years old, kept Henry going at that time.

One very important thing came of the Detroit Automobile Company venture, however. Ford got his first whiff of the thrill of big-time publicity. A jaunty, illustrated article in the February 4, 1900, edition of the *Detroit News-Tribune* told of the ride a reporter took with Henry Ford in that first wagon, under the headline, "SWIFTER THAN A RACE-HORSE IT FLEW OVER THE ICY STREETS—Thrilling Trip on the First Detroit Made Automobile When Mercury Hovered About Zero."

Part reportage, part boys' adventure, this snappy article was served up with several dollops of Henry Ford's folksy musings: "Ever frighten the horses?" asked the visitor. "Depends on the horse. A low-bred, ignorant horse, yes; a high-born fellow, no.... Some are wise, some otherwise." There were several encomiums to this latest form of transportation ("The sooner you hear its latest chuck! chuck! the sooner you will be in touch with civilization's latest lisp, its newest voice"). With this much-noticed article Ford began to see the possibilities that free publicity could bring to him and his enterprises. He would make enormous use of publicity in the coming decades; in fact he would become one of its great masters. The trouble was that he would eventually fall victim to its most dangerous snare: He would start to believe it, forgetting that it was he who initiated and manipulated so much of it in the first place. That blind spot would bring him down many times in the future.

In actuality, the Detroit Automobile Company had not been expending a lot of effort in building commercial vehicles. Ford was not really happy working for hire with only a small profit participation; oftentimes he wasn't around the shop, in essence hiding from his backers. What he really did with the $86,000 the company lost was to investigate the building of a racing car, which he knew could be very important to his future success; as it turned out, it was.

A measure of the faith his backers had in him was that some of them, including Maybury, bought the company's assets at the receiver's sale in May, rented shop space for him in the same building he had been using, and provided him with funds to keep on with his work. Thus Ford was able to keep his crackerjack team of hardworking, brilliant assistants together. Time meant nothing to them, nor did the amount of work they put in. They were a group of men on a mission, happy to be there, rather like the startup dot-commers would be a century later.

One source of revenue was motor-car racing. Ford didn't care much about it, but he got involved out of necessity. The French had attracted considerable attention with races in 1894 and 1895, the second of which, from Paris to Bordeaux, clearly demonstrated the superiority of gasoline cars over their electric and steam rivals. In America, Herman H. Kohlstaat, owner of the Chicago *Times-Herald*, arranged a 52-mile round-trip race between that city and Evanston, Ilinois, on Thanksgiving Day, November 28, 1895. He offered a $2,000 top prize. A field of six entered, and after a harrowing time in cold, snowy weather, one of the Duryeas won, in over ten hours of extremely difficult driving. Enormous publicity ensued, though this demonstration hardly convinced people of the superiority of the gasoline motor car, which was still plagued with so many problems and breakdowns. But the significance of the race cannot be overestimated. As with the first public demonstrations of the steamboat and the locomotive, the public could now see this wonderful new invention with their own eyes, thus legitimizing it in their minds. A door had been opened.

Another Duryea won a $3,000 prize in a race sponsored by *Cosmopolitan* magazine in May of 1896, and in November of the same year, the same car won the prestigious London to Brighton race. Highly publicized races followed. Alexander Winton, an ex-bicycle manufacturer in Cleveland, entered all sorts of speed and endurance tests to boost both his and his car's reputation, and got results.

Things were stirred up a good deal in July 1899 when the 1,428 mile Tour de France caused considerable comment both in the old world and the new. When a Panhard & Levassor won the race with an average speed of 32 miles an hour, people's eyes were opened up to new potentialities in the speed and endurance of automobiles. After that more and more races were scheduled, with vehicles of every sort crowding onto the racetracks, and drivers seeking to beat out one another for recognition. Even William K. Vanderbilt was racing and winning by September of 1900. (The automobile was firmly established as socially acceptable at Newport under the auspices of Oliver Belmont in 1897, and that cachet naturally spread to society leaders in other locations as well.)

Racing had become a craze, and like it or not, Ford knew that it offered the way to ensure his reputation. "I never really thought much of racing," he later maintained, "but following the bicycle idea, the manufacturers had the notion that winning a race on a track told the public something about the merits of an automobile—although I can hardly imagine any test that would tell less. But as the others were doing it, I, too, had to do it."

To do it, he came up with a 26-horsepower, two-cylinder enclosed engine on a minimal frame, with a board on the hind end for the driver to sit on. Though Ford said he designed the vehicle, it might be more accurate to say he conceptualized it; Oliver Barthel claimed that, for all practical purposes, *he* did the actual designing. "I never knew Henry Ford to design a car. I don't think he could," Barthel later said. But as always, what Ford could do was generate the idea for something, then watch its realization like a hawk, contributing many vital suggestions. He always initiated and bore full responsibility for what turned out, perhaps never more so than this time.

Three prominent automobile men, one of whom was the sales manager of the Winton Motor Carriage Company, Charles B.

Shanks, arranged for an auto race to be held at the Grosse Point racetrack on October 10, 1901; the prize would be $1,000 plus a crystal punch bowl that Shanks picked out because he thought it would look good in Winton's bay window. After most competitors withdrew, mostly due to mechanical problems, it became a two-man race between Ford and Alexander Winton, who drove a 40-horsepower beast called the Bullet.

Winton was the most famous and successful of all American race car drivers. Ford had not only never competed before, he had never even been on a racetrack. And the track itself, recently constructed for horseracing, was a treacherous, uneven affair. Ford, with the devil-may-care Spider Huff (a wild but brilliant drunk) hanging on the running board as human ballast to steady the racer, started out at a great disadvantage, but got the hang of it halfway through the race, gradually gaining on his rival. After Winton's car started smoking and slowing down, Ford's car shot ahead to victory. The crowd went wild to see their local boy make good. Clara said he had covered himself "with glory and dust." Henry said, "Boy, I'll never do that again."

Some of the backers from Ford's old company, thrilled by his victory, came forward to enlist him in a new venture, which was incorporated as the Henry Ford Company by the end of November. This one had a paid-in capital of $30,500 on a total capitalization of $60,000. It also had all the problems of the previous venture: Ford was interested in a new racer, to the neglect of developing a salable model for the public, in large part because once again he was a hired hand and felt he was not given enough profit participation to make his efforts worthwhile. He stuck with the race car because, as he explained, "I expect to make dollars where I can't make (cents) at manufacturing."

There was another element now too. The money men had brought in Henry M. Leland, the man who directed what was perhaps the world's best machine shop, Leland & Faulconer. Leland had spent decades at both the Springfield Armory and the Brown & Sharpe sewing machine company perfecting his uncompromising standards of manufacture. Known as the "Master of Precision" because of his insistence on complete inter-changeability of parts in manufacturing, Leland was as organized and methodical a man as could be found in American industry; he could make parts within a 1/100,000th of an inch tolerance. Needless to say, he was the temperamental opposite of Henry Ford, who was a trial-and-error man, if ever there was one. When Leland bore down on him, a clash was inevitable.

The end came quickly, with Ford "resigning" from the company in March 1902, less than four months after it was started. He got the blueprints of his race car, $900, and an agreement that his name would not be used. Leland designed a one-cylinder motor for the regular car that Ford had been working on and changed the name of the company to Cadillac, for the founder of Detroit. Needless to say, that firm became one of the greatest successes in automotive history. Ford may have been free, but he was to harbor a grudge against Leland that resurfaced decades later. As always with Ford, revenge was a dish best served cold.

Luck was with Ford now, however, for Tom Cooper, the world's most famous bicyclist, and one with considerable cash, joined forces with him to build two almost identical versions of Ford's new racer, one called the Arrow and the other the 999, named after a New York Central train famous for breaking speed records. Cooper, almost unnoticed, had competed in a bicycle race at the same track on the day Ford had won his big victory against Winton, and knew that car racing represented the future. They were both lucky that C. Harold Wills, a true genius at industrial draftsmanship and design, went to work with Ford at that time. He would become a vital part of Ford's future enterprises.

The cars the three men developed were stripped down, rough, bone-rattling beasts, and neither Ford nor Cooper wanted to race them. So Cooper secured the services of Barney Oldfield, a hard-living bicycle racer who had never even driven a motor car before. But Oldfield was fearless, learned quickly, and raced against Winton and others in the Manufacturers Challenge Cup on October 25, 1902, winning handily to great acclaim. Later he remarked that he and Ford had been the making of each other on that day, "But I did much the best job of it."

Ford didn't own the car on the day of the race, having sold it to Cooper. But that was fine with him, because by now he was glad to end their association, as he deemed Cooper to be "sneaky."

Once again, however, old associations and the excitement of newfound fame brought Ford another backer, this time for the commercial vehicle that he had long discussed but never fully realized. While Barthel was working on the racers, Wills was developing a new production vehicle. This featured a vertical, rather than a horizontal, engine, which was far smoother and quieter than anything else on the market. (Most cars of the day banged and rattled unmercifully.)

The backer was Alexander Y. Malcomson, an important 36-year-old Detroit coal merchant whom Ford had known since his Detroit Edison days. A plunger if there ever was one, he had expanded his business considerably from his original one (horse coal wagon) through the use of heavy credit. As he fell under the spell of Ford's new car, he agreed to put up some capital for a partnership to be called Ford & Malcomson, which was formed in August 1902. But since Malcomson, ever strapped for cash, couldn't let his bankers know what he was up to, the accounts were opened in the name of James Couzens, his chief assistant, at a new bank. It was in this way that Ford met the man whose contribution to his enterprises would be second only to his own.

Couzens was a meticulous, tough-minded, and extraordinarily smart man with the soul of an accountant, which was exactly what Ford, his polar opposite in financial matters, needed. Equally strong willed, the two men had entirely different spheres of expertise and influence in the Ford enterprises; yet in their mutual respect for each other's abilities, they rarely clashed.

Malcomson proved to be the only entrepreneur to figure out how to make money out of Ford, mostly by assuring that his partner would make good money out of his own success. But he also dreamed that he would eventually leave the coal business for the automotive one, with Couzens assuming the reins of the former. It did not turn out that way, but without Malcomson's appearance at this crucial juncture, who knows what would have happened to Ford?

Four

The Ford Motor Company

One of the problems the automobile faced in 1903 was that not many people owned them (fewer than 10,000), and not many people had ever even seen one. They had heard about them and read about them, but that was all. The automobile caused a lot of excitement, but it was still a novelty.

One reason for the scarcity was that the technology to build automobiles was as primitive as the vehicles themselves. Another reason was that they were so expensive. An average-priced car cost $1,000, when most people did well to earn a third of that in a year. Then there were the roads, which were so bad that it was hard to use a car outside of city limits.

Ransom Olds was the first to lower the price barrier. His Curved Dash Oldsmobile of 1901 was a simple, attractive, and sturdy one-cylinder buggy that sold briskly for several years at prices of up to $650. Olds was the first manufacturer to go into quantity production, with progressive elements in the way his factory was organized. (The reason he went into production with this particular model was not a matter of choice, however. His factory, containing all his models, burned down, and the Curved Dash was the only one that was pushed out the door and saved during the conflagration.)

The Olds factory was in Detroit, the most motorcar-savvy city in the United States. Originally cars were produced in many parts of the country, but gradually, for reasons of supply, transportation, labor pool, and finance, among other things, car manufacturing was to become concentrated in Detroit.

Ford had an advantage by not having to move there, as did Packard and Olds. In November of 1902, he and Malcomson took a step forward in formalizing their agreement by forming Ford and Malcomson, Ltd. It was capitalized at $150,000 divided among 15,000 shares. The two principals kept 6,900 shares in recognition of their contributions in design, patents, capital, etc., and in addition bought 350 shares for $3,500. The other 7,750 shares were for sale to the public. As Douglas Brinkley points out, like it or not, this meant that "until he had a fortune of his own, (Ford) had to depend on the outside capital he so deplored." This time he had to pay more attention to his backers. The automobile business in America was only three years old, and Ford had already flopped twice. He couldn't afford to do it a third time.

The biggest question for the newly formed company was how Malcomson and Couzens would find investors to put up the cash—investors with "serious money" thought car companies were beneath serious consideration. And it was little wonder; scores of companies came and went in those days, often consisting of nothing more than a shiny prototype (often without an engine), a fancy showroom, and a fast-talking salesman peddling impressive-looking stock certificates. Even companies that managed to struggle into business failed with alacrity.

Ford, Malcomson, and Couzens tried everything they knew to sell shares, but they were constantly discouraged. The first break came when Malcomson bought a coal company and wound up with a lease on an old wagon shop, which he persuaded the owner, contractor Albert Strelow, to convert into an auto assembly factory to be leased at $75 per month. Ford and his assistants moved in and set up shop to get started. Then they set out to find other shops to build their cars.

In those days cars were not so much designed and built from scratch as they were designed and then built by contractors according to the manufacturers' specifications. Or they were simply cobbled together from ready-made parts. For example, the Oldsmobile was only assembled at its own plant. It was actually the work of the machine shop of John F. and Horace E. Dodge, two hardheaded, hard-drinking Irish brothers, whose products were considered first rate. "We made everything but the nameplate" for Olds, they said.

Ford and Malcomson approached the Dodge Brothers to supply the chassis, engine, and transmissions for 650 Ford vehicles. The Dodge Brothers were so enthusiastic about Ford's designs for this first car, the Model A, that they agreed, and signed a contract on February 28, 1903, for a total amount of $162,500, to be paid out in a complex step agreement involving delivery of finished goods. In effect they bet the future of their company on the Ford, for virtually their whole capacity was turned over to its production in the spring of that year.

Bodies and cushions for Ford's cars came from the C. R. Wilson Carriage Company, one of many such companies to switch to auto bodies; wheels came from the Prudden Company, and tires from Hartford Rubber. The total cost of parts and assembly was figured out to be $504, with another $150 added for sales costs. It would sell for $750. With a tonneau, an open rear passenger compartment, which cost the company $50, the car would sell for $850.

Finally the money men came around, though Malcomson had to scrounge to find enough of them, and most were relatives or business associates of one kind or another. There was Malcomson's cousin, Vernon C. Fry (who bought 50 shares), his two impecunious lawyers, Horace H. Rackham and John W. Anderson (50 each), and his uncle, banker John S. Gray (105 shares), who advanced $10,000 at a crucial moment when the Dodge Brothers were owed that sum. Anderson wrote a glowing letter about the enterprise to get money from his father, and Couzens (25 shares), as fired up as anyone, borrowed money himself and even induced his sister Rosetta to invest $100, half her life savings, with him. Albert Strelow bought 50 shares, as did C. H. Bennett, of Daisy Air Rifle fame, and Charles J. Woodall bought 10. The Dodge Brothers, who bought 50 each, contributed materials and a note for their shares. Malcomson and Ford each got 255 shares, representing their contribution for the assets of Ford and Malcomson, Ltd, which they assigned to the new firm.

This new firm was the Ford Motor Company, incorporated on June 16, 1903. It had only $28,000 of paid-in capital (aside from what Malcomson and the Dodge Brothers had laid out). But that may have been a good thing. It ensured that eagle-eyed Couzens would watch every nickel.

He would need to. With money going out for parts, salaries, rent, etc., and not all of the capital yet paid in, it was nip and tuck for the first month and a half; by July 11, the bank balance was down to $223.65, and the situation was only saved by Albert Strelow paying in his $5,000 on that day. But on July 15, a check for the first Model A sale for $850 arrived from a Dr. E. Pfennig of Chicago, and thereafter more orders came in. By August 1, there was a bank balance of $3,831.77, which increased to $23,060.67 by August 20.

Late that year Wills designed the Ford logo, a cartouche with the name Ford written in a beautiful, flowing script on a blue background. In a way it exemplified the company then: It looked like Ford's signature, but the work was someone else's, and it was attractive, simple, and durable. In fact it was so good that it has been used ever since. (Ford always said that if something was good it would be used, but even he couldn't have imagined that this logo would last over 100 years.)

The Model A was efficient, simple, and lightweight, three things that would always be important to Henry Ford; and the eight-horsepower engine that had so impressed the Dodges could propel it to 30 mph. It sold well from the beginning, a good thing, as those first 650 cars had to be built and sold quickly to fulfill the Dodge Brothers' and others' contracts. Ford and Couzens were working 16-hour days seven days a week to make it all work out.

And work out it did, though not without certain conflicts between the two men. At first Ford didn't want to ship out the cars, saying they weren't ready. This was undoubtedly true; in those early days everybody expected, and found, loads of defects in any new car. But Couzens was right in that they were good enough to meet customers' expectations, and he personally accompanied Ford and Wills to the train station to make sure they were shipped, so that he could cash the desperately needed checks for them. According to some accounts, Couzens personally nailed the doors to the boxcars shut so Ford couldn't get at them.

In the end, by March 31, 1904, they beat the original quota of 650 by eight cars, turning a profit of almost $100,000. Sales came close to doubling in the next three months. Most importantly, the company's business paid for itself through sales, rather than by going into debt. This way of doing things was at the heart of what Ford was always to believe was sound business practice. "The place to finance a business is the shop, and not a bank," he said, and he stuck to that. "Money is only a tool in business. It is just part of the machinery."

Interestingly, he was later to characterize the period he had just gone through, from the building of his first car to the founding of the Ford Motor Company, as the happiest time of his life. Despite the struggles and setbacks, he was working hard, learning much, and gradually becoming a man of great accomplishment and usefulness to the world. His failures meant little to him. "Failure is only the opportunity more intelligently to begin again," he said. And success? That was the goad to expand in planning and making things better.

Ford had a restless mind, and not just in business. By this period he was beginning to puzzle out "the meaning of it all." Though he went to church, religion still didn't have a profound effect on him. ("Man has made many gods. How do I know I can find out which, if any, is the genuine one?" he once said. "I won't try. I'll just keep busy.") He didn't read a great deal either ("Books muss up my mind," he averred), but he knew his bible.

Then on the day of President McKinley's funeral in September, 1901, as both men were sitting in shocked silence, Oliver Barthel gave Ford a book he had been reading called *A Short View of the*

Great Questions and Eternalism: A Theory of Infinite Justice
by Orlando Jay Smith. It was in two volumes and touched on
such metaphysical ideas as reincarnation and transcendentalism.
Barthel claimed Ford read avidly, and the two of them spent as
much time talking about philosophy as they did working.

What Ford imbibed from Smith's book, and began to believe,
were ideas about the existence of a universal mind that was constantly sending "brain wave" messages to human beings. This
mind and its knowledge were eternal and indestructible. The
universe was illimitable, time without start or finish. Matter and
spirit were one and the same thing, the latter ceaselessly able to
enhance the former in a seamless symbiosis. Add to this a belief
in reincarnation, and one could see that man himself was not
limited to his present physical being. He was the product of what
he had experienced in past lives, and could improve himself by
tapping into that universal wisdom at the heart of the world.
What became of his life, for good or ill, was determined by what
he did with what was available to him. "Ford believed that each
man possessed an individual genius," writes David E. Nye in *The
Ignorant Idealist*, "bequeathed quite literally from previous in-
carnations." His job was to "look for the single spark of individuality that makes him different from other folks, and develop that
for all it's worth." That was what would determine who he would
become in his next life.

Ford worked very hard on organizing his thoughts; it was at
this time that he began to write his musings and observations
down in "jotbooks," little top-opening spiral notebooks that
he kept with him at all times. He ordered them by the caseload
and wrote in them constantly. (In addition to his thoughts, they
revealed him to be an execrable speller.)

Stasis was a bad thing to Ford, as was reliance on old traditions and ideas; constant movement for improvement was the only way to live. So he was not a Calvinist, believing in a predestined life, or a rationalist, believing in the natural laws of the universe. He subscribed to a third view, that something outside us could change us, if only we were attuned to it. His beliefs made perfect sense in their own way, and they had the virtue of simplicity, which appealed to Ford's streamlined way of thinking.

A sidebar to this was Ford's belief that it was self-evident that men were not equal in their native abilities, for which reincarnation also gave a plausible explanation. Likewise it supported Ford's feeling that those of advanced capabilities had the duty to lead others to make better lives for themselves (without being held back by restraints that might be imposed by the envy or shortsightedness of other, lesser beings). A dozen years later, when Ford embraced the philosophy of Emerson, he would agree with him that "the chief want in life is somebody to make us do what we can do." It was crystal clear to Ford by then that this was his position in the chain of existence.

Intuition also played a big role in Ford's philosophical beliefs. If the important notions one had came from the ether, then logic and improvement from strict mental discipline were not as important as they might be in a more rigorous worldview. Instead what was important was that your mind was attuned to intuit whatever messages the universe was sending your way.

This was wonderful when intuition brought you the Model T or the five-dollar day. But it was not so wonderful when it brought you the Peace Ship to stop World War I or "The International Jew" a few years later, which blamed the world's major problems on a secret conspiracy of coreligionists. Where was the universal mind then? Possibly teaching some lesson you needed to know for your personal growth? Or for the world's growth? It hardly seems so. Well, despite these setbacks, there seemed to be enough intuitive successes for him to remain undaunted.

The significance of all of these philosophical ideas is not their depth or consistency, but the fact that in part they provided the basis for Henry Ford's social engineering, which would have a profound effect on the lives of much of the world's population to this very day.

But now Ford's thoughts were turned onto another kind of engineering—that of a succession of car models that his company would bring out over the next few years. Couzens was establishing a strong dealer network, which had to be supplied with a variety of new models to meet the strong competition from other firms like Olds, Cadillac, and Northern. The Model A runabout morphed into the improved, somewhat more expensive Model C, at $800 ($900 with tonneau). The Model F touring car, a first, was sold for $1,000 (both the C and the F had the original two-cylinder engine, with more horsepower). Then there was a bid for the upscale market with the four-cylinder, 24-horsepower Model B at $2,000. Ford disliked this last one intensely and built it only at Malcomson's insistence. Though far less expensive than a true luxury car, it was moving the line in an upscale direction, which was the opposite of what Ford wanted to build—a $500 car for everyman.

Introduced in early 1904, this top-of-the-line Model B would require another big bang of publicity to generate sales. With this in mind, Ford announced he would race a car with an engine almost identical to the one in the new Model B, with the intention of breaking the world's speed record. To accomplish this feat, he hauled out the Arrow racer that had been built at the same time as the 999 three years before, and brought it to Lake Saint Clair near Detroit on the freezing cold day of January 9. As Oldfield wasn't available, Ford had to do the job himself, once again assisted by Spider Huff. The lake ice on which they drove was filled with fissures, so they were either popped into the air whenever they hit one, or skidded around when they landed, but nevertheless they accomplished their goal of a mile in 36 seconds. Ford also achieved his second goal: a boatload of worldwide publicity.

Dealers, signed up at car shows around the country by Couzens and Ford, snapped up all the Ford cars they could get their hands on, and by the end of September 1904, over 1,700 cars had been sold. In the following year sales and profits ballooned again.

By now a new plant on Piquette Avenue was under construction, to replace Strelow's old place on Mack Street. The board of directors foresaw that the company could expand to produce many more cars and thus authorized construction of a new building of three stories that was ten times bigger than the old one.

Fortunately for the company, it was still self-financing, so profits were not being drained by financing costs and no outside directors were interfering with the way business was being done.

Equally important were some of the new men coming into the company at that time. Chief among them was Charles E. Sorensen, a Dane who entered the company as an assistant pattern maker and over the next 40 years rose to become the production chief. A large, handsome man with an explosive temper, he might not have been liked by everyone, but they all respected him. Joseph Galamb, an extraordinarily talented Hungarian engineer also joined then, as did Fred Diehl, a materials and specifications expert who would rise to become purchasing chief, German engineer Carl Emde, and Oscar C. Bornholdt, who would become chief tool designer. These men were vital to the great work that was to come, though all of them acknowledged that it was Ford himself who set them to their tasks and presided over all the work that was turned out.

There were clouds on the horizon, however, despite all the good news and rapid expansion of the company. The first setback concerned the famous Selden patent, which was a major difficulty for Ford from the time he went into business until his major success with the Model T eight years later.

George B. Selden was a Rochester patent attorney with a mechanical bent who had drawn up plans for an internal combustion automobile and patented it in 1879. Since it was useless at the time because no one was manufacturing cars, and the patent would last for only 17 years, Selden kept updating it until 1895, when auto manufacture was finally becoming a reality. It languished until 1899, when a financial whiz named William Whitney, realizing his investment in the Electric Vehicle Company had gone to the wrong technology, bought the patent from Selden for cash and a royalty participation. After a lawsuit with Winton, Electric Vehicle got the major manufacturers to negotiate a favorable agreement and formed the Association of Licensed Automobile Manufacturers (ALAM) to look after their interests. Frederick Smith, a major Olds investor, was its president.

Ford's company was only five weeks old when newspaper ads began appearing threatening lawsuits against any manufacturers who were not licensed. Ford, who had followed this particular patent, did not believe in patents in general because he thought they shackled, rather than promoted, invention. And in any case he thought that this particular patent was worthless because of its lack of novel elements. Nevertheless he applied for a license to remove what could be an expensive nuisance from his business. Smith, who knew nothing about manufacturing, turned him down twice, saying that Ford did not meet the association's licensing standards, because he made assembled vehicles. After a contentious meeting between Smith and the Ford stockholders, the fight was on. (Ford thought the problem was that he and his people were not in the Detroit "in" crowd and were being persecuted for it.) Ford hired Ralzemond A. Parker, one of the country's best patent attorneys to defend the company, and provoked a lawsuit by publicly saying the patent was worthless. The suit began on October 22, 1903, and dragged on, one way or another, until early 1911.

The trial itself did not begin until May 28, 1909, in New York City District Court, with Judge Charles Merrill Hough presiding. It was the luck of the draw. Hough was almost completely without knowledge of automobiles, manufacturing, or patent law, and he proved a dense and difficult man who had little patience for trying to understand what he didn't know. This made things very hard for the defense attorneys in particular, as they tried to explain what was, and was not, covered by the patent. A major defense argument was that the automobile was but a rearrangement of known mechanical elements, and so not patentable. Ford admitted on the stand that his work on the internal combustion engine was based on the work of others for years, even "centuries." "Had I worked fifty or ten or even five years before, I would have failed. . . . Progress happens when all the factors that make for it are ready, and then it is inevitable. To teach that a comparatively few men are responsible for the greatest forward steps of mankind is the worst sort of nonsense," he stated.

But what sort of engine had been patented was at the heart of this trial. Simply put, Selden had patented a two-cycle Brayton-type engine, which nobody used. Ford's, and everyone else's, was a four-cycle Otto-type engine. Selden's expert witness, Dugald Clerk, testified that if the latter could be proved to work, Selden didn't have a patent. The judge allowed an old-design four-cycle engine to be built, attached to a 1903 Ford, and run, which it did successfully. Two Brayton types were built and barely worked, thus demonstrating their impracticality. Judge Hough didn't get it. To him, internal combustion engines were all the same, no matter what their type, and on September 15, 1909, he ruled in favor of Selden.

The Ford lawyers were disgusted, the Selden people got tough with threatened lawsuits, and Ford retaliated by bonding potential buyers of his vehicles against lawsuits by ALAM, and railed against the Selden trust as an enemy of progress. Privately he was so disillusioned by it all that he negotiated to sell his company to William C. Durant's General Motors for $8 million in cash, "and I'll throw in my lumbago." But the cash didn't materialize due to short-sighted bankers, and the sale didn't happen.

A much simplified appeal trial began on November 10, 1910. Each side had only four and a half hours for a summation, with Ford represented by Frederic Coudert, who took over for Parker. He showed that Dugald Clerk had said that no one had developed the Brayton engine further than Brayton himself, which was a blow to Selden's claims. In the end, the three judges agreed that the internal combustion engine was the product of social invention, whose technology should be available to all. Further ruling in favor of Ford, they agreed that his Otto engine was completely different from Selden's. Finally triumphant, Ford was gracious in victory, even attending the annual ALAM banquet and taking a few puffs of a "peace pipe."

But this victory over the Selden patent was really Ford's second. The first, which consolidated his power as absolute controller of his company's fortunes, had come about almost five years before.

It was a victory over some of his partners, particularly Malcomson. As the car company was becoming successful, Malcomson wanted Couzens back at his coal companies and hoped to take over Couzens's role at Ford himself. This had been his original plan. But Couzens wanted no part of it, and neither did Ford, to Malcomson's surprise, and the board backed him up.

In addition to the growing tension among Malcomson, Couzens, and Ford, there was the matter of what sort of motor cars to sell. Ford wanted cheaper ones for the masses, and Malcomson wanted the company to turn out more luxurious models like their new six-cylinder Model K, a heavy, $2,800 car that Ford hated with a passion. Malcomson's preference was not without some justification at that time, for market preference was in the process of reversing from 1903, when two-thirds of all cars were sold in the under-$1,375 category. Prosperity, urbanization, and a desire for heavier, more reliable vehicles all played a role in reversing sales categories, so that by 1906, half of all cars cost between $2,275 and $4,775. But shrewd people, like the Packard sales manager, foresaw that this trend would not last. Indeed by the middle of the next decade, only 2 percent of all cars sold at those higher prices.

Malcomson wasn't the only one who thought that high-end vehicles were the wave of the future. Fred Smith, Ransom Olds's primary backer and the head of ALAM, thought the same thing. Olds, like Ford, had built an inexpensive people's car that was a top seller. But he was forced out of his company because of Smith's objections. Shortly thereafter, Olds's genius of a sales manager, Roy D. Chapin, left also. Smith's policies, which had a lot to do with his sons' snobbish desires, almost sank the company, while Olds went on to found REO (an acronym of Ransom Eli Olds) and Chapin went on to found the Hudson Motor Company. Indeed, an entire book, *Conspicuous Production: Automobiles and Elites in Detroit, 1899–1933* by Donald Finlay Davis, argues that the automotive executives who produced the luxury vehicles wanted to display their own elite status and wound up ruining themselves and their city, whereas non-status-seeking, lower-class outsiders like Ford ultimately won the day.

Olds's troubles didn't visit Henry Ford. From the beginning of the Ford Motor Company, Ford knew what he wanted. In the 1903 money-raising period, he told John Anderson: "The way to make automobiles is to make one automobile like another automobile, to make them all alike; just as one pin is like another pin when it comes from a pin factory, or one match is like another match when it comes from a match factory." One of the purposes of making every vehicle identical was to make them cheaply, so everyone could afford and use them. Ford also wanted to make vehicles simple, so everyone would be able to operate them. He was determined that no one would stop him from this, and he set about to ensure it.

Ford and Couzens decided to get rid of Malcomson, whom they thought of as meddling, impractical, parasitic, and scattered. Their tool was a new company, the Ford Manufacturing Company, ostensibly formed to cut out the profits made by the Dodge Brothers in manufacturing engines, gears, and other sorts of auto parts. Malcomson was not invited to participate, thus limiting his profits now only to the sales, and not the manufacture, of Ford cars. John Gray made it clear to Vernon Fry, one of the other investors, that it was just a ruse to get Malcomson out. It worked. As profits of the new company skyrocketed, and the old one stalled, and a threatened lawsuit went nowhere, Malcomson saw that it was time to get out. After months of icy negotiations, he sold his one-quarter interest in the Ford Motor Company for $175,000. His staunch allies among the other shareholders, Fry, Charles J. Woodall, and Charles H. Bennett, sold out too. Poor Albert Strelow had already sold his shares to Couzens for $25,000, so he could invest in a goldmine, which ultimately failed. Ford now owned 58.5 percent of the company. He was jubilant.

As Nevins and Hill, Ford's great official biographers, point out, he had every reason to be: "The company was his in fact as well as name. He could assert his will in its affairs to an extent seldom exemplified in the greater American corporations, far more completely than Rockefeller had ever wished or tried to do in Standard Oil, more completely even than Carnegie had done in his steel company." Ford bragged to his assistant Fred Rockelman on the way home on July 6, 1906, the day of his independence, "We're going to expand this company, and you will see that it will grow by leaps and bounds. The proper system, as I have it in mind, is to get the car to the people." He saw his automobile as a way of joining together all sorts of peoples, "so they get acquainted with one another, and get an idea of neighborliness...we won't have any more strikes or wars."

Ford's new car for 1906–1907 was to be a $500 runabout, the Model N, much improved over the previous inexpensive models. In the end it cost $600, but it was still probably the best value on the market. It took time to get the bugs ironed out, but when they were, sales of the N, along with slightly snazzier versions of it, the R and the S, plus the slow-selling K, quintupled over the previous year's models to 8,243. In part this was possible through the efforts of Max Wollering, the director of assembly, and Walter E. Flanders, the production manager, who was perhaps the most knowledgeable man in plant design and management anywhere at that time.

The most important thing about the Model N though, good as it was, was that it moved Ford closer to his real dream of a universal car. Already he was down to one type of chassis, and all the other components would soon be standardized too. He was also assembling the staff that would make it possible to build the vehicle he wanted.

He was getting clearer and clearer about what that was. In 1907, he characterized his vision as a four-cylinder car of unchanging standardized design, the production volume of which would steadily grow because its costs were so low that its price could be steadily reduced. As he had told Sorensen, he wanted to produce an automobile his workers could buy.

In the end Ford would achieve his goal, but in 1907, there was no way he could have known how he could turn a company straining every resource to assemble 8,200 cars a year into one capable of building two million 15 years later. True, by now he had an inkling of how this transformation would occur. It was still a matter of vision, observation, hard work, planning, and above all...intuition.

The universal car was still an ideal. Before it could be built it had to be brought from the world of that ideal into reality. Now Henry Ford was ready to do that.

FIVE

THE MODEL T AND THE COMING OF MASS PRODUCTION

There is only one thing stronger than great armies,
and that is an idea whose time has come.

—Henry Ford

THE MODEL T WAS DESIGNED IN A SMALL ROOM—12 BY 15 FEET—on the third floor of the Piquette Avenue factory by a group of top-flight men whom Ford had put together for his company. The idea for the revolutionary vehicle was formulated by Ford sometime in the beginning of 1907 (although it may have started earlier), according to Joseph Galamb, who was in charge of the engineering department. What Ford brought to the Model T was a sense of what it should be. The others worked in their specialties to design and work out various aspects of the car, but the Model T itself was his conception, and he supervised every aspect of it from a rocking chair in that small room hour by hour, day by day. "Ford's genius, if such it was, worked by adding a dimension, namely the sense of a whole machine," as Douglas Brinkley says.

The rocking chair in which Ford spent so many countless hours had belonged to his mother.

About half a dozen men and Ford began with drawings on a blackboard, then blueprints for the new car's parts. The Model T's basis was the Model N, every part of which, except for the dual braking system, Ford thought could be improved. As time went on the little room became ever more crowded with drawings, parts models, drill presses, lathes, and people. Ford sat in the middle of it all, insisting, goading, and guiding his team.

The main thing Ford wanted was a light car. People who wanted heavy cars were wrong, he felt. Weight was good for steamrollers, but only lightness could give you speed and maneuverability. So part of the job was to find a lighter steel, as so much of it was used in car manufacture.

Ford wanted the car to be light, but it also needed to be durable. The solution turned out to be an alloy, vanadium steel, which was stronger, lighter, and more resistant to corrosion than other steel alloys. Ford claimed he had found it himself, picking up a small part made of it from the wreckage of a French racer in Palm Beach in 1905. But others, including Sorensen and John Wandersee, a shop sweeper whom Ford decided to make his metals expert, claimed that it was Wills—the man who had designed the Ford logo—who first heard of it through a consulting metallurgist from Pittsburgh named J. K. Smith, and had it tested. In the long run, vanadium steel proved less than ideal for the various uses to which it was put; often it was replaced by such ordinary material as properly heat-treated manganese carbon steel for various items. But that was done quietly, as vanadium steel had been widely promoted to the public as a star performer. It was indeed strong and lightweight, though, and with 50 percent of it made from vanadium steel, the Model T was a five-passenger touring car instead of a two-passenger runabout, as the Model N was, although they both weighed 1,200 pounds.

Joe Galamb did an incredible job over a six-month period turning the planetary transmission Ford had been using into one that was far better in terms of performance and reliability. Spider Huff made a much better magneto, which supplied the electric spark to the plugs, so much so that the Model T gained a reputation for remaining in operation once started no matter what—quite a novelty then.

The T engine contained several innovations. The four cylinders were cast in one block, rather than two by two, and the cylinder head was detachable. Motor, flywheel (the rotating device that stored energy and had 16 magnets on it, one of Ford's ideas), and transmission were enclosed together, allowing for shared lubrication systems. The lightness and the strength of this design allowed the car to be powerful too, which was the third requirement Ford insisted on for this automobile.

The Model T was designed with a body high off the ground, so it could deal with the muddy, rutted roads that were commonplace at the time. Furthermore, the frame was extremely flexible, which was an enormous asset, as motorcars of the day had to roll over considerable roadway obstacles and drive through holes and ditches. The three-point suspension of the motor was also a help, as it prevented distortion of the motor base on bad roads.

Finally the Model T was the first ordinary production car to feature left-hand steering. As roads got better, it was becoming more important for drivers to see oncoming traffic, rather than perilous ditches by the side of the road.

Once it was completed, Ford was ecstatic. When the first Model T was rolled out into the street, he had an assistant drive him all over the main roads downtown, being sure not to miss a triumphal drive-by of ex-partner Malcomson's office. Grinning from ear to ear, he exclaimed to his associates, "Well, I guess we've got started."

"Started" was exactly the right word for it. They had just started on a project so vast that it would need the Ford Motor Company's constant attention until the last Model T rolled off the line 19 years later.

Ford himself may have been the right man at the right time to do this job, but if he hadn't also surrounded himself with the right men in every department, he might never have been able to realize his dream. When you use terms like "the universal car" and "utility for the common Man," you are making large statements. Such a big mission requires first-rate organization and manpower on a huge scale. So you must be more than a dreamer yourself; you must also be able to weigh and recognize the capabilities of others very shrewdly. You must also be lucky, and Henry Ford was all these things to an extraordinary degree.

Walter Flanders and his assistant Thomas S. Walborn had laid out the machinery in the Piquette plant on a rational basis, according to the operation performed on a part, rather than the type of machine that performed it; Max Wollering had done a great job in supervising production. Everyone learned a great deal from Flanders; he was an old-fashioned Yankee (Vermont) mechanic, with a healthy respect for interchangeability of parts. That respect was conveyed to, and avidly appreciated by, Ford, who insisted it become a mainstay of his operation. He immediately understood the virtue of this kind of simplicity. Factory layout was another of Flanders's many areas of expertise. Even Sorensen paid tribute to Flanders, noting that even though he left Ford before the Model T, "he had created a greater awareness that the motorcar business is a fusion of three arts—the art of buying materials, the art of production, and the art of selling."

But despite their success at Ford, by early 1908, all three—Walborn, Wollering, and Flanders—had left for the chance to get involved in producing cars at a new company called E-M-F, which was Flanders with two partners, William A. Metzger and Barney F. Everitt; this firm would be absorbed into Studebaker before very long. P. E. Martin and the up-and-coming Sorensen replaced these men at Ford, with great competence.

Sorensen played a key role when it came time to consider making some parts out of pressed steel, rather than from castings. He had known the John R. Keim Stamping Company, which made bicycle parts in Buffalo, where he grew up. When William Smith, one of the owners, suggested to Henry Ford that stamped rear axle housings could be better and cheaper than common cast ones, Ford agreed, and set Sorensen to using pressed steel whenever possible in the cars. The arrangement worked out so well that in 1911, Ford purchased the Keim Company and shipped all the machinery to Highland Park. With the company came several more talented engineers, most notably William Knudsen, who would run Ford's assembly plants in other cities and one day become president of General Motors.

Another key individual to go with the E-M-F group was E. Roy LePelletier, who had come to Ford in 1907, and was an extremely creative advertising man. The phrase "Watch the Fords Go By," which the firm used successfully for years, was his idea. But he found Ford's way of doing business disconcerting. LePelletier had just a tiny staff and no defined budget. (Ford detested the strictures of accounting; one day he walked into that department, threw the bills out the window, and told the workers to put the money in a barrel and reach in to pay what was necessary.)

And then there was Norval A. Hawkins, an ex-con embezzler of such charm that people waited outside the prison to wish him well when he emerged. Hawkins was hired in 1907, when the responsibility for both finances and marketing became too much for Couzens. The Ford Motor Company learned about Hawkins through his own company, which gave efficiency advice to big firms; nowadays we would call him a consultant. He began the *Ford Times*, a house publication chock-full of articles about everything from car design, the work of branch managers, and buyer testimonials, to uplifting editorials on hard work and enthusiasm. He also encouraged rivalry among the various Ford sales agencies; this was very successful in moving autos out of the showrooms.

In an era of expansion, Hawkins's success in this area was vital, for sales estimates determined production schedules. Because he was so good at what he did, he was given a free hand in organizing the rather chaotic and fast-growing Ford enterprise. As Nevins and Hill say, "Hawkins did an important work in promoting plan and order throughout the whole business area—purchasing, stockpiling, distribution, bookkeeping and selling." He even paid meticulous attention to how many of various Ford parts could be loaded into boxcars, a great financial savings when figured out correctly. But the main thing Hawkins did was to market the cars, which he did so well that even the crusty Couzens grudgingly approved of him. After all, not only did he sell the cars, he also took the greatest pains to see that things were done as cheaply as possible throughout the business.

Hawkins was lucky that Couzens had been his predecessor, for it was Couzens who had established the Ford network of much-sought-after dealerships. These dealerships were spotlessly clean and well thought out. The service areas were enclosed and separate from the showrooms, so that customers never had to see defective or broken-down cars being repaired. Parts were plentiful and mechanics were well trained. Dealers had to pay 50 percent down on cars they ordered, with the balance due when they arrived at the dealership. But there was such a demand for them, and deliveries were so reliable that everyone wanted a Ford franchise. If a dealer didn't do what he was supposed to do, Ford would replace him with someone else. Hawkins may have had to find ways to whip those dealers into a selling frenzy, but he didn't have to start from scratch.

Couzens had his hands full keeping the Ford financial house in order, though he was lucky to be aided by Frank L. Klingensmith, an accountant of the very best quality. Couzens had both foresight and determination to keep things running well in good times and bad. In the fall of 1907, when a panic swept out from Wall Street to the rest of the country, Couzens came up with a neat trick. He shipped cars from the factory to the dealers, whether they had ordered them or not, insisting they be paid for. (Ford had been financing itself though advance payments all along, but never before on unordered merchandise.) The dealers naturally complained loudly, but Couzens's financial pressure made them sell cars as quickly as they could, which made for prosperity for both them and the company. Henry Ford would remember this during another downturn years later, to his great advantage. It was not for nothing that Sorensen called the first six years of the Ford Motor Company "the Couzens years."

From the date of the announcement of the Model T on March 19, 1908, it became apparent that the company had a tiger by the tail. Agents were astonished at what was on offer. When the public saw the first ad for the five-passenger, four-cylinder 20-horsepower touring car, and its amazingly affordable $850 price, they went crazy over it, placing some 15,000 orders in a matter of days. And therein lay a big problem. The Piquette Avenue plant was an old-fashioned assembly factory, not tooled for Ford parts manufacturing, which was being done at another plant on Bellevue Avenue. Piquette couldn't produce the new model in sufficient numbers to match the orders for it. All the rearranging and expansion that could be done at Piquette wouldn't make it up to the task. If the orders were going to be filled at the rate they were being placed, a new factory would have to be built.

But actually Ford had been planning this for years, realizing the necessity of a proper facility to accommodate his new product. It was an enormous help that by the time the need became a reality, he had decided to build only one chassis (for the Model T), which made it much easier to for Sorensen, et al., to design and build or procure new single- or special-purpose machine tools. This, and the accuracy and speed with which these tools were made to work, was the essential element of mass production. Martin and Sorensen were to lay them out with meticulous attention to detail when they were installed in the new factory, in a progressive, if not yet integrated, manner.

In 1906, Ford bought 60 acres in Highland Park on Detroit's northern edge, on the site of the Highland Park racetrack. When he was ready, he turned to the leading architect of automobile factories of the day, perhaps any day, Albert Kahn, to design his new plant. A few years younger than Ford, he had turned to industrial design in 1903, when he received the commission to design a 40-acre complex for the Packard Motor Car Company on East Grand Boulevard in Detroit. He probably got the commission in part because leading architects of the day thought designing factories was beneath their dignity. But Kahn loved the spare logic and aesthetics that went into designing them, as he loved machines, "for the absence of all not absolutely required for the performance of its works."

It was with the tenth building on the Packard site that Kahn made his mark. It was made of poured concrete reinforced with steel rods, and consequently very few interior columns. A good deal of window space made it very light and bright, very much the modern sort of factory building that would become pervasive in the 20th century.

Kahn was just the sort of man for Ford: flexible and forward-thinking, glad to meet the challenges of the rapidly expanding automotive industry. When the two first met at the Highland Park site, Ford talked about some sketches he had made, and Kahn threw out some of his own notions, but as was his usual practice at this stage with a client, he mostly listened. What Ford wanted was something that had never been done before, and together, with great mutual enthusiasm, they figured out a way for Kahn to give him what he wanted. Kahn told Ford to make a layout of his machinery and the flow of his materials, and then said that he would construct a building around it. In doing that, he said he would make sure that "all noses should be pointed in the same direction."

It would be known as the Crystal Palace, a four-story, 865-foot long, 75-foot wide building with huge windows (50,000 square feet of them) in every wall (75 percent of the wall space was glass) and an enormous glass roof. The main reason Ford wanted a glass structure was practical: to eliminate wasted movement, for if there is lots of light in a building, you can put machines closer together, and operations take up less time, energy, and space; hence they cost less. As a side bonus, this design permitted much better ventilation for the workers, increasing their general health and well-being.

The building was also rationally designed, with raw materials entering on the top floor, and gradually descending to the lower floors where they were forged and machined into parts. On the bottom level, they were joined with bodies and assembled into cars. Shortly after opening the plant, Kahn built a single-story, sawtooth glass-roofed building, 840 by 57 feet, next to it; this served as the principal machine shop. A huge glass-roofed craneway (860 by 57 feet) was between them, and all floors in both buildings were open to it, so that materials could be easily moved from one building to the other. The craneway was the major distribution point of raw materials for the Model T.

The Highland Park factory would be the first of some 1,000 commissions Ford would give to Kahn, despite the fact that after 1920, Kahn, who was Jewish and the son of a rabbi, wouldn't go near the Ford works. Ford's Antisemitism truly revolted him, though it did not prevent Kahn from working for him, nor did Kahn's being Jewish affect Ford's decision to hire him. They were both practical, hardheaded businessmen, and they needed each other.

Ford threw open the doors to anyone who wanted to see his new factory (it opened on New Year's Day of 1910), and to his credit he was glad if businessmen would get ideas from it to apply to their own companies, which many did. As his fight over the Selden patent had shown, Ford believed in the free dissemination of new ideas, as he thought they were catalysts for social growth. Also, opening his Crystal Palace to visitors was great free publicity. The crowds who streamed through his factory became enthusiastic promoters of Ford products and Ford ideas. He also welcomed journalists and other writers to educate the public about his operation. In 1913, Fred Colvin wrote an invaluable series of articles, liberally illustrated with photographs, for *American Machinist,* describing the Ford works in great detail. Two years later, Horace L. Arnold and Fay L. Faurote wrote a study called *Ford Methods and Ford Shops*, which became a of its kind and had a wide contemporary influence.

Though customers were enthralled by the Model T from the start, in no small part because of its $850 price tag, that price was somewhat deceiving; if you wanted such niceties as a windshield, top, and lights, they would cost $135 more. But within a year, these items were standard for $950 total, in effect a price reduction. It was the beginning of another principle of Henry Ford's: to use the savings from economies of scale to reduce the price of his car so that it could be put into the hands of an ever-widening public. To be the universal car, Ford knew that it had to be universally affordable. He thought that every time he cut the price by one dollar, he gained a thousand new customers. Ironically, though this meant he was making less money per vehicle, the economies of scale worked there for him too, for his total profit on operations grew exponentially. Essential to it all was that the cost of every aspect of production had to be minutely inspected and rigidly controlled.

Production and sales began a rapid ascent in 1910 as, true to Ford's word, prices nosedived. As the price of the Model T skidded from $780 down to $360 between 1910 and 1916, sales increased from about 20,000 to nearly 600,000. The Model T was clearly transforming the motorcar from a rich and middle-class man's prerogative to a utilitarian commodity for everyone. And Ford and his stockholders made money like never before. Profits rose from $4.1 million in calendar year 1910 to $57.1 million in fiscal year 1916. But though production expanded rapidly through 1912, it was in 1913, when various aspects of assembly line technique were introduced, that production and profits began to explode.

According to Sorensen, the assembly line began as a series of Sunday experiments at the factory in July 1908, with Sorensen, Martin, Wills, and Charles Lewis, an assembly foreman, pulling a chassis along an improvised line with a rope and adding things to it at stations along the way until it was completed—all under the watchful eye of Ford. If true, and various contemporary accounts confirmed it (albeit with differing dates), this experiment in assembly line production was quite primitive. Wills and Martin were opposed to it, and it was left to languish as an idea for some time. Finally it was required, when close to 200,000 cars needed to be built in 1913.

In any case, it was hardly a new notion. Some historians argue that the pyramids were built on a form of assembly line, and it is well known that in the 15th century ship hulls were outfitted in a progressive way in a short period of time at the Venice Arsenal.

The modern assembly line did not spring full blown from the head of Zeus. Apart from those early predecessors, it was figured out by studying various processes and techniques that had been used in other industries for quite some time. Oliver Evans's Automatic Flour Mill, which managed a complete flour-milling operation with such things as gravity feeds and chutes, came into being in the late 18th century. Edwin Norton, who organized both the American Can Company and the Continental Can Company in the early 20th century, created automatic can-making machinery by 1885, using both special-purpose machinery and a conveyor system. In 1890, Westinghouse Air Brake developed a process for moving molds to pourers along a conveyor system, thus integrating manufacturing and conveyance. Breweries did something similar. Perhaps most influential of all was the meatpacking industry, which was like the assembly line in reverse, disassembling pigs into pork products by using first trolleys, then gravity-operated conveyors, slides, and strategically placed workers in a progressive manner. Whether at Ford's initiative or his own, William Klann, the head of the engine department at Ford, certainly studied this kind of operation at Swift & Company in Chicago.

As to the matter of conveyors, chutes, and slides, many men, including Wollering, claimed they existed at Ford as early as 1908. But David Hounshell notes that Colvin's exhaustive illustrated articles on the Ford plant in 1913 show no evidence or discussion of such things. This suggests that these items were introduced rather late, and wholesale, as the need for them became clear when various moving assembly lines began to appear throughout the factory. Ford himself said the company did not keep records, as he didn't believe in them. Events simply progressed too quickly to waste time memorializing them. Nevertheless, it is clear that to keep production moving quickly and smoothly, these items were essential and had to be omnipresent by the time lines were pervasive throughout the plant. They alone were estimated to save 30 percent of assembly time.

Though accounts differ, it appears that the first assembly line at Ford was a flywheel magneto subassembly, which began operation on April 1, 1913. For the first time, instead of each worker assembling a complete unit at his own bench, he performed only one operation before moving an item down to the next worker, who did the same, and so on, until the item was complete. Everyone at Ford knew they were onto something, although it took awhile for them to work out the flaws in the system. The height of the line had to be adjusted to keep workers from developing back pain; safeguards had to be installed (there was a bad accident on the second day when one of the pieces fell off the conveyor belt); items had to be properly spaced; and most important, because this was a coordinated group effort, the pace had to be the right one: to speed up slow workers and slow down the swift; this was done by moving the line along at a set pace on an endlessly moving chain. Immediately, the time of assembly for each piece dropped from 20 minutes to 13 minutes and 10 seconds. Within a year, the number of workers assembling flywheel magnetos on the line dropped from 29 to 14, and the time of assembly dropped to five minutes.

Soon other aspects of transmission assembly went on the line, with similar results. The technique was so successful that it began to spread like wildfire throughout the plant. By November, the complete engine assembly was put online, cutting assembly time by 60 percent. By August 1913, experimentation began on Sorensen's old dream of chassis assembly on the line, which is what most people think of as *the* assembly line. It took 12.5 hours to assemble a chassis before it went on the line; the very first crude attempt reduced that number to 5 hours and 45 minutes. By April 1914, the time was down to 93 man minutes. From the beginning, there was never any hesitation about using this technique. As Klann said, "There wasn't any discussion on whether this would work. You couldn't go wrong because the first one worked."

Perhaps the most important man in figuring out how it all would work was Clarence Avery, a high school shop teacher who had instructed Edsel Ford. Under Sorensen, he spent eight months mastering every type of manufacturing operation at Highland Park, complete with motion and time studies, and once he had done this, he and Sorensen began to lay out the chassis assembly. It was Avery who came to be called "The Father of the Assembly Line." As he said, "It was my good fortune to have (been assigned) the problem of developing the first continuous automobile assembly line." (And to have had the brains to figure it out.)

For close to a hundred years, there has been debate over whether the work of Frederick W. Taylor influenced Ford, because his techniques seemed to be essential to the development of the assembly line. Taylor was the man who created time and motion studies intended to eliminate wasteful motions in factories through rational study of the work, and selection of workmen for certain tasks in a scientific manner, in a process that came to be known as "Taylorism." On the surface of it, Taylorism seems to be exactly what Ford was doing, especially since Taylor's *Principles of Scientific Management* (which was closely studied by Avery and others at Ford) appeared in 1911, just a short time before the assembly line began at Highland Park. In reality, however, Ford's assembly line really wasn't the same thing. Under Taylor, one studied an operation to see how it could be done better. Under Ford, one studied whether or not it should be done at all.

At Ford, nothing was a given. There was constant experimentation, with materials (why worry about cast metal if a better job could be done with pressed steel?), machinery (why worry about how to make a machine tool function better if you could develop a better, more efficient machine tool?), and labor (why worry about how a man could do a job better if a machine could do it more efficiently than he could?), among other things. As Hounshell puts it, "Taylor took production hardware as a given, and sought revisions in labor processes and the organization of work; Ford engineers mechanized work processes and found workers to feed and tend their machines." Taylor also thought workers should be given an incentive to efficiency through piece-rate payments. Ford abhorred this, believing it disrupted the manufacturing process with unequal performance of work. In fact, as far as he was concerned, how people should be compensated for their labor shouldn't be guided by human elements. Rather, it was machines that should determine it. Taking this to its logical conclusion, he was to come up with a system of pay that was far more generous and forward-looking than anything that had existed before.

Ford came from a world where mechanical skill was highly prized and compensated. It made for great inequality in the workplace. One of his greatest innovations was to reverse that state entirely. He did not want skill in the great majority of his employees. He wanted a few men of exceptional abilities (toolmakers, experimental workers, machinists, and pattern makers) to put skill into machines so that, with highly skilled planning and management, people of unequal skills or even no skills could operate them. A job was not left to chance, because it was standardized; there were to be no fitters in the factory.

Ford wanted democratization of work. He held it to be self-evident that all men were *not* equal, but that every man had the right to work and to participate equally in the economic benefits of his labor. And by "all men," he meant "all men," even the ill, disabled, the criminal, the unintelligent, the unschooled, and those who could not speak English, and yes, even women. "I think that if an industrial institution is to fill its whole role, it ought to be possible for a cross-section of its employees to show about the same proportions as a cross-section of society in general," he said. This egalitarian notion of work was only possible because he and his system had created the most egalitarian type of work. One man had one part of one job to do, and no more. People could be brought in off the street and taught a job, in semaphore if necessary, in as little as a few hours, and presto, they were a part of the workforce. Because there was no skill in it, only repetition, each job on the line was just as valuable as any other.

But there were problems, severe ones, in the Ford factory. The men hated the work, finding it soulless and dehumanizing. Then there was the matter of the plant atmosphere. Writer Julian Street described it as "but one thing, and that was delirium"; the sound alone was like "a million sinners groaning as they were dragged to hell…at the very edge of Niagara Falls." By 1913, Ford had to hire 963 men to add 100 to his workforce. Like Lincoln emancipating the slaves, it took some time, adjustment, and observation in a period of crisis to lead him to come to the right conclusion.

It would seem the old Zen maxim that when the student is ready, the master is at hand applies in this instance. During 1912, Henry became acquainted with the works of the dean of American naturalists, the 75-year-old John S. Burroughs, an author and poet who was a great follower of the philosophy of Thoreau and especially Ralph Waldo Emerson. In a burst of enthusiasm for the old man's works, out of the blue, Ford sent him a Model T at Christmas (one of some 200 or so cars he gave away during his lifetime). When the men shortly became very good friends, Burroughs introduced him to Emerson's essays. Ford found an immediate connection with Emerson's idea that God is innate, that we each have our own genius within that can be released by retreating from too much rationality and giving in to our more erratic, but also more creative, impulses. This was a blueprint for how Ford had lived his life. Building on ideas he had begun to develop as a young man reading Orlando Jay Smith, Ford devoured more and more of Emerson's works, including *Self Reliance* and *On Justice*. Though they all seem to have had a profound effect on him, it was the essay *On Compensation* (which addressed labor and wages) that affected him most deeply.

"Human labor, through all its forms...is one immense illustration of the perfect compensation of the universe. The absolute balance of Give and Take, the doctrine that everything has its price—and if that price is not paid, not that thing, but something else is obtained," Emerson wrote.

Ford was well aware that huge profits were being made and distributed to his investors, of which he was the largest, and that concerned him. Until reforms went into effect in 1913, pay scales for different jobs were still unequal, and as a result jobs were for the most part underpaid. On October 1, 1913, a pay raise averaging 13 percent across the board was announced; minimum pay was set at $2.34 a day. It didn't do much good. By December 31, a bonus of 10 percent of yearly salary was given to any employee who had been with the company more than three years. Only 640 out of a workforce of 15,000 qualified— just 4 percent of the total. Ford was getting "something else" for the wages he was paying if he couldn't hold on to his laborers. Something had to be done.

"Always pay," Emerson admonished. "For first or last you must pay your entire debt.... He is great who confers the most benefits. He is base—and that is the one base thing in the universe— to receive favors and render none.... Beware of too much good staying in your hand. It will fast corrupt, and worms worm."

Did Henry Ford use *On Compensation* as his primer as he approached his labor problems in late 1913? Nobody knows for sure, as he didn't start writing about Emerson until some time later. But considering how well this reading applied to what came next, it seems likely. That was the spectacular, world-shaking five-dollar-a-day wage, perhaps still the most important piece of social engineering ever instituted in the field of labor. It was also the final step in the process of creating the system of mass production.

Henry Ford of course claimed the credit for thinking up this overhaul of the pay system. So did James Couzens. Important figures at Ford, including John R. Lee and John Dodge, backed up Couzens's claim in court testimony. So did the Reverend Samuel S. Marquis (about whom more shortly) in his writings. But Sorensen claimed it was Ford who started it, with some of his own help; he backed this up by saying that he was there when the idea was first floated. It certainly fit in with Ford's ideas at the time. As Brinkley says, both camps may have been right, each in their own way. Ultimately, whoever's idea it was initially, what matters most is the enormous change that resulted from it.

In the first few days of 1914, either Ford came to Couzens with the notion of increasing wages dramatically; or Ford consulted with Sorensen, who showed him how ever-expanding production could pay for this; or Couzens brought the idea to Ford. At any rate, a meeting was called among Ford, Couzens, Martin, Sorensen, Wills, Lee from personnel, and Hawkins to discuss the labor problem. (In addition to the turnover among employees, there was a growing threat of unionization.) It was here that the wage increase was discussed. Figures from $3.50 a day to $5 a day were put on a blackboard and talked about. Some of the new figure was to be derived from wages, and some from profit participation for the workers, paid in advance; if that didn't work out, wages would revert to the status quo ante. Additionally, the new figure was a minimum wage; highly skilled employees would earn more. At last Ford agreed to or proposed the five-dollar figure, and on January 5, 1914, at a meeting consisting of Ford, Couzens, and Horace Rackham, it was adopted, along with a cut from a nine-hour day to an eight-hour day, plus a policy about hiring handicapped workers. All this was to take effect on January 12, 1914.

There was something else happening with Henry Ford at that time. In the next few years he would be concerned about bettering the lives of those who worked for him, in a proactive, egalitarian way. He wanted men to receive compensation in the truest Emersonian sense, beyond the value of money alone. "We want to make men in this factory as well as automobiles," he would later say. Some have argued in retrospect that it was paternalism designed purely to manipulate the lives of his workers, to control their wages though the application of a company-determined standard of personal conduct.

Nevertheless, David Hounshell would one day be able to say that the Model T was arguably the most influential piece of new technology to appear since the printing press, because its effects were so pervasive throughout society.

Six

Peace and War and Consolidating Power

THE ANNOUNCEMENT OF THE FIVE-DOLLAR DAY FOR EIGHT HOURS of work on January 5, 1914, created pandemonium. Business leaders around the country were shocked. A board meeting at Packard broke up when the news came in; directors despaired of being able to match these wages. Others predicted bankruptcy from such a policy. The *Wall Street Journal* wrote that what Ford had done was "to apply Biblical principles into a field where they do not belong." The more popular presses saw it differently, however. "World Economic History Has Nothing to Equal Ford Plan," proclaimed one; "A Magnificent Act of Generosity," said another; "God Bless Henry Ford," opined a third.

By the following morning 10,000 men, some raggedly dressed in a depression- ravaged city, were lined up in 10-degree weather outside the Ford plant looking for jobs. By mid-January, 15,000 people were assembled there daily, more and more arriving every day from other cities hoping to find work at Ford. Eventually a near riot took place, and the Highland Park police department resorted to turning fire hoses on men in 9- degree weather.

Everybody wanted the kind of prosperity that Ford offered. Workers got a big wage boost. Ford in return got their loyalty and their new enthusiasm to do a better, more efficient job. However, it was not entirely a workers' paradise. The new wage was accompanied by a speed-up on the line, and some prospective employees could be hired for six months at a much lower rate; it also took some time for the five-dollar wage to be implemented. Ford was justified when he later said he thought it was the best cost-cutting move he ever made. And he also got a new market among his own workers for his products. Industry got a new way to produce goods at a much faster rate. And merchants and real estate people in Detroit got a bonanza from the newly prosperous workers.

Some of the merchants complained though. When various local stores got too greedy and jacked up their prices, Ford established a group of 11 commissary shops near his factory to sell high-quality goods of all kinds—from food to clothing and household items—at bargain prices. As with everything else at Ford, this progenitor of both the modern supermarket and the Wal-Mart style of super discount store made a profit. As word got out, not only Ford employees but people of all kinds descended on the shops to take advantage of what they offered. After awhile, however, many local merchants complained too loudly, and the stores were restricted to Ford employees.

Ford made money on everything in his plants, including the waste products of the industrial processes. Gas from the coke process was used to dry paint. Benzol was used as a motor fuel.

Ammonium sulfate was used to make fertilizer. Small pieces of coke were sold to the employees to heat their homes. Even the sweepings from the factory floor had a use: The charcoal briquette was invented by Ford workers trying to figure out a use for them. And Ford himself knew every dollar that such things created. It all fit in with one of the cornerstones of his business philosophy and his personality—an abhorrence of waste of any kind. Waste, whether human or inanimate, meant loss, and that to him was a terrible shame. Worst of all was a waste of time, for there was no recovery from that.

Ford's paternalism was also apparent from the start. Employees had to meet certain standards to obtain the new five-dollar wage, and the Sociological Department set up by John R. Lee insured that those standards were met. First off, workers had to be local residents for a minimum of six months, and then they had to work for the company for six months. The wage was to be paid to three categories of workers: married men living with their families and known to be taking good care of them; single men who were at least 22 and known to be thrifty; and men under 22 years of age and women of any age who were the sole support of next of kin or blood relatives. Men under 22 also had to prove they were "sober, saving, steady, and industrious." Because all workers were thoroughly investigated by a force that eventually grew to 150 people who visited their homes to make sure they met the standards, it actually took until the summer of 1914 for the new wages to go into effect for 70 percent of the workers.

Ford had good reason for this sort of oversight. The objective of the five-dollar day was to create an alert and efficient workforce. The circumstances in which many of the Ford employees lived were conducive to anything but this. Many were housed in terrible hovels or slums. They squandered their money on drink, gambling, and prostitutes, leaving their families without any means of support for their daily needs. Overcrowding was conducive to crime and sickness, which were rampant in Detroit's working-class neighborhoods. And because many spoke little or no English, they were constantly exploited by predators looking to take advantage of the new prosperity flowing from the Ford Motor Company.

Hence these visits were made by the Sociological Department—inquiries were opened, and standards were enforced. If they were not met, the profit-sharing portion of the wage was impounded until such time as improvement could be seen. If that never happened, those sums were supposedly given to charity. In any event, the daily domestic lives of those who did comply were improved. And within two years 90 percent of all Ford workers qualified for the full five-dollar-a-day wage, including women.

Another paternalistic Ford policy encouraged the immigrant men working there to learn English and become naturalized citizens. Knowledge of English was essential for the latter, which went a long way to discourage workers from remaining in the ethnic enclaves that circumscribed their lives, often in conditions of poverty, isolation, ignorance, and exploitation. It meant they could participate more fully in American life. It also helped maintain factory discipline, for a great deal of time was saved by a workforce who understood orders in English. (At one point 58 nationalities of Ford workers spoke over 70 languages and dialects.)

Non-English-speaking workers were therefore required to take group lessons, either before or after their shifts. They participated in a program set up by Dr. Peter A. Roberts from Berlitz. He trained office and supervisory personnel from Ford, who taught on a voluntary, uncompensated basis. At the conclusion of the course, a ceremony took place in which the workers in the garb of their native countries descended from a stage into a symbolic "melting pot," from which they emerged dressed as Americans in stiff collars, ties, and suit jackets to receive a certificate attesting to their newfound status as English speakers. As they did this they carried little American flags and sang "The Star Spangled Banner."

The program worked out very well. Two-thirds of Ford workers were non-citizens in 1914; two years later, in a much larger work force, half were U.S. citizens. Home values of Ford workers increased 900 percent in the two years after the beginning of 1914, and the amount of home equities and bank accounts combined rose from $196 to $750.

In time John Lee was succeeded by the Reverend Marquis, an urbane, compassionate man completely committed to the uplifting ideals of the Sociological Department. Marquis was one of Ford's closest associates and admirers for many years, until he became disillusioned by the shabby practices that led to his departure from the company. In 1923, he would write a rather unflattering portrait of Ford entitled *Henry Ford: An Interpretation*, the first of many to note the underside of Ford's nature and the changes, many of them sadly disheartening, that success had wrought in his character.

In the beginning, however, it was very different between the two men. Ford had spoken to Reverend Marquis of his considered ideas of the importance of giving his employees not just money, but also a chance at living better lives. Clearly he had thought a great deal about their living conditions and, as always with Ford, thoughts led to action. His life improvement ideas were a further development of his Emersonian ideals. The thoughts he expressed in 1919 at the Dodge trial about the purpose of a corporation showed that these ideals were never far from his mind in this period. Business wasn't about charity, it was about making money, but making money without sharing would have led to disaster in the balance of life, and Ford was not about to let that happen.

Several curiosities about the reputation of mass production linger in the collective conscience today. One is that it was all about the assembly line. This misconception is probably due to the fact that the most famous statement about it came in the 1926 article on the subject that appeared in the *Encyclopedia Britannica* under Henry Ford's name (ghostwritten, of course). After noting that it was not just about quantity or machine production, the article stated: "Mass production is a focusing upon a manufacturing project of the principles of power, accuracy, economy, system, continuity and speed." True enough, but if enlightened employment policies had not been simultaneously put into place, it would not have been possible to sustain the system, and if a large enough market had not been created, there would have been no point to mass production in the first place.

The second curiosity is that at its moment of greatest fame, mass production was already dead, as Hounshell has pointed out. The market had matured to the point where variety, and not utility, of product was foremost, and it was therefore imperative that manufacturers respond to this with *flexible* mass production, which could be adjusted in a multiplicity of ways at any time. Within a year even the creator of mass production, stalwart Henry Ford himself, would be forced to recognize this.

But by 1926, Ford was long a world figure. The announcement of the five-dollar day in early January of 1914 had made him a universal celebrity overnight. Partly this was because of the image he projected: that of a simple, smart, hardworking, unpretentious, and folksy friend of the common man who seemed to know that man, and care about him, like a brother. If Henry Ford did something or said something, everybody assumed it was good.

Over time, however, this image began to change. Ford started making public pronouncements on issues that strayed far from his own areas of knowledge and expertise. He was contentious, and many of his notions were unpopular, eventually alienating him from large segments of the population. Stung and then bewildered by such reactions, Ford began to retreat from wide contact with people. This was exacerbated by the fact that as his company's success, and hence his fortune, began to grow at a dizzying pace, his desire to keep more of the gains of his enterprise for himself also increased. The result was that, one by one, he began to rid himself of the people, many from the earliest days of the Ford Motor Company, who had contributed so much to making him successful in the first place. This in turn made him even more isolated. As Ford's legendary self-confidence turned toward megalomania, and he began to be rebuffed, even humiliated, because of some of his actions and statements, paranoia began to develop. With fewer and fewer people around who could provide checks and balances, he became dictatorial and absolute, often with disastrous consequences.

The first great controversy came over Ford's attempt to end World War I by his own personal intervention. The war had begun in June 1914, with the assassination of Archduke Franz Ferdinand in Sarajevo. In a few days much of Europe, which had been lining up in various sorts of alliances with or against Germany for quite some time, was drawn into the conflict. As bands played and banners waved, nations great and small marched off to war, believing it would all be settled quickly and at little cost. By the autumn of 1915, however, it was apparent that this war was of a monumental awfulness on a scale that the world had never experienced before, and this was even before the heart-stopping carnage of the battles of 1916, such as those at Verdun and the Somme.

Henry Ford had always hated war with an almost visceral passion. In this he was not out of step with the times. By the end of the 19th century a number of societies had been formed to foster the cause of peace. Czar Nicolas II was very influential in the movement, helping to codify the laws of war and establish the Court of International Arbitration at The Hague, which accomplished a great deal during the next 15 years. Then there was the creation of the Nobel Peace Prize, which lent enormous prestige to the cause of world peace. (Theodore Roosevelt had been awarded one in 1904 for his efforts to end the Russo-Japanese War.) In retrospect it seems ironic that just before the beginning of World War I, people were seriously thinking that war would soon become a thing of the past.

Ford said he inherited his pacifistic attitude from his mother, who had lost one brother and saw another injured during the Civil War (none of the Dearborn Fords had volunteered for it). Certainly another influence came from those *McGuffey Eclectic*

Readers, one of which contained an essay entitled *Things by Their Right Names*, which equated soldiers with murderers. Forty years on, still using this as a point of reference, Ford was saying the same sort of thing.

On August 12, 1915, he made his definitive statement on the subject to the *Detroit Free Press*: "I hate war, because war is murder, desolation and destruction, causeless, unjustifiable, cruel and heartless to those of the human race who do not want it, the countless millions, the workers. I hate it none the less for its waste, its uselessness, and the barriers it causes against progress." Presciently, he expounded to Rose Wilder Lane in 1917 on the futility of an arms race. If America begins on such a path, he said, "We must make something worse...and worse still, and then something still more horrible, bidding senselessly up and up and up, spending millions on millions, trying to outdo other nations which are trying to outdo us. For if we begin to prepare for war we must not stop. We cannot stop." Calling upon "the only real, practical value in the world...the spirit of the people of the world," he instead proposed that because people, unlike animals, have minds, they should use them to do useful, constructive things. After all, "There were animals on the earth ages ago who could kill a hundred men with one sweep of a paw, but they are gone, and we survive."

There was something else he deemed sinister about war too, something that would figure prominently in his thoughts and actions in the future: Ford thought that war was caused by insidious financial interests, which sought to profit from it. He even went so far as to say that he would rather burn down his factory than supply any matériel to belligerents. In the increasingly jingoistic wartime atmosphere in the United States, especially after the sinking of the *Lusitania* in May 1915, his ideas were grating to many. But many were vociferous in their support of him too.

Suddenly, as so often was his wont, all of Ford's peace talk turned to peace action. In November of 1915, he met a dynamic Hungarian woman named Rosika Schwimmer, who was at the forefront of a movement to promote mediation in the war by neutrals. She had gathered evidence that both neutrals and belligerents were amenable to such ideas, and having read in August 1915 that Henry Ford had said he was prepared to devote his life and fortune to achieving peace, she set out to catch his attention for her cause. This she did and secured an interview with him through Edwin G. Pipp of the *Detroit News*, who would later work for Ford. She met him at a luncheon, in company with Louis P. Lochner, another influential peace worker who was trying to get Woodrow Wilson to convene a Washington peace conference to appoint a commission of neutral nations that would work in "continuous mediation" for a peace acceptable to all belligerents.

It was proposed that Ford suggest to Wilson that he would support an official commission abroad for this purpose until Congress could fund it. If this was not acceptable, he was urged to suggest that he would pay for an unofficial body to do the same thing. Ford bought into the idea, which was also supported by his wife Clara. Ford and Lochner set off to New York to launch the proposal in the press (by this time Ford's instinct and appetite for press attention were keenly developed). At a luncheon meeting with a group of influential people (including Jane Addams from Hull House) at the McAlpin Hotel on November 21, the plan of action was approved. At one point, when Lochner offhandedly suggested hiring a ship to take the delegates to Europe, all the bells and whistles went off in Ford's mind. This idea would surely get a lot of attention and press, which he knew would cause people to take the peace plan a lot more seriously. By the end of that day, through Madame Schwimmer, he had chartered the liner *Oscar II* from the Scandinavian-America line.

Ford and Lochner duly went to see President Wilson, who liked the idea of continuing mediation, but wouldn't let himself be tied down to any one plan of approach, including Ford's. After the meeting the auto magnate dismissed the president as "a small man."

Nevertheless, Ford persisted. At a big press conference on November 24, he announced his plan to bring a group of major peace advocates to Europe on the ship "to try to get the boys out of the trenches by Christmas." For the next couple of days screaming headlines ensued, with no editorial comment. When press responses came, they ranged mostly from condemnatory to satirical, although some stood behind Ford's noble intentions.

Ford plowed on ahead, backing up his words with actions—he had said Christmas, and Christmas it would be. The departure date was set for December 4, leaving only nine days to get things organized. As it turned out, that was not nearly enough time. Had he postponed the trip until the new year, he might have been able to get some of the commitments from the major figures that he sought to join him and which might have given an air of competence and seriousness to the whole venture. But that wasn't Ford's way. Always anxious to stay in motion, he wanted as little time as possible to elapse between any idea and its execution.

Unfortunately, he left Madame Schwimmer in charge. A difficult, imposing person who was rather off-putting despite her attempt to stay in the background, Schwimmer was also an enemy alien in America—Hungary had sided with Germany in the war. This sat badly with many. In the end, even though there was some support from important people, not a single major figure among the many invited signed on to go with the expedition. Even the highly touted Jane Addams fell ill and could not sail, which was quite a blow to the prestige of the entire operation. Desperate, Ford offered a million dollars to Thomas Edison, who came to see the expedition off, to accompany him; but Edison was quite deaf and didn't hear Ford's words, so the offer literally fell on deaf ears. On the other hand, the pleas of Dean Marquis and Clara Ford, who both saw things falling apart and were now against the whole business, didn't prevail either. Ford was determined to do this, and that was that.

The many reporters on board sent out dispatches on the goings-on during the voyage, including what turned out to be active dissension among the participants. A good deal of ill feeling was caused by the acerbic, autocratic ways of Madame Schwimmer. But the real main attraction of the trip—the opportunity to get to know Henry Ford better—was a big success with the press. They all liked him, finding him friendly, folksy, and admirable. One approvingly quoted Ford's "faith in the people" as a faith that brought him to this venture. "I have absolute confidence in the better side of human nature," Ford told them. "People never disappoint you if you trust them." The reporters all felt that such statements were made with evident sincerity.

They were far less approving of the squabbling and often eccentric delegates, however. Part of the dissension had to do with Ford's Declaration of Principles of the Ford Peace Party, which was an anti-preparedness document that every delegate was expected to sign. (Ford had sent it to Congress, where it was read aloud). To his credit, however, he never tried to censor any press dispatches, no matter how critical.

Not long after setting sail, Ford caught a very bad cold, which led him to take to his bed, after which he was little seen by delegates and reporters. This may have been to his advantage, as he found the arguing among the members of his party irritating and was eager to avoid it. Aside from the cold, the other significant thing that happened to Ford on the ship, he later claimed, was that his eyes were opened to the sinister manipulations of "international Jewish banking powers," who had started the war and were financing it for their own benefit. He said that the source of this revelation was Herman Bernstein, the socialist editor of the Jewish publication *Day*. He said that this information disillusioned him and changed his attitude toward his project to end the war. (Bernstein, who was Jewish, later brought a lawsuit against Ford, denying he had ever said any such thing to him.) At any rate, Ford, who was no fool when it came to knowing which way the wind was blowing, kept to his sickroom when the ship landed on December 18, granting only one interview four days later in which he expounded on his new tractor, emphasizing that he would convince arms manufacturers that they could make more money with tractors than with guns. Reporters were stupefied at this. The next day, under a veil of secrecy, he began his voyage back home.

With Ford's disappearance, some of the bloom was definitely off the rose, but despite quarrels and backbiting, a peace conference was convened, working very hard to accomplish its mission in Europe for more than a year, and Ford, though he had given up a direct role, maintained that he was proud of its achievements and continued to support it. After he pushed Lochner to intervene directly among the belligerents in the autumn of 1916, Ford's prayers were answered, but in a way that St. Teresa of Avila would have recognized: "Answered prayers are the worst." First, Kaiser Wilhelm indicated a willingness to negotiate, but in an alienating and infuriating manner, which embarrassed Wilson, who was prepared to act. When Wilson sent a note to the Allies dictating peace terms, the Germans accepted, but the Allies would not, which made the Germans redouble their submarine strikes. After Wilson's "peace without victory" speech in early 1917, Ford thought the president was doing all he could for peace; but he also recognized that the enhanced German war effort meant that America could be drawn into the war, whether it wanted to be or not. Both factors made his peace commission unnecessary, so by February 7, it was shut down.

Launched on a sea of ridicule, the Peace Ship ultimately sailed into a safe harbor of influence and respect. People talked more seriously about peace because of it, and the Treaty of Versailles, among other things, was influenced by its ideas and workings. In the end, few disparaged Ford for the nobility of his effort despite the lashing he took in the press.

As for Ford himself, he took the bad press with equanimity, noting that "the best fertilizer in the world is weeds." He never wavered, then or later, in his conviction that he had done a good thing. If anything, his self-confidence grew ever stronger, as he felt himself to be unquestionable in the rightness of his cause. Later on, though, his same sense of conviction was brought to bear on far less noble causes, with far more questionable results.

On the practical side of things, Ford thought that the $465,000—a fortune then—he spent on the peace crusade got him a million dollars worth of publicity. And as he said, "I didn't get much peace, but I learned that Russia is going to be a great market for tractors."

Ford increased his self-confidence by relying on himself, and only himself, more and more. As Brinkley points out, it was the opposite tack from people like Carnegie or Rockefeller, who drew trusted associates close to them and relied on their efforts and judgments. As the 1910s and 1920s went on, Ford got rid of most of his associates one by one. Sometimes it was greed that led him to do it, sometimes it was paranoia, but underneath it all was the desire to run everything by himself, on his own responsibility.

The first ones to go were the Dodge Brothers who had built all the important mechanical components for Ford cars from the beginning. But when Ford opened the new Highland Park plant in 1910, they began to see that Ford was increasingly building his cars out of components he was manufacturing himself. Because Ford was virtually their only customer, the Dodge Brothers clearly had to do something else to ensure their survival.

That something else turned out to be their own car (a bigger, more expensive and more sophisticated car than the Model T) that they brought out in late 1914. Their statements indicated to potential customers that their vehicle was the right one to choose if they wanted "a real automobile." (It was indeed a very good vehicle; publicists coined the word "dependability" to describe its virtues.)

The previous year the Dodge Brothers had expanded their own factory in Hamtramck—now part of Detroit—in preparation for their entry into the marketplace; eventually they cancelled their contract with Ford; this actually played into his deepest desires. As Ford became more autocratic and difficult, they may have found him impossible to take. But on his part, he found the money they were making as both Ford suppliers and investors intolerable, especially as it was their profits from manufacturing parts for Ford and their dividends as Ford shareholders that allowed them to go into business as his competitors.

Ford would eventually do as much as he could to thwart them from using what he thought of as "his" money to become his competitors. In 1914, however, he was still too wrapped up in worrying about how to sell his own cars, and producing them to fill the orders, to do anything about this situation. In fact, to go along with his five-dollar day, he offered a $50 rebate as profit-sharing to his customers, provided he could sell 300,000 cars in the 1914–1915 model year; he beat that goal by almost 8,200 cars, and Ford was a hero to the public once again. Though he huffed and puffed to get the cars built, build them he did, Dodge Brothers or no.

He could not have done it without the one person in the Ford Motor Company who was just as responsible for its success as Ford himself: James Couzens, who was the next to depart. He was as much of a genius in business as Ford was in everything else. It was because of him that Ford stopped experimenting with improvements on the Model A and got it into production, which started the meteoric rise in the company's fortunes. It was Couzens's tightfisted and brilliant guidance of those fortunes that turned the company into an unprecedented business success in under a dozen years. Part of the reason for that success was that Ford and Couzens never interfered in each other's bailiwicks. But beginning in 1914, relations between the men began to go awry, eventually deteriorating to the point where they were seen in public arguing. In August of that year, a commercial bank-run rumor caused Ford to order all his funds withdrawn from the Highland Park State Bank, which Couzens had started as a tool for financial manipulation to Ford's advantage. Ford summarily put all his money into a savings bank, without first discussing his decision with Couzens, who was forced to comply. Things went downhill from there. Ford started checking up on Couzens's absenteeism from the factory and found that he wasn't there half the time, because he was concentrating his efforts on a growing interest in politics. "I don't believe in absentee control," Ford groused.

But Couzens's poor attendance wasn't the issue that brought matters to a head. It was Ford's aggressive pacifism that did it. In pamphlets and public statements, he began blaming bankers and sometimes "the Jews" for fomenting preparedness and war sentiment (this before his supposed revelation from Bernstein about the Jews on the Peace Ship). He was even very hard in his attitude toward the sinking of the *Lusitania* in the spring of 1915, saying that the passengers were "fools" for sailing sail on her, because they had been publicly warned beforehand.

Couzens's views were the opposite of Ford's; he believed that preparedness and military intervention were the best way to end the carnage. When strong pacifist editorials under Ford's name began appearing in the company's house organ, the *Ford Times*, Couzens argued that this was alienating customers and losing sales. Ford was sure of the opposite: that his editorials were boosting sales because so many people believed in his pronouncements. Finally, on October 12, 1915, Couzens had had enough and resigned; the proximate cause was that Ford wouldn't stop putting peace propaganda in the *Ford Times*, which was supposed to be under Couzens's control. Frank L. Klingensmith, a very capable man, though without the genius of Couzens in business affairs, replaced him.

Almost immediately, Couzens went into politics, never to return to the auto industry. First, he became a police commissioner, known for taking tough measures to clean up all sorts of corruption in Detroit. Later, he became mayor of the city, and finally, in 1924, he was elected to the U.S. Senate as a Republican from Michigan. He served with distinction and was much admired for his service to the poor and unemployed, especially during the Great Depression. Over the years he maintained considerable contact with Ford, though they were often at odds. It is telling though that, at his funeral in 1936, Ford served as a pallbearer.

The departures of the Dodge Brothers and Couzens were perhaps the most significant ones, both in themselves and as harbingers of the future. Each spoke to a different, vital area of expertise. Ford was willing, even happy, to be responsible for each of these areas on his own, but most of the replacements he put in place, no matter how competent, were never quite as good as the people he had lost. Only in one instance did he ever acknowledge this fact, but this reluctance spoke to the essence of his nature. Once you had a job up and running in the plant, anyone could do it. But at this level, nothing could have been further from the truth. It would take awhile for all this to play out, as we will see when we deal with each successive departure in its turn.

In addition to his relentless desire to consolidate power in his own hands during this period, the simultaneous world war revealed one of the very oddest things about Henry Ford: his ability to have a stranglehold on an idea, and then in an instant completely reverse himself, contradictions be damned. As Nevins and Hill put it, "The transformation of Henry Ford from peace angel to Vulcan took less than a week." On February 3, 1917, President Wilson severed diplomatic relations with Germany. Two days later, believing that the president must be supported, Ford said, "in the event of a declaration of war [I] will place our factory at the disposal of the United States government and will operate without one cent of profit."

Startling as this sudden reversal was in its speed, it was quite understandable in its substance. The world had changed considerably in the previous year, and Ford had too along with it. Anti-German feeling was on the rise, because of increased U-boat attacks and sinkings. Despite his thoughts about the victims of the *Lusitania*, Ford became increasingly convinced that Wilson had shown himself to be a committed man of peace, until peace was no longer an option. So Ford reasoned, if "militarism can be crushed only with militarism…I am in on it to the finish." Ford may have been the first diehard pacifist to fall in line behind support for the president's war effort, but he was not the last. After the declaration of war on April 6, people fell all over themselves to demonstrate their willingness to put their support behind president and country.

Actually, Ford was already in the war business, not as a supplier of armaments but of farm implements. Britain, an island nation, had a desperate need for food for both troops and civilians, and lacked the means to produce it. Ford had been trying to create a cheap, lightweight, and efficient gas tractor for years. As we have seen, it had been his dream to produce such a machine before he ever wanted to produce a car, in order "to lift farm drudgery off flesh and blood and lay it on steel and motors." Try as he did with many different models, he didn't have what he wanted until 1917, when his new tractor, designed by a brilliant

Hungarian immigrant named Eugene Farkas, took shape. It was a 20-horsepower, four-cylinder, three-speed-and-reverse vehicle that used 42-inch rear wheels for driving power and 28-inch front wheels to steer. Farkas's design eliminated a frame through precise casting and allowed the engine to be enclosed to protect it from dirt. It was the English who got Ford into tractor production with this model.

Percival Perry, head of Ford's highly successful English operation, prepared to have the tractor produced in England according to Ford specifications. But a heavy German bombing campaign, which caused more panic than destruction, led British industry to focus almost exclusively on strengthening its air power, so the tractors had to be made in America. Ford already had a tractor company called Henry Ford and Company, which he changed into a new company, Henry Ford and Son, separate from the Ford Motor Company, incorporating it on July 27, 1917, to produce the tractors. With a firm order for 6,000 units, the company began manufacturing them in Dearborn. It was very slow going at first, with only 254 produced by the end of the year. But by April 1918, over 7,000 of Britain's expanded order were delivered. Ford then began selling the tractors to the U.S. market. He received 13,463 orders and delivered 5,067 by June.

In addition to the tractors, there were ambulances. In England Perry built and delivered thousands of them, set on Model T chassis; similar vehicles were constructed in France. Though Ford wouldn't officially sell to belligerents, the company began to do so when the U.S. government placed orders on May 30, 1917. (For some time it had been producing helmets, eventually numbering a million, which were not considered objectionable.)

Much more was produced for the war effort by the Ford Motor Company. There were the Liberty Motors—V-12 airplane engines designed by J. G. Vincent of Packard. Ford solved an intractable cylinder-manufacturing problem on them and manufactured over 415,000 cylinders during the war, at an enormous cost savings. Eventually the company also built about 4,000 complete engines.

In 1915, Ford purchased a large site for a new plant for tractor production on the River Rouge. The site was near several railroad lines and on a river that, when dredged out, would make an excellent place for moving raw materials in and finished products out. The project languished for quite some time, and indeed there was no factory there by the time Ford began producing tractors, which is why they were built in Dearborn. But just as the government finally got Ford into tractor production, it now provided the impetus for him to develop the Rouge site into what would eventually become the largest manufacturing site in the world.

It came about because the government wanted Ford to produce boats, specifically a 204-foot submarine chaser eventually called the "Eagle." They figured that if Ford could mass-produce cars, he could do the same thing for boats. It took a lot of time, effort, and money on his part to find this out, and by that time the Rouge was started.

Actually, Ford had solicited the business. The Navy simply couldn't find a large enough facility to build the boats, and Ford said that if the River Rouge were properly dredged out and a factory was built, he could launch Eagles directly on a path to the Atlantic. With no real alternatives, the government agreed and Congress appropriated the money for the work, with the understanding that the facilities would be sold to Ford at the conclusion of the war.

On January 17, 1918, the secretary of the Navy, Josephus Daniels, sent a telegram ordering 100 of the boats, and the project was begun. Albert Kahn designed the assembly building, a 1,700-foot wonder that went up with lightning speed as various aspects of construction took place simultaneously. The first keel was laid on May 2, and the first completed boat was launched on July 10, 1918. Great cheering ensued.

And then the troubles began. The basic problem was that boats and cars are built in different ways. Cars are assembled by bolting them together, whereas boats use rivets and casting. The workforce had great difficulty adjusting to new techniques, and the Navy's constantly changing specifications didn't help either. Though at its peak the program employed 8,000 workers and cost $46 million in the end—the most expensive of all Ford's war contracts—only 60 Eagle boats were ever built, and only one was commissioned before the war was over. (They were quite seaworthy, however.) The whole episode cast Ford in an unfavorable light, for it showed him as someone willing to take on a huge project that he did not understand and on which he could not deliver.

Moreover, another controversy hung over his war work, and that involved his promise to give any war profits to the government, likening them to "blood money." When Secretary of the Treasury Andrew Mellon read in Sarah T. Bushnell's *The Truth about Henry Ford* (a flattering biographical portrait published in Chicago in 1922) that Ford had given $29 million in wartime profits to the United States, he examined the government's books and found no record of payment. He then wrote a polite note to Ford mentioning this and requesting payment, which Ford did not make. Many think this incident shows him up as a cynical liar and a skinflint, but the truth is far more complex, as Nevins and Hill point out. In the first place Ford's wartime profits totaled only $8.15 million and, after taxes were deducted, they were only $4.35 million, with his own share at $2.5 million; after deducting his personal taxes, only $927,000 remained. Ford made a good-faith effort to determine the proper amount, but even after he did, he could have been liable to a reopening of the whole matter until 1924, due to government regulations. Then too, he had clearly refrained from billing the government on some large items and probably came to feel resentful of government red tape and the loss of profits (perhaps $40 million) caused by the restrictions on his regular auto production. But he could have and should have paid what he promised, or at least what he actually made, and the fact that he didn't casts another kind of shadow over his ambivalent wartime record.

Another aspect of the war that affected his reputation concerned his son Edsel, who was drafted in August 1917, along with eight million other able-bodied Americans. His father was determined that he wouldn't go to war, confiding to Pipp his fear that Edsel would have been targeted for death by "certain interests" if he went. Accordingly, over Edsel's protests, Ford lawyers wrote an appeal to the local draft board, pleading that as his father's only son, he was indispensable to the war effort at home. Indeed, that, and the fact that by now he had a small child (his son Henry Ford II was born in September of 1917) kept him out of the service, and both were legitimate claims. But it did not shield him from a sort of national raspberry, for he was ridiculed as a draft dodger both privately and in the press. Ohio Republican Congressman Nicholas Longworth famously remarked that, of the seven young men assured of escaping the war unscathed, six were the sons of the Kaiser, and the seventh was Edsel Ford.

Meanwhile, Henry Ford was getting richer and richer. In a telling incident, the day Edsel turned 21 in November 1914, his father gave him a million dollars and took him to the bank so he could see what it looked like in gold bullion; afterward, Edsel was so giddy that he put in the worst day's work of his life.

It was an odd thing for Henry to do, considering his self-avowed contempt for money as an end in itself. "Money valuable?," he said to Rose Wilder Lane, a journalist and daughter of the author of *The Little House on the Prairie*, and also credited as one of the founders of the American libertarian movement. "Money itself is nothing, absolutely nothing. It is only valuable as a transmitter, a method of handling things that are valuable." This was a typical statement. But this incident with Edsel showed perhaps a truer picture of his actual values. He may have wanted to use money to create a better standard of living for humankind, but he clearly also wanted as much of that money as possible to be his and no one else's, for him to decide to use as he saw fit. At this moment, he was passing those values on to his son. But Edsel was a very different sort of man. He used his wealth to indulge in many of the finer things of life for which Henry had nothing but contempt—beautiful architecture and art, fine wines, and clothes. And there was little Henry could do to stop him, except complain, and that was useless. Edsel was his father's most devoted employee—he became secretary of the company in 1915 and president in 1919, a post he held until his death in 1943—but in his private life he was his own man and used money in his own way. Had Edsel been more of a tough guy at work and lived a more subdued, private life, there might have been much greater harmony between father and son. But as it was, there was much unpleasantness and anguish.

That the money was there, however, was not in doubt, as were the power and influence that went with it; profits in 1916 were to bring Henry, as owner of 58.5 percent of Ford stock, almost $35 million. This didn't prevent him from openly characterizing stockholders as parasites, because he felt they were not productive members of the corporate team. And God help anyone whom he felt was unproductive or who challenged him.

In the late 1910s, he pursued two such instances like a dog in a manger, and the results, for good and ill, in both instances had a profound effect on Ford's nature for the rest of his life. Both involved lawsuits and revolved around incidents that began in 1916 and ended in 1919. As in the Selden patent lawsuit, Ford was more than willing to take his time to achieve his goals.

The first involved his minority stockholders and was precipitated by the Dodge Brothers in particular. As has been previously noted, they had been making huge amounts of money as both parts suppliers (they charged Ford top-of-the-line prices) and stockholders, using the money earned from Ford to go into business on their own. By 1916, Ford was fed up with this, and in January announced that henceforth all but $1.2 million of profits per annum (a paltry fraction of actual profits) would be plowed back into the company so that he could expand production and lower the price of the Model T to $220. It was the beginning of a cat-and-mouse game. That August Ford announced a price cut to $360 and a suspension of special dividends. John Dodge, the senior brother, had already asked Ford why he didn't simply buy out the minority stockholders, to which Ford replied that he had no intention of doing anything of the kind, whether they liked it or not. All had been quiet for some time until this announcement. Now the game was on.

On the night of November 2, 1916, Edsel married Eleanor Lothian Clay, the niece of J. L. Hudson, the late Detroit department store magnate who was also the namesake of the Hudson motor car. The Dodges were guests at the event, and John had even chatted amiably with Henry. But the next morning, Ford received a terrible shock, for newspaper headlines announced that the Dodge Brothers were suing him for mismanaging his business, sacrificing shareholder interests through expanding production, lowering prices, and acting in a philanthropic manner with the purpose of monopolizing the auto business. (Ford's expansion was not news to them, as they had long known about the River Rouge land purchase, but they had previously been relying on Couzens to keep Ford in check.)

The next night, the tables were turned in an article with a bill of particulars that made the Dodges seem like greedy hoarders expecting Ford to keep production down and prices high. As to their contention that he was trying to create a monopoly, Ford said, "The bane of monopolies, as I understand it, is in getting control of goods, and making the price unreasonably high. Think of it. Trying to make us a public menace because we sell our goods at too low a price to suit them." He also pointed out that for every $10 profit the Dodge Brothers would lose, he would lose $58 as majority stockholder. He was giving as good as he got. But the underlying basis of the suit was clear: whether or not Ford was acting in a manner opposed to the best interests of the stockholders.

The suit ostensibly began on November 14. The early days were most important to Ford, however, for one of the first things the court would establish was whether he could begin his Rouge expansion, and how much he could spend on it. At first Ford was enjoined from continuing work on a smelter he had started to build, though later he was allowed to continue to the extent of $10 million, as long as he posted a bond for it.

The suit itself was equally notable for what Ford revealed of his business attitudes on the stand. Regarding profits, he said his purpose was "To give employment, and send out the car where the people can use it." Later, he added, "and incidentally to make money.... Business is a service, not a bonanza." When asked if his purpose was "to employ a great army of men at high wages, to reduce the selling price of your car, so that a lot of people can buy it at a cheap price, and give everybody a car that wants one," he expressed in one sentence the revolutionary nature of his business philosophy, which so shook up his peers: "If you give all that, the money will fall into your hands: you can't get out of it."

The case didn't go to court until June 1917 and wasn't settled definitively until February 1919, but before it was, Ford startled everyone in November 1918 by announcing that he was resigning as president of the Ford Motor Company at the end of the year in favor of his son, explaining that he was interested in becoming a newspaper publisher. Eventually the decision came down that Ford could legally continue his expansion, but that he had to pay $19.3 million to his shareholders in dividends and interest, which he proceeded to do. But on March 6, he startled everyone again, this time by announcing that he and his son Edsel would start a new car company, to build a more modern and much cheaper car than the Model T. And what of the Ford Motor Company? "Why, I don't know exactly what will become of that."

This was one of Ford's cleverest business moves ever, because it manufactured the one thing he needed most of all: panic in his shareholders, who didn't know what would happen to the value of their shares. Then he quietly set about tendering offers to buy out the remaining stockholders, through the Old Colony Trust Company of Boston. His one stipulation was that he would buy all the shares or nothing. Since they couldn't be sold on the open market, the shareholders came and sold to him, one by one. He got his wish, paying some $106 million for all the remaining shares in a deal reached in July 1919. The only cloud in the transaction was that he had to borrow $60 million from the banks to do it; this would later come to haunt him. But it was still good business; the shareholders could have sold for double that amount on the open market, if that had been possible, and some years later Ford turned down $1 billion for the same shares. It was said that he danced a jig when he heard of the final agreement.

Carol Gelderman in *The Wayward Capitalist* best sums up the significance of this event: "Never before had one man so completely controlled a company; John Rockefeller controlled at most 2/7ths of Standard Oil. Never had anyone risen so meteorically: in 1902 Ford had yet to design a car for the market, but seventeen years later he owned a complex of factories worth at least a billion dollars. Henceforth he could act with no restraint upon his massive power."

And what of the new company and car? A short time after the buyout, Edsel told the *New York Times*: "Of course there will be no need for a new company now."

The other lawsuit was not about money but rather *amour propre,* and the results were far less clear cut or favorable to him. The *Chicago Tribune*, once very partial to Henry Ford for his progressive, labor-friendly policies, had grown indignant over his anti-war and anti-preparedness views and in 1916 went too far in condemning the man. Or rather, Robert McCormick, its 35-year-old editor, a decorated ex-soldier, both dashing and jingoistically conservative, and once described as "the greatest mind of the fourteenth century," did. He published an editorial on June 23 calling Ford both an "anarchist" and an "ignorant idealist." This was done under the belief—mistaken as it turns out—that Ford would not keep jobs for National Guardsmen called to fight in the famous border incident involving Pancho Villa and General Pershing, or support their families. When the paper would not retract its statement, Ford sued for libel to the tune of $1 million.

It took almost three years for the suit to go to trial, which it finally did in the tiny town of Mt. Clemens, Michigan, after impartial juries could not be found in either Chicago or Detroit. During that period America had gone to war, and neither the *Tribune* nor anyone else was willing to pay the salaries or hold the jobs of anyone who was then fighting the war. So the paper changed its tack. Now it said that its editorial was part of a public discussion on preparedness, and took the view that Ford's anti-preparedness ideas were inimical to the security and best interests of the country.

The whole business turned into a media circus. McCormick had nine lawyers and a large entourage, and Ford had eight, with a complete retinue of 63. Ford established his own news bureau to hand out daily summaries to the hundreds of small-town papers he knew would be favorable to him; this was to ensure they would not pick up the bias of big city papers, which he knew would oppose him. As in the Selden and Dodge cases, Ford wanted to use this suit as a platform for expounding his views, this time on peace rather than business.

For his part McCormick hired an entire law firm to pretend it was representing Ford, so that his team would figure out any possible strategy of his opponent. To give an idea of how convoluted the case eventually became, the *Tribune* by now maintained that "anarchist" didn't refer to a "person who advocates anarchy, or absence of government," but instead "anyone who advocates placing the government in a position where it cannot properly discharge its duty toward its citizens to protect their lives and property."

The *Tribune* side brought in Texas rangers to testify to the awful things the Mexicans were doing on the border, and Ford's people brought in Mexicans to testify to the terrible things the Americans were doing. Finally the judge, an incredibly dense man named James G. Tucker, ruled on limitations of testimony. He deemed that anything Ford did or said that could justify the criticism in the editorial was relevant, and since pacifism and anti-preparedness were the essence of the case, anything related could be introduced. And it was. Everyone from Tolstoy to Saint Paul was cited to support one side or the other. Whether Ford disdained or distributed the flag was discussed, as was whether or not he had returned his wartime profits to the government, etc., etc. Everything was dragged into the proceedings, until everyone was sick to death of these tactics.

Eventually Elliott Stevenson, the head of the defense team, called Ford to the stand to testify as to whether or not he was an "ignorant idealist."

Under questioning, Ford stuck to his characterization of war as murder ("Killing anybody or anything. I don't know what else war is"). He suggested that a far better way of going about things was "to educate people. To teach them to think for themselves." Stevenson took his opening: "You call yourself an educator. Now I shall inquire whether you were a well-informed man, competent to educate people." He then proceeded to harass Ford mercilessly, exposing his basic ignorance on a wide variety of historical and civic topics, ranging from the date of the American Revolution ("1812" was Ford's answer) to the identity of Benedict Arnold ("a writer," said Ford, obviously confusing him with Arnold Bennett) to the basic principles of the government ("justice, I think"). When asked to read something, he refused, even when told that it might give the impression that he could not read.

The big city press had a field day with this, but oddly, Ford came off rather well. For one thing, he never lost his composure under the grilling, and for another, many ordinary Americans sympathized with him—they were like this too, and recognized one of their own. In the end though, he would not admit to being ignorant about everything, and defined an idealist as "a person that can make people prosperous. I believe I can do it a little."

When this phase of testimony was finally ended, Ford's lawyers, led by Albert Lucking, took over. (Stevenson and Lucking had also faced one another in the Dodge Brothers trial.) They talked about Ford and the Mexican situation and introduced one of Ford's most striking comments, considering the tenor of the times. "We mustn't go down there with a rifle," he said. "We must go down there with the plow, the shovel and the shop. If we could put the Mexican peon to work, treating him fairly and showing him the advantage which is sure to come from working fairly and treating his employers fairly, the Mexican problem would disappear from the continent as steam fades from the windowpane.

There would be no more talk of revolution. Villa would become a foreman, if he has brains."

By July 25, Ford's testimony was over, and he left the courtroom vowing never to enter one again. In addition to being made to seem a fool, he was particularly put off because he thought everything had been discussed during the trial except the issues of the case.

In the summaries, Stevenson said he had exposed the mind of Henry Ford "as bare as was necessary to show you that what we said about him was true." Lucking countered by reminding everyone that Ford had erected "one of the wonders of the world," with 14,000 machines and 40,000 men in one factory: "a marvel." How ignorant could such a man be?

Judge Tucker delivered his charge to the jury on August 14, 1919. Stupefyingly, though he had allowed weeks of testimony on the preparedness issue, he now charged that it was irrelevant. The only issue was whether the editorial was true; furthermore, if it was written with malice, the jury had to consider extra damages. The jury reached a verdict ten hours later. It found for the plaintiff and awarded damages of six cents. It seems that none of the jurors thought Ford was an anarchist, but four of them thought the editorial was "fair comment." One was rankled by the fact that neither Henry nor Edsel had ever served in the armed forces. The six-cent damages award was a compromise to avoid a mistrial.

Over a million dollars and the efforts of some of the finest legal minds in the country had been spent on a sideshow. The big newspapers were against Ford, as he had predicted they would be. The *Herald Tribune* called Ford "deliciously naïve and omniscient and preposterous." The *Nation* said, "Now the mystery is finally dispelled. Henry Ford is a Yankee mechanic, pure and simple: quite uneducated...but with naturally good instincts and some sagacity....He has achieved wealth but not greatness; he cannot rise above the defects of education, at least as to public matters. So the unveiling of Mr. Ford has much of the pitiful about it, if not the tragic. We would rather have had the curtain drawn, the popular ideal unshattered."

Ford himself couldn't get over the fact that nobody commented that an incompetent judge had dragged out a trial that should have lasted no more than a week, had it been held to the real issue—anarchism. He eventually got rid of Lucking because of this and never trusted lawyers again.

Rural and small town America rallied to him. The Ohio *State Journal* summed up their ideas best: "We sort of like old Henry Ford, anyway." Of course they did. His court testimony showed him to be just like millions of other Americans you could see and hear holding forth at cracker barrels in small towns all over the country. And that goodwill stuck with him for a long time.

Nonetheless, the whole affair stung him and made him even more suspicious and isolated. His personality was changing because of what was happening to him, and not for the better. He was becoming much darker in his views.

Seven

Modern Times

Henry Ford was fond of saying that mankind had three basic occupations: growing things, making things, and moving things. He began his life growing things, hating the drudgery and waste involved in farm work. A desire to change the farmer's lot led him to become a maker of things that moved other things, transforming not only farm work, but taking all sorts of work in directions that had never been taken before. In the process the rural world of the farmer turned into something resembling the urban world of the factory worker. Ford foresaw the benefits that the changes he instigated would bring to the life of the common working man. But he did not see the ways in which the common man himself would change into a new sort of modern, industrialized urban being, filled with urges and desires for fulfillment that were the antithesis of those that guided the life in which Ford grew up and held dear. He was aghast at this transformation and spent a good deal of the last part of his life trying to instill the virtues and values of old-fashioned country life into this new 20th-century city creature he had done more than anyone else to create.

Ford was in motion all his life. In fact, motion, ceaseless and ever-more refined, was the guiding principle of his existence. Despite this, it took him a remarkably long time to figure out what he was going to do. As we have seen, his first 28 years were inchoate, an undecided shuttling back and forth between the farm and the city. He was 30 before he began serious work on a motor vehicle, 35 before he made a business out of it, and 40 before he made a success. But even that success was not a mature one, in terms of his real goals. He knew he wanted to make a vehicle that the masses could afford, but it took him until 1908 to refine his ideas and develop such a vehicle. Then it took him another five years to figure out a system to make and deliver that vehicle to the masses and, furthermore, create his dreamed-of mass market for it. So Ford was 50 years old when he got where he wanted to be in his own life's project.

Not that he stopped then. Like a hummingbird or a shark, he had to keep moving. To rest on your laurels was to stagnate for Henry Ford, and wasting time was a cardinal sin. For the rest of the second decade of the 20th century and the beginning of the next, he started a hospital; organized a peace expedition in the midst of World War I, then did an about-face and became a major supplier of war matériel to his country; began what was to become the world's largest industrial complex, completely integrating it; took over and became publisher of a highly controversial weekly news magazine; lived through a devastating libel case; saved his company and made it stronger during the worst crisis the auto industry had ever seen; and at last became, with his family, the sole owner of his vast enterprise.

He broached all these challenges with his usual energy, brain-power, and vision, but for several of them, he was not prepared in terms of background or sophisticated reasoning. He had a series of stumbles that would grow and eventually haunt even the success of a man as extraordinarily accomplished as he was.

His candor and spontaneity could be endearing. When a reporter asked him how it felt to be the world's first billionaire, he squirmed in his seat and replied, "Oh, shit!"

His attention wasn't only on business, legalities, and money, however. Robust health and good nutrition were lifelong concerns of Ford's; far ahead of his time, he urged consumption of fruits, vegetables, and legumes instead of meat and sugar. "Most men are digging their graves with their teeth," he admonished. He referred frequently to the works of Luigi Cornaro, a 17th-century Italian nobleman who became completely dissipated through bad diet at the age of 35, but then changed his eating habits entirely and lived to 102. Eat and drink only what agrees with your stomach, not your palate, and eat only small amounts, was Cornaro's advice, and Ford heeded it. Exercise was another part of Ford's "clean living" lifestyle, which he publicized as an example to others. That lifestyle excluded liquor in all forms, which he thought of as the major enemy of self-control, without which a man could not utilize his talents to create success for himself and prosperity for others. "Liquor never did anybody any good," he said. "Business and booze are enemies."

Ford was particularly prescient in his condemnation of cigarettes, becoming one of the first major figures to attack the smoking habit by publishing a pamphlet entitled "The Case against the Little White Slaver" in 1914. In addition to what he saw as a dulling of the senses, ("with every breath of cigarette smoke [boys] inhale imbecility and exhale manhood"), he quite correctly saw that smoking debilitated such major organs as the heart, kidneys, and lungs.

There may have been more than a whiff of old-fashioned moralistic reform wafting off his jeremiads against the evils of tobacco, and especially alcohol, but nearly a century later, in an age of public smoke-free living and awareness of the effects of alcohol abuse, there is still a pervasive echo from his pronouncements.

For the sake of improving the farmer's lot, Ford worked on making tractors better and more widely available, an initiative that began in 1910 and continued into the 1920s. But at the end of that decade, when he was already over 65, he began to think about agriculture and the new possibilities it offered farmers in ways that have had profound consequences even to this day. "What were the unsuspected uses of crops that could be discovered?" he asked, sponsoring numerous and sometimes vast experiments to discover them. In the process, he was enormously influential in creating the modern soybean industry, converting this humble legume from cattle fodder to a crop with a thousand uses, just like corn and peanuts. Today nobody knows this, but it is second only to the creation and sponsorship of the system of mass production in his achievements. It alone would have given great importance to his life.

In the 1910s his major industrial challenge was to expand production, and thus it remained until the mid-1920s when Model T sales reached their peak. For Ford it was all about making more Ts in an ever-more efficient way. (The Model T itself was changed and improved over its 19-year lifespan, especially after the war; however, when significant parts of it were modified—just look at a 1908 model compared with a 1927 one—it was usually done very quietly and without fanfare. Ford was wise enough to make the T better without undermining its basic appeal as a timeless product.) Wages went up (the five-dollar day became the six-dollar day by 1919), prices went down, the market ballooned, and Ford took steps to meet its demands, as we shall see.

The six-dollar-per-day wage of 1919 came about for reasons similar to those that created the five-dollar-per-day wage. Thanks to the prosperity created by the latter, the workforce was once again becoming unstable, as inflation was up over 100 percent in Detroit in a five-year period, and the five-dollar wage wasn't even worth half of what it had been. Even with the six-dollar rate, Ford workers were still falling behind, especially as more money could be earned at other employers' establishments by this time. So the six-dollar day was a foregone conclusion when 1919 began. Once again, it was accompanied by a speed-up on the line to accommodate ever-increasing production.

Ford's production kept breaking records over the years, with growing momentum in the period following the introduction of the assembly line and the five-dollar day. He saw more clearly than anyone else that even the tremendous Highland Park facility, with an annual capacity of 500,000 cars, would soon become too small. Accordingly, early on, perhaps as soon as 1913, he began to formulate plans for a much bigger facility. He wanted it to be a fully integrated operation, capable of taking in iron ore and other raw materials at one end and putting out fully finished vehicles at the other to be sent to points all over the world. (Ford's first foreign sale took place in 1903 when the sixth vehicle he made was shipped to Canada. Though production there began in 1905, it was negligible for another decade. There were many other foreign sales, extending the reputation of the Model T throughout the world, but most of those vehicles were assembled from knock-down kits shipped to and put together in other countries, along with a certain amount of local parts; Argentina alone made over 100,000 Model Ts in this way. But real foreign production, aside from that in Canada, was not a factor until after the Dagenham works in England were completed under Percival Perry in 1931.)

The first thing he needed was a site, and he got the one he had wanted on the Rouge River for some time, buying up 2,000 acres there through agents in mid-1915. As we saw, he used the development of the site as a ploy in his efforts to rid himself of his "parasite" investors, while actually getting the government to foot the bill for it.

Although Albert Kahn designed the astonishing main B-building, much of the planning of the complex, which had many striking architectural elements, was left to William B. Mayo, who worked with a staff of 250. It went up beginning in January 1918, and the first Eagle boat keel was laid in May of that year, rather a remarkable achievement. Knudsen even set up the factory with three assembly lines, allowing multiple ships to be constructed at the same time.

The government didn't get much for this project, which cost some $46 million; only one of the 60 boats that were eventually built was commissioned by the time of the armistice, mostly because of inexperienced Ford workers and endlessly changing Navy specifications. But Ford, in addition to all that taxpayer money spent on the Eagle, got what he wanted most: the basis for his vast, new plant, which became the world's largest, exactly according to his plan. Eagle production ended in mid-1919, and by late 1919, production of cars in the B-building was growing by leaps and bounds. On May 17, 1920, after a coke plant and sawmill began operations, blast furnace A was inaugurated with a match thrown by Ford's grandson, two-year-old Henry Ford II.

There was a boom in civilian car production after the war ended. So much of the American automobile industry was involved in creating war matériel in 1917 and 1918 that auto production was way down, and everyone assumed that a huge pent-up demand would exist for cars at the war's end. Government spending, high wartime wages and savings, and a low discount rate permitting easy credit did indeed lead to a soaring demand for cars. Only a lack of materials and supplier strikes slowed down production. Nevertheless, enormous amounts of parts were manufactured and assembled into vehicles as quickly as possible, though many of them were constructed from outmoded prewar designs.

Eventually, supply caught up with demand. Jobs decreased, incomes fell, and the Federal government raised interest rates, in part because of a surplus of easy automobile credit. As sales declined, concerned dealers asked manufacturers to lower prices, which the manufacturers refused to do. The public wouldn't buy at high prices, and by the fall of 1920, sales began to nosedive. Unsold cars and parts were piling up all over the country, which was beginning the sharp, and as it turned out, quick inventory recession of 1920–1921. The effects were felt throughout the industry.

William C. Durant, the smile-and-a-shoeshine salesman who founded General Motors in 1908, lost control of his company through overexpansion in 1910 and regained it through brilliant manipulation of Chevrolet stock in 1915. But he overplayed his hand through speculation in GM stock in late 1920 and almost ruined the entire company. The duPonts had to step in to bail out both Durant and the company, and as a result, he was out of GM again, this time permanently. This left the reluctant Pierre S. duPont, and eventually Alfred P. Sloan, in charge of a completely reorganized and stronger firm. Their business model of horizontal, rather than vertical, integration would create much more flexibility, because responsibility for decision- making would be much more departmentalized and rationalized than in the past. Their system affected all business administration profoundly from that time on.

John North Willys, another auto pioneer in the Durant vein, ran what was for a while the second most successful car firm in the United States, Willys-Overland. But he, like many others, got caught up in the inventory pile-up, made even worse by the fact that he had erected an enormous new plant in Elizabeth, New Jersey, to manufacture an all-new vehicle that had not yet been fully designed. The bankers who backed the firm brought in Walter P. Chrysler, the charismatic former head of Buick and vice-president of GM, who rolled up his sleeves and saved the company largely through a ruthless program of cost-cutting. He did this so well that most of the same bankers hired him on to save the venerable Maxwell-Chalmers Company, which was in many ways worse off than Willys-Overland. Maxwell cars were so badly built that the first thing Chrysler had to do was send mechanics out into the field to fix problems like gas tanks that were falling off the vehicles. Then he had to recapture dealers to sell them and cobble together better vehicles from the acres of parts sitting on demurrage on railroad sidings all over the country. He christened these new models "The Good Maxwells," a name that made him choke but nevertheless moved the merchandise. This time, however, the bankers gave him the chance to take over Maxwell-Chalmers and create his own company. He did this by hiring three brilliant engineers from Willys—Fred Zeder, John Skelton, and Carl Breer—and setting them to work to create a revolutionary middle-class vehicle that was in many ways the most important new car since the Model T. This was the Chrysler, the first truly modern car, and out of it came the Chrysler Corporation. Such were the auto business stories of late 1920.

The crisis of 1920–1921 could not have come at a worse time for Henry Ford. He had borrowed $75 million from a consortium of banks in order to complete the buyout of his minority stockholders in 1919; this came on the heels of a court order to pay them almost $20 million in dividends and interest. In addition, he had spent $60 million developing the Rouge factory and nearly another $20 million buying and developing other properties. Though he had actually used only $60 million of his credit line and repaid $35 million, he still owed $25 million, due in April 1921. Furthermore, Ford would not renege on $7 million in bonuses due to employees in January 1921, and he owed somewhere between $18 and $30 million in taxes. He said his total obligations amounted to $58 million, though this may have been overstated. Against this, the company had some $20 million in cash in the autumn of 1920.

Ford's financial situation was well known, and most assumed he would have to resort to more heavy borrowing from banks to get by, especially after sales dropped in November and the Highland Park facility was closed. All activities switched to the Rouge facility in December, causing a shutdown that would be much longer than the usual midwinter break. Later Ford said he never contemplated borrowing, but others in the firm investigated that possibility with his knowledge, if not his active participation. In January, when Joseph Bower of the Liberty National Bank of New York offered a financial plan to him, contingent upon the appointment of a new treasurer chosen by the bank, Ford literally showed him the door. He was shocked by this turn of events, which deepened his distrust of and contempt for bankers. And anyway, Ford had his own plan for reviving the company.

He did this in several ways. First, to move inventory, he reduced prices of his products by a huge percentage on September 1 (e.g., the Runabout was reduced from $550 to $395), declaring that "The war is over and it is time war prices are over," because "Inflated prices always retard progress." This move worked pretty well for a while, bucking up sales and maintaining profits on replacement parts, which were not reduced in price. Starting in October, there was a program of severe economy applied throughout the company based on studies and practices instigated by Edsel Ford and Ernest C. Kanzler in the spring of 1919. Henry Ford pushed it to extreme lengths as time went on, eliminating whole departments (he took special glee in getting rid of anything to do with accounting, which he loathed as a parasitic activity) and eventually selling off all the idled equipment caused by employment reductions, down to each and every pencil sharpener (from then on, you sharpened a pencil with your own knife). It was said the sale netted the company $7 million. Hiring was frozen, with laid-off white-collar workers being offered the chance to work in the factories. Even top executives were kept on only as watchmen in abandoned facilities.

Indeed, while all this was going on, Ford was eliminating key personnel, as well as ordinary workers. Now that he was sole proprietor, he did not want anyone around whom he saw as a threat to his authority. For instance, Frank Klingensmith, who had taken over Couzens's responsibilities, left over the issue of bank loans. Charles A. Brownell was dropped as head of advertising. Dean Marquis, in charge of the sociological department, left over what he saw as increasingly callous behavior on the part of Ford, and his department pretty much went with him. Most important of all was William S. Knudsen, the brilliant production man who had an increasingly grating rivalry with his fellow Dane, Charles E. Sorensen, an equally brilliant man in these areas, but gruff and unquestioning of Henry Ford's orders. Knudsen had always been accommodating to his subordinates and more reserved and balanced in his response to Mr. Ford. (This last loss Ford was later to regret, as Knudsen was hired within a year at Chevrolet, where he was to create production methods that would in 1927 make Chevrolet the nation's number-one selling brand, a position it was to maintain almost exclusively for 80 years.) These men all left in January 1921. Previously, in 1919 and 1920, important associates like C. Harold Wills, Ford's right-hand man and greatest designer, the charismatic John R. Lee, in charge of the Sociological Department, and Norval A. Hawkins, in charge of sales, had left. But even so, Ford had a depth of talent second to no one else's. (Wills's departure in particular could have been foreseen. In a private deal to lure him onboard, Ford had paid him 10 percent of his profits since he joined in 1903, and there were suggestions of Wills making money in shady metals deals, so it was no surprise that when Ford got rid of his stockholders, he got rid of him too.)

Though effective in the short run, some of Ford's personnel cuts were haphazard, slash-and-burn tactics, not considered ones. Had he left this in the far more capable and organized hands of his son and Kanzler, the company might have come up with a far better, and reliable, method of organizing employment and responsibility at Ford, in the manner that Alfred P. Sloan and duPont were then beginning at GM.

Ford's better-idea take on Taylorism was continuous in his factories, no matter the cost of throwing out machines and systems that proved to be outmoded, for he knew that nothing was more cost-efficient than increased work efficiency. Thus, on the day the armistice was declared in 1918, he had all the equipment used to make tanks hauled outside the factory in Dearborn, to prepare for peacetime production. There was never a moment to spare. And this helped cost efficiency in the long run too.

As unnecessary personnel were let go and old machines were sold off, the whole operation became streamlined and more economical. This was much better than Taylorism.

Despite all his efforts, Ford, like everybody else, was forced to close down for inventory adjustment by November 24, 1920, and didn't resume production until February 1, 1921. It was then that his true financial acumen became apparent, with a stroke of what can only be called genius.

No doubt remembering Couzens nailing new Fords into a boxcar to ship them and receive payment, when the factory reopened, Ford did essentially the same thing. Because cars had to be paid for when the dealers received them, he simply shipped them to dealers without orders from them, knowing he was guaranteed payment by contract on all cars shipped; otherwise, dealers were at risk of losing their very valuable Ford franchises. The dealers were furious, as they already had unsold merchandise on their lots. However, Ford sent men into the field to help them move the stock and secure loans for the new merchandise, which after all would increase their liabilities, not Ford's. So when Ford began producing again, he was using their money to pay for parts, since he had been paid immediately, and he paid his bills on a 60-90-day basis, giving him much better cash flow. It all worked. Sales nationwide began to pick up for all manufacturers in early 1921, and by the time Ford resumed production, there was a real market for his vehicles. Thus, through a combination of all his efforts, he was able to pay off his obligations to the banks on time in April 1921 and still have a surplus of nearly $30 million.

During this period and for some time into the future, Ford was considering safeguarding his means of production by controlling the acquisition and flow of raw materials into his factories. In 1919, Ford, along with the naturalist John Burroughs, Thomas Edison, and Harvey Firestone, close friends with whom he made a series of highly publicized summertime camping trips in the 1910s and 1920s, went on a trip through upstate New York and New England. On the way home, he discussed forest, mining, and lakeshore properties in Iron Mountain, located in the Upper Peninsula of Michigan. Ford had made it clear to E. G. Kingsford, a real estate agent from the area, that he wanted to buy large tracts of timberland, iron mines, lakeshore property, and other facilities to furnish his factories with raw materials. And in fact, over the next two years, he purchased over 850,000 acres of timberland and 2,200 acres of ore- bearing land; erected sawmills and chemical plants to convert the residue of timber production into usable products; and purchased port facilities, ships, and shipping equipment to accomplish his goals. Beginning in

1920 and continuing until 1923, he also bought up coal mines in Kentucky and West Virginia to ensure himself an uninterrupted supply of that material.

The last venture turned out so well that by 1928, Ford sold off one-quarter of his coal production to the public. Ford had a long-standing policy of selling excess coke and coal to his employees at bargain prices; when even they couldn't use it all, the rest was sold to all comers.

The ore venture was another matter, not actually producing anything until 1929. This didn't matter given that, until then, wood was used extensively in the production of car bodies, and Ford could have supplied 80 percent of it. But in fact, he used others to supply it, keeping his own holdings in reserve. In this respect, essentially, he got things backward, because in a few years, metal would increasingly be used in the production of motor cars, and wood would almost disappear. No matter though, for all this activity accomplished one major goal: He created the impression of self sufficiency with regard to raw materials, and that in itself was enough to assure that his suppliers would keep prices down.

One of Ford's big successes was glass manufacturing, which he got into because of high prices, scarcity, and unreliable quality in the postwar years. Clarence Avery hit on the idea of simplify-ing Model T glass production by eliminating a whole pouring process, which speeded up and cheapened its manufacture enor-mously. By 1926, with production having ballooned to previously undreamt-of heights, Ford was producing 26 million square feet of one-quarter-inch glass, more than ample for all his cars.

At the same time, he acquired the Detroit, Toledo & Ironton, a broken-down railroad begun in 1874 that had never paid a dividend. Its rolling stock, tracks, and roadbeds were badly neglected; its employees were demoralized; and its lines went through remote areas not much frequented by other railroads. Yet it was precisely this last feature that made the railroad especially attractive to Ford, for it meant that his southern coal could be brought to Dearborn in half the time. He purchased the line for the knockdown price of $5 million from owners eager to be rid of it, and proceeded to do his usual reclamation job, cleaning and fixing it up in every conceivable way. In two years he turned a $1.9 million deficit into a million dollar profit, which rose to $1.7 million in 1924. But by 1928, sick of federal laws and regulations, Ford sold out for $36 million, more than seven times what he had paid and, in the process, just missed the devastation of the coming Depression.

Beginning in 1923, Ford commissioned a fleet of huge lake steamers that would connect with his railroad and haul coal and iron ore across the Great Lakes. The steamers, along with barges he purchased, made substantial profits in the period from 1925 to 1929, as they enhanced Ford's ability to produce more cars.

And produce he did. Having just missed the mark of building a million cars in 1919, he surpassed that goal with the ever-expanding Rouge factory in 1921, and then doubled it between 1923 and 1925, while still reducing the price of his vehicles down to an all-time-low of $260 for a touring car with no options. If people couldn't afford a Ford at that price, it wasn't his fault. In little more than a dozen years, he had managed to turn a plaything for the rich into an appliance for the masses.

Once again, however, the workers paid a price. As Ford rehired them in early 1921, he doubled production out of 20,000 fewer workers by means of yet another speed-up. And because he knew the labor market was greatly to his advantage, he tightened wages. The age of paternalism was over, which was becoming apparent to more and more people as Ford was raking in huge profits in the early 1920s. He even admitted as much when he claimed in 1922 that too much attention was being paid to do-gooders.

Ford's self-confidence—many now said arrogance—led him to make some huge mistakes. One was the establishment of Fordlandia, a 2.5-million-acre rubber plantation founded along a tributary of the Amazon in 1928. His hope, at Harvey Firestone's urging, was to break the British monopoly on rubber production. The plantation was intended to eventually provide 38,000 tons of creamed latex a year for the Ford plants. In addition, true to Henry Ford form, it was conducted as a social experiment consisting of small housing developments run as if they were situated in the clean-living (no alcohol or tobacco) Protestant Midwestern United States, which, in the Amazon, was about as wrongheaded as it could be. But despite much energy and a $20 million investment poured into it over almost two decades, it failed, mainly because of the difficulty of planting viable trees and the invention of artificial rubber during World War II. In the mid-1940s, it was sold to the Brazilian government for next to nothing. (The book *Fordlandia* by Greg Grandin is a brilliant analysis of this entire debacle.)

Worse still was the most expensive mistake that Ford ever made, and it was entirely his own fault. Remembering his days at Detroit Edison, he insisted that direct current, rather than alternating current, be installed in his plants. Alternating current had been perfected by 1920, and its superior virtues—greater efficiency and safety—were apparent to all. All, that is, except

Henry Ford. Direct current's woeful inefficiency was eventually so self-evident that even Ford had to concede and install alternating current throughout his plants, at an estimated cost of $30 million. Typically though, he insisted that GE and Westinghouse invent completely enclosed fan-cooled motors for him, which they proceeded to do.

While continuing to build and consolidate his empire with well-publicized success—and simultaneously hiding or disguising its shabby underpinnings and failures—he was also doing something revolutionary to the venerable American work ethic. For the rank-and-file Ford workman, the work in the plants was less backbreaking than before, with less human energy wasted bringing the work to the worker and, wherever possible, machines utilized to perform strenuous tasks. And the workplace itself was clean, light, and airy as it had never been before. But the work itself was impersonal in the extreme. The individuality of the craftsman was bled out of it on purpose. Brainpower was put into the creation of the type of work that each person would do, breaking that work down into the smallest possible unit of effort. For the worker, repetition of the task was key, and that was brain-deadening. It was not for nothing that when *Modern Times*, Charlie Chaplin's satire on factory work, with its scenes of Charlie at the mercy of the mechanical routines of the modern plant, was first shown in Pittsburgh to audiences of steelworkers, nobody laughed. It was simply too true to be funny. In essence, this endless repetition of one single task had little to differentiate it from the work of machines; those jobs in fact were done by men in part because there were not yet machines that could do them. Nothing else mattered than showing up on time to do the miniscule, endlessly repetitive task that was assigned to you. Nothing could have been more demoralizing. The ordinary worker's goal of pride in craftsmanship was gone.

Henry Ford had unfortunately convinced himself that the great mass of workers were too lazy or dimwitted to want to do anything more than this every day. In his mind there were only a few creative types who could focus their thoughts and energies into designing products, machines, and systems for the work. So how could Ford make the work of the common laborer appealing?

He did it by giving them the fruits of success at the same time as they did their work: paradise now, in the form of the five-dollar day, which lifted them up into a realm of better living, not in the hereafter, but in the quotidian. They could know exactly why they put up with the drudgery of routine and the din of the factory every week when they got their paychecks. With the money they earned, they could buy the same nicer, more valuable homes, furnishings, clothes, and machines that previously belonged only to the God-fearing, industrious middle class. They didn't have to be better than anyone else at what they did to prove their worthiness, just reliably good enough and decidedly no better, because anything else could ruin the entire production scheme, over which they had no control. The Messiah wasn't the Messiah anymore; the Machine was the new Messiah, granting its bounty to all who performed its rituals. And Henry Ford was its high priest and intermediary.

Ford had created prosperity for all; it was the end product of his complete system of mass production. But what Ford didn't realize was that he was making his workers into something they had never been before: free men in their private lives. When you took the horse away from people and replaced it with a machine, you took away all the time, care, and effort that went into keeping the horse, and left people with much more time to think and act for themselves, in new and unconventional ways if they so chose. And when you took them away from the farm and farm life and brought them to a factory in the city, you opened them up of necessity to an entirely new way of life: urbanization. The Jazz Age of the 1920s was not a rural phenomenon, and both its blandishments and its sickly come-ons were out in the open for all to see and experience. Work in itself had been devalued for the masses. It was the material fruits of that work that were now prized above all else, and Ford, to his dismay, had no way to reverse what he saw as the soulless materialism of the new age.

Ford tried in many ways to revive old-fashioned country ways and values. His most ambitious plan was to build a series of villages on bodies of water that would give people pleasant homes in the open, fresh air, with opportunities for manufacturing during part of the year, and outdoor work, preferably in agriculture, during the rest of it. His thinking for planned communities along the Tennessee River and in Fordlandia occasioned some of his notions for these towns. Several small ones were built, starting in rural Georgia in the 1930s; these were interesting, well-thought-out experiments that went on for some time, but they died out with him. He used to say that the only thing more powerful than great armies was an idea whose time had come. Sadly, he didn't recognize the cultural idea of the modern world when it came along. The great irony of this was that he had done so much to bring it into existence.

EIGHT

HAS SOMETHING COME
BETWEEN US?

The past is a foreign country: they do things differently
there.

—L. P. Hartley

FROM THE TIME HE ANNOUNCED THE FIVE-DOLLAR DAY AT THE
beginning of 1914, Ford became an international celebrity,
mobbed by people eager to hear anything from him or even
touch him on the sleeve. This unnerved Ford deeply at first, until
he began to realize that he liked his newfound status with the
public. He started to see that he could create a mythical Henry
Ford for them, cut and sewn to measure from materials he himself supplied, and that this creation could make weighty, albeit
homespun, pronouncements on the issues of the day. The problem was that he began to believe he actually was this creation,
and then he began to believe in the validity of what he had to say

even more than his most ardent admirers did. Ford was the most quoted man in America by 1920, holding forth in little roadside interviews and expounding his philosophy in books and articles written by others.

This carefully crafted public scenario didn't always work according to plan. The hasty, ill-considered Peace Ship scheme in late 1915 made him a laughingstock for awhile. Then there was the black eye he got in the press for keeping Edsel out of the war when so many other boys were proudly marching off to join it; Henry and Edsel never quite lived that down.

The 1919 libel suit against the *Chicago Tribune* caused further humiliation. In the presses of the influential urban centers, the "ignorant idealist" looked like a fool; this shattered the carefully constructed myth. From then on he saved his pronouncements for intermediaries to make, mostly through the medium of his own publications.

In 1918, Ford bought a failing hometown publication called the *Dearborn Independent* and transformed it into a nationally circulated weekly megaphone for his views. He even had "Mr. Ford's Own Page" each week to be sure he would have the chance to put forth his "ideas and ideals . . . to the public without having them garbled, distorted, or misrepresented." The aforementioned E. G. Pipp, editor of the *Detroit News*, was induced to become his first editor, due to Pipp's strong belief in their shared idealism. Ford bore all production costs himself, since he didn't want to be beholden to any advertising interests. His fame prompted tens of thousands to subscribe to it immediately. Through various ploys, including forced sales through Ford dealerships, the circulation of the *Independent* reached a 1926 high of 650,000.

The *Independent* at first consisted of rather innocuous editorials on subjects from science and industry to education and agriculture, and fiction from respected writers such as Booth Tarkington. But from the first edition containing "Mr. Ford's Own Page" in January 1919, this became the most important feature in the paper. Ford spoke in his editorials ("with plain Americans in a way that we can understand each other") about his favorite themes concerning opportunity, hard work, and public service, as well as profits for industry, and the evils of war, absentee ownership, and speculative capitalists.

A year later, however, the *Independent* published a hair-raising series of Antisemitic articles that were eventually collected into four volumes called *The International Jew*. These diatribes went on for 91 weeks, and their tone and substance outraged much of America. They also poisoned the atmosphere at the *Independent*, which became torn apart by factions at the paper with their own axes to grind. Pipp himself quit in April 1920, soon after learning of the planned series of Antisemitic articles, which were more than he could bear. He was shortly to write a scathing attack on Ford in a book called *The Real Henry Ford*.

It is important to note that nothing in the *Independent*, not even "Mr. Ford's Own Page" or *The International Jew* series, was written by Henry Ford. Nonetheless, the paper published no opinion except by his instigation and with his approval. There is considerable evidence that each issue was read to him before it was published. But the words were always someone else's, so when it became convenient and necessary to deny his own authorship, he was able to do so fairly easily.

The "someone else" who was writing articles under Ford's name was mostly William J. Cameron, a brilliant editor and writer who arrived at the *Independent* at the behest of Pipp, for whom he had worked at the *Detroit News*. During the early 1920s, Ford came almost daily to the magazine's offices for chats on various issues of the day, which were turned into articles. But his statements required an understanding of his thought processes, which jumped from one subject to another without prelude and the expressions of which were cryptic to the point of incoherence to all but those closely initiated into the mysteries of his syntax and ideology. "Mr. Ford has a twenty-five track mind," Cameron explained. Later on, either Cameron or Fred L. Black, who also worked at the *Independent*, were present at any Ford press interviews, interpreting for journalists "what Mr. Ford meant" by his often garbled words, as the man himself sagely nodded his approval. On the rare occasions when Cameron or Black was not present during an interview, journalists were left wandering around in a haze of seemingly unconnected thoughts and epigrams. (It is interesting to note that Cameron was so important to Ford that even though he was a world-class drunk, Ford turned a blind eye to this hated foible.)

In short, Ford didn't actually write any of the articles attributed to him in the *Independent* both because he didn't have the journalistic skills to do so and because he was canny enough to know that they could never be pinned on him directly if he did not. But even though they were pushed through a journalistic mix-master, there is little doubt that the ideas expressed therein, including those in the Antisemitic series, were Ford's own, and nobody else's.

"Antisemitism" is actually not a term of recent coinage. (Scholars have now returned to this original spelling from the more recent "anti-Semitism" because they believe it better emphasizes the most important part of the term.) It appears to have been invented by Wilhelm Marr in Germany in 1879, when he founded the Antisemitic League, an openly political organization. But diffuse anti-Judaism, or Judeophobia, the fear and hatred of Jews, was ancient, dating in Egypt to at least 700 years before Christ and 1,300 years before Mohammed. Jews were attacked and massacred in Alexandria in the first century CE and devastated by a series of Jewish wars that began in 66 CE and ended in 136 CE. Philo of Alexandria tells us that there were a million Jews in that part of the world around the beginning of the first century CE, but by the end of the Jewish wars, very few were left, and those were scattered in various cities of the Mediterranean littoral. Until that time, attacks on Jews were based on their legalism, perceived unpleasantness to others, and stubborn adherence to their own god in a carnal religion, coupled with a closeness to powerful elites and a willingness to do their bidding.

In the Christian mindset, "The Jew" not only became synonymous with carnality, physicality, and picayune legalism (as opposed to the greatness of what Saint Paul calls, in direct contrast with Judaism, "things of the spirit"); Jews were also taxed for their pervasive xenophobia, clannishness, and above all their supposed secret hatred of Christianity, of which there is little evidence. But beyond all this, as David Nirenberg shows in his magisterial work *Antisemitism: The Western Tradition*, anti-Judaism became, over the next two millennia, a widely disseminated mentality, a generalized way of thinking about *anything* one was opposed to, not just Jews and Judaism. In short, anti-Judaism, or Judeophobia, entered into and has remained in the vocabulary of Christendom as a form of denigration. In the first seven centuries of Christianity's rise, intense debates arose about the meaning of Judaism in relationship to Christianity. But little or none of it occurred with actual Jews present in society, even where there were a few to be found. The opponent was rather the negative mental construct, "The Jew." Saint Augustine, for example, who provides a defense of Jews in *The City of God* (one that still remains authoritative in the Church) encountered only one Jew in his lifetime, in a court case. It was, in short, the Christian idea of Jews that was being debated, not the actuality.

What about Antisemitism? What *is* Antisemitism? When Wilhelm Marr coined the soon-to-be-ubiquitous term in Germany in 1879, he intended to break with what he considered to be the "religious" and "medieval" tradition of Christian Jew-hating, and instead founded a new ideology based on sociological observation against Jews not as a faith, but as a separate "nation" or culture, or (later) "race." "Jewification" he argued, was threatening to overtake Germanness as the dominant national force. He aimed his brickbats at the recent rise of Jews in many leading areas of professional, artistic, and business life (especially banking) now that the recent laws of emancipation were making participation in these livelihoods possible for them. Antisemitism offered palpable action for change, unifying all strata of society. By its self-severance from its "medieval" past, it offered people an opportunity to hate Jews "scientifically" without Christian guilt.

The Antisemites' claim that "the Jew is everywhere" was in a sense modern, but it was also in reality a preservation of the *longue durée* of Judeophobia through the ages, as any historian of it in medieval or ancient times could easily show. In fact, no speech act of Antisemitism could ever be completely free of religious significance, intended or not. But now it was to be the socioeconomic, cultural-racial, and secular that counted, not the religious. The old Jew-hatred had to disappear, so Antisemitism could be (supposedly) empirical, not personal or irrational.

But "The Jew" in Gentile eyes is never what he appears to be or is said to be; he is always attendant on the gaze cast at him. This gaze was not a steady one. Marr's organization attracted few adherents and soon disappeared. Others, from the Berlin Movement, took up the term and spread it, both in Germany and other countries. It became trendy throughout Europe, and many used it as an attachment to other ideas, to show a certain social conservatism. But Antisemitism was a weak doctrine compared to competing ones like Marxism, Social Christianity, or National Liberalism, all of which could be converted by better thinking in their own ranks. Antisemitism was a one-trick doctrine that could not evolve, and it failed utterly to convince large numbers of people that its view of "The Jews" was based on a realistic assumption. By the eve of World War I, it was a marginal political view, more mystique than politique to the general public.

But whatever its shortcomings, Antisemitism was definitely a political act, not a set of inchoate feelings or unsuspected attitudes. It was a public, political position that disseminated its position, had organization, and attracted money and commitment from its adherents. After the war, its strength would be resurgent.

Somehow, when he was in his early 50s, Henry Ford allowed pylons of this deadly prejudice to sink deeply into his mind. Unschooled as he was and unreflective, he seems to have imbibed a considerably greater degree of semiconscious antipathy to Jews than what was felt by most Americans, who were only moderately Judeophobic, compared with Europeans, in the 19th century. (Americans had other prejudices and *bêtes noires*.) It is hard to know or measure these early feelings, for no contemporaneous documents speak about his youthful attitudes toward Jews; we can only judge after the fact, when he "came out" suddenly and unexpectedly as an Antisemite in 1920. In any case, neither he in his lifetime nor his reputation a hundred years later would ever be free of this poisonous taint again.

At the time of Ford's birth, there were about 400 Jews in the state of Michigan. Like everyone else around him, all Ford knew of them in his childhood were the Shylock and Fagin stereotypes he read about in the *McGuffey Readers*. Later, as a typical farmer from small town America in the 1880s, Ford was a firm believer in the ideas of the Greenback Party, which advocated money backed by silver rather than gold. Cheap money would make credit more available and loans easier to pay back. Who advocated the gold standard? Why, bankers and Wall Street financiers. And who were they? One common perception in the United States was that they were " all Jews," though here again, this prejudice was far less extensive or evident than in Europe, not least because there were far fewer Jewish bankers here than there. Ford, like many others, adhered to this stereotype. (It was said he called all Wall Street bankers Jews even if they weren't, like Jay Gould.) Then too, Ford had an abiding nostalgia for an idealized, healthier rural past. He saw modern culture, with its jazz, flappers, bootleg liquor, and liberal urban press as the enemy of his social dreams; he thought Jews, in large measure, were behind these social depredations. One could perhaps say as much for later Nazi Antisemites, but there was an enormous difference. Ford was nostalgic for a social past that had actually existed, one in which he had happily participated. To him, the country would be better off if all men returned to espousing and living the values of that past. This was a far cry from the Nazi commitment to a mythical, exalted racial past of gods and heroes to which the German people should return, and on whose behalf the Third Reich was willing to enslave and eventually annihilate subhuman and mongrelized races, whose modern ascendancy they attributed to the efforts of Jews to take over the world.

Ford's deep animus toward Jews appears to have moved into overt and willful consciousness at the time of the Peace Ship debacle in 1915, his first major public defeat. Despite all his talk about the Emersonian notion that defeat was important in life because of what you could learn about yourself from it, Ford immediately began looking for a scapegoat. Madame Schwimmer, the Hungarian Jewess who had organized the expedition for Ford, was startled to find him blaming Jews and their financial interests for starting and maintaining the war. He pointed to papers in his pocket that constituted "proof" of his charges, proof that he would reveal when the time was right. Later, he alluded darkly to a Jewish journalist on the trip who had revealed to him that it was indeed Jewish financiers who were behind the war. When Herman Bernstein, who had been on the Peace Ship as a journalist, published an expose of *The Protocols of the Learned Elders of Zion* as a complete forgery, Ford "revealed" that Bernstein had been the man who had told him of the Jewish conspiracy, occasioning Bernstein to launch a $200,000 lawsuit against him that dragged on for years.

In a way, Ford's history with Jews up until that time was not much different from that of many Americans who had a generalized prejudice based on old stereotypes that were received "wisdom," little examined, as Jews themselves were little experienced in life in many parts of the country. Their prejudice could boil over into hateful acts, such as the Leo Frank trial and lynching in Atlanta in 1915. But Antisemitism as an organized movement, with principles and doctrines, did not exist here as it did in Europe. Americans knew mainly age-old Judeophobia and anti-Judaism, the private sentiment, only somewhat acknowledged among its believers, often hidden or disguised in the larger society.

Ford's associates were convinced that the origins of his decision to move from personal Judeophobia to public Antisemitism had been encouraged by Ernest Liebold, a passionate admirer of his own German heritage and a rabid Antisemite himself. He came to Ford through James Couzens, who, in 1912, saw and admired his hard work and abilities in a banking position. Liebold rose through the ranks to become Ford's private secretary, handling everything from his correspondence to his personal banking; in addition to Ford's checkbook, he had a million dollars of his boss's money in a safe in his office. Due to Ford's inattentiveness to detail, not to mention his reckless disregard for it, Liebold was often left on his own to make important decisions for him with little or no guidance. One of Liebold's functions was to keep Ford away from unwanted appointments and almost all of his correspondence. Thus Ford, who received millions of letters during his lifetime, was prevented from seeing the contents of almost all of them. So, in this way, perhaps the most important businessman in the world was basically unavailable to just about everyone. Many were quite sure that Liebold's unique position allowed him to fill Henry Ford's receptive ears with Antisemitic ideas.

Ford had a simplistic, Manichean, good-versus-evil view of the world. For a man who could not or would not see the true causes of disorder and evil in himself and the world around him, blaming the Jews in a public and socioeconomic-racial way (i.e., Antisemitism) was perfect as a form of action and explanation. In a previous century he might have said "demons" or "witches" caused these things, and called on priests or elders to confirm it. Now he could rely on books and pamphlets to "confirm" his deepest suspicions.

But it is one thing to have private ideas and prejudices against Jews and quite another to make those ideas public. And if you are Henry Ford, a man with an all-but-unique renown and prestige in 1920, and you openly espouse Antisemitism, it becomes an enormous political act with tremendous ramifications. Did he realize what he was getting himself into? Perhaps not. In any case, in 1920, there was a renaissance of Antisemitism in post-war Europe that might have led American Judeophobes to wonder if the time hadn't come for Antisemitism to work in the United States as well. Then too, the megalomaniac in Ford might well have convinced him that his great and newfound fame entitled him to speak on any subject to the public, which was clamoring for whatever he said anyway. In any case, it surely seems that he came to believe that the world needed to be shown the hidden problem of the Jews in full daylight. Perhaps a public posture was Ford's revenge against the people he thought were behind the despised World War I he had spoken against so vociferously. Perhaps those New York bankers who imposed onerous terms on the loan he sought in the 1920–1921 Depression fueled his desire to carry on the Antisemitic series for so long. But even before he started the series of articles against Jews, he came up against an obstacle he did not foresee: Pipp quitting as editor of the *Independent* upon hearing of these articles. There would be much more opposition to come.

No matter who influenced whom, in the spring of 1920, Henry Ford gave the go-ahead for the articles on the Jews to appear in the *Dearborn Independent*. Liebold, for once showing some restraint, suggested the title *The International Jew* to distinguish those people from other, better kinds of Jews, but Ford, though agreeing to the title, didn't think there was any such distinction.

Predictably the articles inveighed against all sorts of perceived deleterious effects of the Jewish influence on American life, from jazz to flappers with rolled stockings, from immoral books and films to flashy jewelry and the consumption of liquor. Jews were making money by sapping the strength of the American character, foisting such cultural phenomena on the public through the media of Jewish-owned publishers and film studios, etc. These pieces, 91 in all, were mostly written by Dr. August Muller, who had found a position at the *Independent* through Dr. Edward A. Rumely, a close friend of Ford's who had been a member of a German propaganda ring in the United States during World War I.

Shortly after the articles began, another influence was brought to bear on them. *The Protocols of the Learned Elders of Zion* in an English translation reached Liebold's hands through an anti-Bolshevik Russian émigré named Boris Brasol. This infamous forgery had an immediate effect on Liebold and, through him, on Ford.

The document purported to be a record of a secret meeting in the Jewish cemetery of Prague among a select group of distinguished descendants of the Twelve Tribes of Israel. The head of each tribe was supposed to report on its contribution to an imminent takeover of world society by Jews. In one hundred years, their descendants were to reconvene to report the results of the previous century's accomplishments. Supposedly this document was read at the World Zionist Conference in Basel in 1897, which was strange because not a single journalist present reported this. In reality it was crudely concocted in large measure from a French pamphlet of the 1860s that had nothing to with Jews. *The Protocols* were written in French, and after a comic opera of mysterious translation and cross-border smuggling, appeared in Russian in 1905. But it was not until the Russian Revolution that they became widely known and translated.

Shortly after Liebold became aware of *The Protocols* (although excerpts had been printed in Philadelphia the previous year, he did not know of them until meeting Brasol), references were made to them in *The International Jew* articles. First appearing in the tenth of this series, they were used to condemn amusement parks like Coney Island as "centers of nervous thrills and looseness" and to equate Negro music with "Jewish moron music." Supposed Jewish control over all sorts of important aspects of American life was constantly hammered home in the series, which also warned that Jews would triumph not through acts but by words, literally talking a path to hell.

It was no surprise that Ford would give currency to these ideas at that time. The Russian Revolution and World War I had caused tremendous upheavals in people's lives, and they were willing to listen to outrageous notions about what might have been behind these events. Ford's anti-Judaism had been growing since 1915, and *The Protocols* fed into his gullible, paranoid fantasies about what might be causing what he saw as the breakdown of American life. So printing them was an easy decision for him to make. No one could tell him not to, and he was not wise enough to tell himself not to.

Later in 1920, collected *International Jew* articles were printed in book form by Ford's Dearborn Publishing Company to keep up with the supposed demand for reprints. Perhaps as many as 500,000 copies of this first volume were printed, and it was followed up by three more volumes of collected articles over the next year and a half, each selling for 25¢; in addition, many were distributed free of charge to "influential people." When these books began to be translated and reprinted overseas, Liebold was able to claim that he could not prevent this, because none of the articles had ever been copyrighted, which was true. Thus, the book could be distributed worldwide by anyone who wished to do so, and it was read by millions in 16 languages, including the six editions published in German by 1922.

One of its biggest fans was Adolf Hitler. Ford was the only American mentioned by Hitler in *Mein Kampf* and, according to his American editors, he even copied some sections of *My Life and Work* (about which more later) verbatim into the unexpurgated edition of his book. Hitler was also said to have a full-length portrait of Ford in the headquarters of the National Socialist Party.

Ford had no sooner printed up and made available an edition of *The Protocols* when a series of articles in the *London Times* by Philip Graves appeared in August 1921, exposing *The Protocols* as a fraud. Liebold had already said the previous January that the *Independent* could not vouch for the truth of *The Protocols* and simply made them available to let the public make up their own minds about the claims therein. Ford himself stubbornly insisted, despite the Graves exposure, that they seemed to be an expression of the way things had been and still were in the 16 years since they were originally printed.

Cameron, who told Pipp he had a personal distaste for the *International Jew* articles, nevertheless was responsible for having them written, and he did his boss's bidding in researching every Antisemitic allegation, no matter how outlandish and chimerical. Perhaps the most hare-brained was the assertion that Jewish bankers were behind the plot to assassinate Lincoln because of his support of the Greenback Party. Though exhaustively researched, proof of any of these allegations was never found.

There was something of a market for these articles in America at the time, although they did not get the popular play they got in central Europe, where the hammer blows of a disastrous war and political destruction had battered the broad public into considerably more paranoia and gullibility than in the United States, at least as far as Jews were concerned. This is hard to imagine today. If they were to appear now, they would be considered the ravings of a lunatic fringe. But things were different then. (L. P. Hartley was right; the past *is* a foreign country.) At the close of World War I, Bolshevism was considered a foreign threat to order and the American way of life, a belief that added to a rising tide of xenophobia and the severe immigration quotas that followed. The Ku Klux Klan, which was anti-Jew, anti-Catholic, anti-Negro, and in fact anti-anything that was not white, Anglo-Saxon, and Protestant, was swelling its ranks by the millions. By 1920, there were close to a million Klansmen in Michigan alone. Paranoia was epidemic in the American public, especially in rural and small town areas where Ford found his greatest popular strength.

On the other hand, and this cannot be stressed strongly enough, the American political and social scene, with its primarily Protestant liberal elites, however marked they were privately by anti-Jewish beliefs and attitudes, did not cotton to overt Antisemitism as it was reemerging in post-war Europe. This sort of thing was considered vulgar and "foreign," not native to a country that had opened its arms to a million Jews in the 19th century and had manifestly battened on their industry and achievements. Various forms of racism, nativism, and know-nothingism (anti-Catholicism) flourished in the United States, but not organized political Antisemitism as the Europeans knew it.

Then too, American Jewish associations reacted and were heeded by other elites. In November of 1920, a coalition of Jewish organizations co-signed a withering response to *The International Jew*, written by Louis Marshall of the American Jewish Committee. Then, an incensed social critic, John Webster Spargo, having previously published a vigorous rebuttal of Ford's views, composed a statement called *The Perils of Racial Prejudice*. It denounced those views once again and was signed by more than 100 "citizens of Gentile extraction and Christian faith," including Presidents Taft and Wilson and President-elect Harding, nine secretaries of state, a cardinal, university presidents, and other luminaries such as Clarence Darrow, William Jennings Bryan, Jane Addams, and Ida Tarbell. On January 16, 1921, it was published in newspapers across the country.

For a time, deaf to all complaints and criticisms, Ford continued to publish his articles. He even went so far as to hire a group of agents in New York to attempt to unmask the operations of the hidden international Jewish government specified in *The Protocols*; all they came up with was a Jewish community organization called the Kahilla, the chief function of which was to educate and protect Jews.

And then one day almost a year later, Ford told an astonished Liebold to stop the articles, and nobody really knows why. Some say it was because he was told that Model Ts were boycotted by Jews in big cities like New York and Cleveland, which seems to be true. But Ford's sales were booming at the time, with the public snapping up everything he could produce, especially in rural and small town areas. Some said Ford stopped publishing the articles because of the importuning of Edsel and others close to him who were deeply embarrassed by the whole situation. But then again, he never listened to Edsel unless he wanted to.

The most likely explanation involved money and politics. At the time, Ford was promoting an "energy dollar," a new kind of currency that derived its value from energy, which could promote production and economic growth; he considered traditional reserves of gold inert and inherently useless. As we shall see, the idea of an energy dollar fit in with his protracted attempt to create a basis for his takeover of the Muscle Shoals power project from the government. Then too, Ford's popularity was attaining new peaks, in part due to a number of books that had been burnishing his image for the public, an effort soon to be crowned by an "autobiography" ghost-written by Samuel S. Crowther, *My Life and Work*, which would become a major best-seller (and which contained the Antisemitic remarks that would so impress Hitler). Ford told Liebold he needed the support of Jewish bankers for his energy dollar, but perhaps even more importantly, because he knew he was a serious contender for the presidency of the United States and had warmed to the idea, he didn't need to be harassed on this issue by the sort of very important people who disagreed with him, Jewish or otherwise. So the articles came to an abrupt end, as Ford realized, perhaps for the first time, that

Antisemitism was a political act that could have disastrous personal and economic consequences. In 19th-century Europe, Antisemites had suffered arrest, aspersions, legal retributions, and social rejection for their "bold public initiatives." Hitler would presently be put into jail—not the first Antisemite to suffer this fate. Henry Ford suddenly realized that he would not be willing to go through any of this sort of public opprobrium, particularly when doing so would also harm his precious corporation. So, while mean-spiritedly suggesting that open-minded Jews should be grateful for the articles because they exposed truths about themselves that needed to be expressed and that could therefore be rectified, he nonetheless brought his Antisemitic campaign to a sudden halt.

There was to be another, more definitive, confrontation between Henry Ford and Jews a few years later, but for now Ford put the kibosh on his fulminations against "The Jew." His popularity returned to dizzying heights, and he was soon seen again as the all-American symbol of success in an age that worshipped success. His presidential ambitions were not so far-fetched after all. In fact, he turned out to be the most-written-about figure in 1920s American journalism next to Calvin Coolidge, and most of the press was favorable. In our more enlightened time, his virulent Antisemitic spasm would surely have buried his popularity, but then, it didn't.

But, as Shakespeare said, "The evil that men do lives after them." Both *The Protocols Of The Learned Elders Of Zion* and, to a lesser extent, *The International Jew* remain widely published, read, and believed today, mostly in Arab and other Islamic countries. Perhaps tens of millions of people, maybe hundreds of millions, have no doubt in their minds that they are true. Thus, they contribute to the continuing misunderstandings and tensions between a major factor of the world's population and the rest of humanity. And for his contribution to this, Henry Ford is much to blame. It is fair to say that next to Hitler, Ford was the most influential Antisemite ever, with the possible exception of Martin Luther.

Unlike Hitler though, Ford never advocated violence toward Jews, much less genocide. He never had anyone killed or suggested that they should be. In fact, Ford's views were based in part on the myth that Jews were providing money for armaments to promote the violence and destruction of war, the human activity he abhorred most of all. To him, violence was only acceptable for the sake of self-defense in wartime; this was consent to unavoidable violence, not promotion of it. In the end, one can only accuse him of what Victor Hugo called "the sins of the inkwell," which may be despicable but remain a far cry from materialization or action. And despite his well-known dislike for the Jews, it is also true that in 1938, when the United States displayed indifference to the plight of European Jews seeking refuge from the Nazis, Ford was advocating for it on humanitarian grounds.

Judeophobic references continued to percolate through the *Independent* for the next couple of years, concentrating on such issues as cultural affairs and, of course, banking. But the firestorm of public Antisemitism didn't return until April 1924, after Ford had definitively lost out on Muscle Shoals, and the idea of his running for the presidency was behind him, hence obviating the idea of his need for Jewish political support. It was then that the *Independent* began an attack on a young Jewish lawyer named Aaron Sapiro from Chicago.

Sapiro was a charismatic former rabbinical student who, after thinking deeply about the plight of the farmers, became prominent in 1919 by urging them to organize into cooperatives to protect their interests in the marketplace. Sapiro suggested that each cooperative should be centered around one specific crop and have a central price setting and payment schedule for its members in a generalized system covering all, to avoid a dilution of specific farming interests. He was smart and his assessment was correct, and as a consequence he was highly successful and respected for his ideas.

By 1924, Midwestern wheat farmers had become discontented with their lot, and Sapiro was trying to gather the growers into a super wheat marketing combination, a highly controversial notion then. Some politicians accused him and his associates of using the support of the farmers for political ends and cheating them on payments. (Sapiro did indeed bill very high fees for his legal services to farmers' cooperatives, and in 1924, there were charges from Canadian wheat and apple growers that he was misappropriating funds from the cooperatives to pay those fees.)

The ever-vigilant staff at the *Independent* noted that many prominent supporters of the cooperatives were Jews, including Bernard Baruch, Eugene Meyer, and Otto Kahn. They then cooked up an increasingly noxious stew of articles claiming that Goldman, Sachs, in providing a $10 million revolving line of credit to farmers, was colluding with the Federal Reserve (which, it stated, was invented by Paul Warburg and other Jews) to prevent farmers from obtaining credit elsewhere, in order to keep agriculture in their hands. Sapiro was involved, they said, because the money for the loans went through his banking institutions; he was also charged with cheating his clients.

Sapiro filed a million dollar anti-defamation lawsuit against Henry Ford (but *not* the *Independent*) in early 1925; it came to trial in March of 1927. Though Sapiro's lawyer, William Henry Gallagher, tried to get Ford's attacks on the Jewish race in general read into the trial, the judge agreed with Ford's lawyer, Senator James A. Reed of Missouri, that since only Sapiro had brought the suit, only Ford's alleged attacks against him were relevant.

The defense proposed that Ford had nothing to do with these attacks, as he had nothing to do with the articles. The lawyers maintained that Ford left all the details of the magazine to subordinates and was too busy a man to pay any attention to them. William Cameron became the fall guy, swearing on the stand for five days that he was solely responsible for what appeared in the magazine, including any articles about Jews; that Mr. Ford had never seen any advance copy; and that in fact he had never even seen Ford read a copy of the publication. Liebold's part in all of this, as both general manager of the Dearborn Publishing Company and Ford's secretary, never came up.

Given that the suit was against Ford, Sapiro's attorneys were determined to make him appear on the stand. Remembering the disaster of his testimony in court during the Mt. Clemens trial in 1919, Ford did everything he could to avoid a subpoena, until one finally fell into his lap as he watched planes at the Ford airport. But subpoena or no, he never showed up in court.

The night before his scheduled appearance, Ford was involved in a mysterious car accident. As he drove along Michigan Avenue in his Ford Coupe, another car sideswiped him, sending his car down a 15-foot embankment and into a tree near the River Rouge. He showed up dazed and bleeding at the gatehouse of his home, Fair Lane, and was taken to the hospital two days later. All sorts of confusing versions of this event were bruited about, including a possible attack by Detroit gangsters and a cover-up engineered by Ford himself to get out of testifying in court. But the most likely explanation was a bit of road rage on the part of a couple of teenagers in a Studebaker touring car who were incensed by Ford's refusal to get out of the fast lane as he drove along pokily in his Model T. In any case, there was a continuance.

Shortly thereafter, one of the jurors, accused of accepting a package that may have contained a bribe, lashed out in self-defense to a reporter, blaming the defense counsel for anxiously trying to keep the case from going to the jury. The judge could not avoid declaring a mistrial, and the case was adjourned for six months.

It was enough time for Ford once again to turn tail and settle, on the advice of his attorneys and in his own self-interest. Characteristically, he went further than anyone could have expected to rectify the situation. On July 7, 1927, he published a personal apology to Sapiro and a retraction of all the attacks on Jews that had appeared in the *Independent*. *The American Hebrew* announced that this was the first time in history that anyone publicly apologized to Jews for Antisemitism. (It wasn't. Wilhelm Marr did the same in the later 1890s after he recanted and attacked Antisemitism.) Ford expressed regret that Jews regarded him as their enemy and disavowed "charges and insinuations" against them published in the *Independent*. He further expressed mortification for giving currency to *The Protocols*, which he admitted were "exploded fictions" charging that the Jews were "engaged in conspiracy to control the capital and industries of the world," besides laying at their door many offenses against decency, public order, and good morals. "Had I appreciated the general nature, to say nothing of the details, of these utterances, I would have forbidden their circulation, without a moment's hesitation," he said.

This apology was Henry Ford's idea alone and was truly astonishing in its range; but it came about through negotiation with two important Jewish leaders, Louis Marshall and Nathan D. Perlman. Once again, Ford did not write a word of it. That was done by Marshall, in consultation with Joseph A. Palma, a Ford man attached to the New York field office of the Secret Service. When it was finished, the apology was brought to Ford's New York office, where his lieutenant, Harry Bennett, attempted to read it to him over the phone, cautioning him that it was "pretty bad." "I don't care how bad it is, you just settle it up," Ford replied. "The worse they make of it, the better." He added, "When my real views are explained to the proper people, they will know I am prepared to act honorably and to repair the damage as far as I can."

No one, including Louis Marshall, who wrote most of it, could believe that Ford would let such a strong statement go under his signature without changing a word. But he did let it go, and when it was released through the offices of the widely syndicated columnist Arthur Brisbane, who had brokered the deal, the entire world was astonished at this complete and utter reversal. Ford settled with Sapiro for $140,000 for expenses and legal fees (Sapiro claimed it was much less), and the now-admiring Herman Bernstein also settled his long-term $200,000 lawsuit for an undisclosed sum. In addition, Ford dismissed both Cameron and Liebold from their posts at the *Independent* (they stayed with the company, however), and at the end of the year, closed the magazine down completely. Even Brisbane's $1 million offer on behalf of Hearst for the magazine did not derail Ford's determination to close it down. In all, he lost nearly $5 million on it in the eight years of his ownership.

Ford emerged from this latest public fiasco of Antisemitism as everybody's darling. He showed up at several testimonials for important Jewish men and at Jewish fundraisers. On one such occasion, 2,000 people stood up and cheered for a full minute at the very mention of his name. He even went to Marshall's office expressing his desire to do anything Marshall might suggest to "minimize the evil that has been done."

That Ford would be forgiven his attempts at organized political Jew-hating so readily is a statement about how little Antisemitism as a formal public movement could get a strong purchase in the United States. It also probably reflects another important influence in America at that time: old-fashioned Protestant revivalism. In tents and houses of worship, millions of people all over the United States were confessing and repenting their sins, in order to be forgiven and reborn in Jesus. In this pervasive national atmosphere, Ford's apology and offers of restitution were a reflection of daily events in the lives of the American multitudes, and they probably saw the meaning of this act as a normal American's expression of guilt and remorse, and the promise to initiate better behavior in the future. Though this was a Jewish situation, not a Christian one, and Ford never framed his actions in any religious terms, shouts of "Hallelujah!" to a repentant sinner were understood by all.

Why did he do this? People can have a change of heart, of course. But Ford's transformation was so startling that it seems too good to be true. It would be nice to think that his about-face was sincere, especially since this period of reconciliation went on for almost six years. But 20 years later, Liebold said, "Mr. Ford...was supposed to have apologized to the Jews, but I think everybody knows about that. He never even read that or ever even knew what it contained. He simply told them to go and fix it up."

What made others question Ford's change of heart later on was that reprints of *The International Jew* began cropping up in different parts of the world in 1933, and Ford made only the weakest of passes at trying to stop them. Liebold gave tacit permission for them by noting the lack of copyright on the articles and following up complaints about them in a desultory manner. Thus, they even proliferated in America, where the German American Bund—an organization formed in the 1930s to promote pro-Nazi views—distributed both English- and German-language editions of *The International Jew*. Scholar Victoria Saker Woeste suggests that if Marshall had lived beyond 1929 to see this, he would have taken a very different view of Ford's apology and spoken out strongly against its sincerity.

Privately, Ford did not discontinue his Judeophobic ravings, as several people attested. In the mid-1930s, he began complaining about "international financiers" and "money lenders" contributing to the rising tensions in Europe. He was accused of contributing money to Nazi coffers in exchange for Hitler's promise to print *The International Jew* and of paying over $300,000 to Prince Louis Ferdinand, second grandson of the late Kaiser, to funnel money to Hitler when the Prince was in Ford's employ in South America. Neither charge was substantiated. In 1934, Kurt Ludecke, on a fundraising jaunt for Hitler in the United States, arranged a meeting with Ford through the efforts of Winifred Wagner, the daughter of Richard Wagner. But despite talk of "those cunning Jews" on Ford's part in this meeting, no evidence has ever arisen that he gave one cent, then or ever, to Hitler. But we will never know for sure. Ford Motor Company archival records pertaining to these questions were destroyed in the 1960s.

It is worth noting that Ford rebuffed Hitler's attempt to get him to construct a second Ford-Werke plant in Germany and become involved in building the Volkswagen. Furthermore, despite enormous Nazi pressure he refused to fire prominent half-Jewish Erich Drestel as head of Ford-Werke for three and a half years, finally letting him go only for incompetence. No one was going to tell Ford how to run his business.

However, we also know that in 1938, Ford accepted the German government's highest civilian award for a foreigner, The Order of the Grand Cross of the German Eagle, on the occasion of his 75th birthday. A huge brouhaha ensued, with Ford defending himself by stating that he was accepting the honor on behalf of 70 million German people, not Adolf Hitler.

Perhaps he only fully understood the consequences of his beliefs in 1945 when, according to his secretary, Josephine Gommon, he saw the first films of the liberation of the concentration camps in an auditorium at the Rouge. He apparently fled from the room in great agitation, shortly thereafter to have a stroke from which he never recovered.

There is a deep sense of remorse and effrontery that stirs in the American soul when one is shown to be a dupe and a fool, especially if one's actions are proven to have had malicious consequences. For a man with Henry Ford's sense of pride and self-worth, it is easy to see that this must have been unbearable.

The simplest reason for his change of heart in 1927 was business. Sales of the Model T, which peaked at over 2 million per annum from 1923 to 1925, declined by 20 percent in 1926 and much more the following winter and spring, despite more modern designs and colors. The general public considered the Model T an old-fashioned, cheap utility car by then. It couldn't compete with the much more modern-looking designs of competitors who were selling cars for well under $1,000, especially the Chevrolet, the production of which was relentlessly ratcheting up thanks to William Knudsen, the man Ford had let go six years before. Under relentless pressure from close associates like Sorensen and his son Edsel, Ford had decided to end production of the Model T on May 27, 1927, and replace it with an all-new Model A within six months. Since the A itself, not to mention the tooling for it, didn't yet exist, even in Ford's mind, this was unquestionably the biggest challenge of his life. The last thing he needed was hostility of any kind, especially from Jews, who (his sales staff had told him) were avoiding his products in increasing numbers, not just in the East, but in the Midwest and California as well. Ford's goodbye to Antisemitism was a perfectly timed gesture.

But there was something deeper here. This was the second time he was forced to give up support for Antisemitism, and this disavowal was much more far-reaching in its scope. In fact, he realized that he had to retract his position against Jews in a spectacular fashion to finally rid himself of the taint of it. It was a period of painful change and growth for him, in which he could no longer afford to be seen as backward in his social thinking, any more than he could in his business thinking. Antisemitism had sunk its poisonous fangs into the hand that fed it, and he had to pull them out to survive. There was never to be a public statement against Jews from him again, no matter what he may have thought or said about them in private. He went back to being the man of private prejudice he once had been, but no longer was he a public Antisemite, visiting his prejudice on the body public, to the detriment of all.

Ford's relationship to Jews was therefore peculiar and complex—in a word, ambiguous. He often pointed out that he never employed fewer than 3,000 Jews in his organization (though he assiduously kept them out of his offices), and he had no trouble doing business with them. As previously noted, he frequently praised Albert Kahn, the architect of most of his buildings, as the best architect he had ever known. Ford even had no qualms about describing Rosika Schwimmer of his doomed Peace Ship expedition as having more brains than all the rest on that trip put together.

Ford also had many warm personal friendships with Jews. In fact, there appears to be no record of his ever having a personal animus against any Jewish individual. He seems to have dealt with "The Jews" completely in the abstract, as he came to do with labor over the years—as if these terms had nothing to do with living human beings. Ford failed to realize this in any meaningful way, which is an explanation for his behavior but not an excuse.

The most poignant illustration of this involves his relationship with Rabbi Leo M. Franklin of Temple Beth-El, who was Detroit's most influential and respected rabbi. Ford and Franklin were neighbors, and the rabbi often visited Fair Lane. Each year, Ford gave him a custom-built Model T. But in 1920, after *The International Jew* series had commenced, Franklin was deeply dismayed, saying that Ford's "publications have besmirched the name of the Jews in the eyes of the great majority, and especially in the small towns of the country," where his word was taken as gospel. "He has also fed the flames of Antisemitism throughout the world." In light of this, he returned the latest car that Ford had sent him. Ford, taken aback at this, phoned the rabbi to ask, in all innocence, "What's wrong, Dr. Franklin? Has something come between us?"

NINE

A BODY IN MOTION TENDS
TO STAY IN MOTION

YOU WOULD THINK THAT THE DEVELOPMENT OF THE SYSTEM OF
mass production and the implementation of the five-dollar day;
the Peace Ship excursion; attaining the status of the most powerful living businessman, the world's richest man, and the first
billionaire; and the building of the Rouge facility, the world's
largest and most modern plant, among other things, would be
enough to satisfy any one man, especially one over 50. But not
Henry Ford.

Ford claimed not to believe in charity, because, he argued, it
took away a man's ambition and self-respect. Instead, he believed
in fairly remunerated work, because it gave people a sense of
self-worth rather than a servile dependence on others. He took
great pains to employ the handicapped at a time when others
thought of them as family burdens or candidates for the poor-
house. If you were blind, deaf, dumb, or even if you lacked one or

more limbs, or were confined to a hospital bed, Ford would find work for you. He even employed 1,000 victims of tuberculosis in a separate space, feeding them a diet designed to help restore their health. In fact, as early as 1913, 7.5 percent of his workers were disabled in some way. John R. Lee maintained a long list of jobs that could be done by people with various specified disabilities, unheard of then. Social disadvantages were no barrier either. Just arrived from Europe and couldn't speak English? Were you black, a woman, or a young man and the sole support of your family? Just out of prison and no one would hire you? Henry Ford would, and treat you well besides. But in none of these instances would he let the whiff of charity permeate his activities. Just good business, he would say, because he got good, productive, and motivated workers through his policies. "Charity becomes unnecessary as those who seem to be unable to earn livings are taken out of the non-productive class and put into the productive."

Despite his stated policy, there is plenty of evidence that Ford and Clara gave away a fair amount of money to benefit private individuals during the course of their lives, many millions in all. Often this money went to cases brought to their personal attention. It certainly fit in with Ford's pattern of interaction with people: warm and generous individually, abstract and often cold with humanity in general.

Ford's first significant involvement in public charity came with what would become the Henry Ford Hospital in Detroit. It started as the Detroit Hospital Association in 1909; Ford was first a member and later the chairman of the board of trustees. When ground was broken for the new building in 1911, only one-third of the necessary cash was in hand, and progress was slow. By mid-1914, things were going so badly that the trustees were considering handing over control of the hospital to the city of Detroit, which Ford thought a bad idea. He proposed taking over the whole thing, returning all monies to anyone else who had contributed to the hospital, provided that he could have a completely free hand in running it. All agreed, and it became a for-profit corporation in 1915, with Henry as president and Edsel as vice-president.

Ford ran the hospital on a completely scientific basis, asking the doctors and health care professionals what they needed and taking full responsibility for catering to those needs. Everything, from the size of the rooms and the amount of air required for each patient, to the kind and amount of instruments that were necessary, was methodically calculated. Doctors and nurses were well paid, but could take no outside work, and though outside doctors could refer patients to the hospital, they could not treat patients there. Costs were also calculated on a rational accounting basis, and everyone, from common laborer to millionaire, was expected to pay, but no more than the services actually cost. The hospital looked into its patients' finances before they were admitted to determine if they could pay their bills. Otherwise, they paid in advance. True charity cases, however, were treated for free.

Mr. and Mrs. Ford made a considerable contribution to the design of the hospital, but it was given to Liebold to supervise the actual construction and running of it until Edsel took over in 1921, in part because the staff did not like the autocratic Liebold. By 1926, Henry Ford had spent over $11 million on the hospital, no mean amount for a man who didn't believe in charity. (Years later, after an appendix operation there, Ford got out of bed and began walking on the second day after the procedure, to the horror of his doctors. When they saw he had no ill effects from this, they began to reconsider their post-operation protocols. This allegedly was the beginning of the modern practice of getting patients ambulatory as soon as possible after an operation.)

In addition to charitable enterprises, Ford was also involved with social and educational reforms. Ford's first foray into education reflected the pedagogical values and methods he thought were worthwhile. There was no question that education had merit in Ford's eyes. Reynold Wik, the author of *Henry Ford and Grass Roots America*, points out that "he often said he was more interested in education than manufacturing." Ford thought people did little reflective thinking. "Thinking is the hardest work there is," Ford would say, "which is the probable reason why so few engage in it." It was his opinion that most individuals needed education from knowledgeable people to guide them through life.

Ford's educational ventures began in 1916 with the Henry Ford Trade School, which educated young boys in the practical skills that would be applicable to their daily living. They were taught traditional academic subjects and shop work in the Ford plants on an alternating weekly schedule. A boy was given a scholarship upon entering the school and paid wages of between 19 and 35 cents an hour for his work; this was deposited for him into a savings account. Starting with a small number of students, the school enrollment quickly grew into the several hundreds.

This was to be the first of many educational ventures in which Ford would be involved, and not just in the United States, for he opened schools in other countries where he was involved in business, like England and Brazil. In the United States, Ford began schools in Greenfield Village in Dearborn—today the home of the Henry Ford Museum—and elsewhere in which boys were educated in traditional subjects, but also given a rake, a hoe, and a plowed plot of ground, on which they were taught to grow produce. They were paid for their crops and helped with their savings plans. These schools were tailored to Ford's ideas about allowing people to combine indoor and outdoor living in their daily existences. By 1938, the model village schools, foreign schools, and various one-room schools he created at certain of his factory towns, along with those at the Henry Ford Trade School, Apprentice School, and Training School for High School Graduates at the Rouge, had 20,000 enrolled students.

Ford had another large philanthropic interest in education, one that didn't have anything to do with the Ford enterprises. It was in Rome, Georgia, at the Berry Schools, founded in 1902 by Miss Martha Berry, a socialite who made education her cause at a time when there was practically no education available to the rural poor in that state. This group of schools took students from the primary grades through college. What attracted the Fords, beginning in 1922, was the institution's emphasis on self-reliance, and the fact that it featured instruction in agriculture and the trades for all its students. After a Berry School college was started in 1927, the Fords stepped up their donations dramatically, providing a quadrangle of several stone buildings. In the end, Ford gave over $2.75 million to the schools, possibly more, and Clara nearly $1.1 million of her own.

The Fords did not create or support traditional, elite institutions of higher education, as did John D. Rockefeller (University of Chicago and Rockefeller University) or Andrew Carnegie (Carnegie Institute, later Carnegie Mellon). In business, Ford distrusted experts and elitism, often choosing untrained men from his shops to be major leaders and department heads. So it was in keeping with his views that his money and efforts went to support education on the practical, basic, and as he saw it, most democratic level.

Beyond educational pursuits, Ford maintained an intense and philanthropic interest in history throughout his life. Everybody knows a version of his famous remark to the *Chicago Tribune* in 1916 that "History is more or less bunk...the only history that matters is the history we make today," and many still remember the shocking ignorance of this subject he showed on the witness stand during the Mt. Clemens trial in 1919, when he couldn't correctly identify Benedict Arnold or the dates of the American Revolution. Deeply embarrassed by this episode and firmly believing that the history of kings, battles, and treaties was not important in the grand scheme of things, Ford began to formulate a plan to give the public his own notion of a tangible history that reflected the lives of real people. While figuring out his ideas, he bought and set aside acreage in Dearborn for future buildings and exhibition space.

He also bought and restored the Wayside Inn in Sudbury, Massachusetts, made popular by Longfellow decades before in his *Tales of a Wayside Inn*. Starting with 90 acres and the inn itself, for which he paid $90,000, he eventually restored and built a 2,667-acre complex around the inn with farms, schools, and restored buildings of many types, from grist mills to a little red schoolhouse, in order to give the public an understanding of an old-fashioned American locality. Ford was to do something similar, albeit on a much smaller scale, with the Botsford Tavern near Detroit, where he had courted Clara 40 years before. The Wayside Inn project cost him over $1.6 million to purchase and restore, and he lost an additional $2.8 million on it during the 22 years between 1923 and 1945, mostly on the farms and schools connected with it. The Botsford Tavern cost him another $600,000.

But this was just a prelude. While the restoration of the Wayside Inn was going on, Ford was refining his museum idea. He decided he wanted to show more than a generalized idea of life in this country: "We shall reproduce the life of the country in every age," he said. To do this, more than a typical museum building was needed, and the idea of a village that would display fully equipped buildings related to major eras of American history began to develop; eventually, this would turn into Greenfield Village, an outdoor museum complex in Dearborn. Everything from Edison's Menlo Park workshops (Edison said all that was missing was the dirt on the floors) to Steven Foster's home would be set up there (the latter was completely unconnected to Foster, as it turned out, which didn't bother Ford, who said his purpose wasn't so much accuracy as drawing attention to the composer). Ford filled the former Dearborn tractor factory with industrial and domestic artifacts he collected ravenously, if somewhat indiscriminately, from all over the country and even abroad through his agents. Naturally, though Ford supervised the creation of the museum, he didn't do it alone, with Edsel, Cameron, and the ubiquitous Liebold among many Ford people working hard on the project. When it came to obtaining the artifacts, some people sold to Ford, and some donated. When it was suggested to one old man that he donate his superb collection of old carriages, wagons, and automobiles to the museum, he dropped dead. Eventually his widow was cajoled out of the collection, and 56 freight cars brought the artifacts to Dearborn. As word got out, all sorts of people offered items to Ford, who had already collected so much that his warehouses were laden with many duplicates of various items. With his abhorrence of waste, it is hard to see why he allowed this, "unless," as Charles Voorhees speculated, "it was so he could have what there was, and there would be no more left."

The one aspect of American life that was completely left out of the Henry Ford Museum was war. Not a trace of it was to be found anywhere. Ford started his museum to counteract the notion that history was only an accounting of violent confrontation and conflict, reflecting the biases of the academic professionals who taught and wrote about it. But in his history, he was no less selective than they and no less prejudiced.

The museum itself, which covered eight acres under its roof, was designed as an adaptation of Independence Hall in Philadelphia, though on a much larger scale. The museum and Greenfield Village were to be connected as types of libraries to the Edison Institute, where young men were to be educated in the industrial trades.

The grand opening of the Henry Ford Museum and Greenfield Village took place on October 21, 1929, a date chosen to commemorate the 50th anniversary of the illumination of Edison's first lightbulb. No expense was spared, and a day-and-night-long celebration of the event brought luminaries, including Madame Curie, Orville Wright, Will Rogers, Walter Chrysler, Albert Einstein (by telephone hookup from Berlin), and even President Herbert Hoover, to offer their congratulations. The celebration was called the Golden Jubilee of Light, and millions in the United States and abroad listened to it on the radio. People had been asked to turn off their electric lights just before the exact moment of the illumination of the first lightbulb. Edison walked into the Menlo Park replica, and when he reached up and illuminated a lightbulb with two wires, lights were turned on all across America. The great man himself was so exhausted and moved by all of this that he could barely pull himself together to speak.

A gigantic painting depicting all the celebrities present at this event, resembling in no small measure the monumental Jacques-Louis David painting of the coronation of Josephine by Napoleon I, was commissioned to commemorate it. Considering that Ford's grand opening celebration took place just eight days before the stock market crash of 1929, which heralded the start of the Great Depression, it could be considered the last major event of the Roaring 20s. At the time, the illumination from the Golden Jubilee of Light only reached backward, its meaning understood today as retrospection, not prediction. For the world was on a gigantic liner navigating into the dark ocean of the future; standing on the rearmost section of the top deck, one could only wave and salute this sparkling event through one's tears of nostalgia for what would soon disappear into the night.

It took almost four years before the public was admitted on June 12, 1933. Ford officially spent over $10 million on this project, and his wife and son in excess of 10 percent more in addition to that. The real sums were probably greater. In today's terms it would be close to a billion dollars, maybe more. What he got for his investment was a cavernous warehouse of historical artifacts, some well chosen and curated, others not. The problem was that there was no clear central idea among the tremendously varied exhibits. Comparing it with the Deutsches Museum of History in Munich, which was focused on science and technology, Ford scholar Keith Sward called Ford's museum "a hodge-podge, despite its core of excellent restorations. It has the appearance of an Old Curiosity Shop, magnified 10,000 fold."

It was also interesting that while Walter Chrysler, only two years younger than Ford, was building the famed Art Deco Chrysler Building in New York as an architectural symbol of the Jazz Age, Ford was turning all his energies into denying that age through this reconstructed view of the long-gone past.

"I have no patience with professional charity or with any sort of commercialized humanitarianism," Ford said in *My Life and Work*. "The moment human helpfulness is systematized, organized, commercialized and professionalized, the heart of it is extinguished, and it becomes a cold and clammy thing." Nevertheless, of the approximately $139 million he earned between 1913 and 1947, Henry Ford is estimated to have spent somewhere between $25 and $37 million on philanthropy, educational projects, and public works. (The amount is hard to determine because some of it appeared under the rubric of "business expenses"; we do know that over $15 million was deducted from his taxes for charity during this time.) Clara and Edsel together contributed $3.8 million more, and Edsel millions more of his own money. And that is quite apart from the monies that went into the Ford Foundation after the deaths of father and son.

In the end, the Ford Foundation, headquartered in New York City, remains the most enduring and significant philanthropic activity begun by Henry and Edsel, with a vast scope and reach that has affected the lives of millions of people in the over 75 years since it was established. Benefits notwithstanding, the foundation was originally conceived as a necessary tax dodge. Legislation passed in 1935 during the New Deal would have meant that new inheritance- tax rates would have removed ownership of the

Ford Motor Company from the family's hands after the deaths of Henry and Edsel, who owned 97 percent of it. The thought that the money Ford had earned could wind up supporting Roosevelt's social spending galvanized the old man into finding a way to prevent this. He set his lawyers to work studying the new law so they would come up with a plan that would both comply with it and keep the family in control of the firm.

They devised a brilliant scheme in which 95 percent of the company's stock was to become non-voting class A stock. The other 5 percent was to be voting class B stock, and both types were to be privately held. Upon the deaths of Henry and Edsel, the class A shares were to be given to a foundation, which would be tax-exempt as a charity under American law. But the control, that voting class B stock, would remain in the hands of the family.

Accordingly, on January 15, 1936, the Ford Foundation was established "to receive and administer funds for scientific, educational and charitable purposes, all for the public welfare and for no other purpose." Less than a month later, Henry and Edsel signed new wills that left their stock, already divided into the A and B shares, to the foundation and their families in accordance with this plan. Through this extraordinary piece of economic foresight, the payment of some $321 million in inheritance taxes was averted, the Ford Motor Company remained in family hands, and the work of what turned out to be one of the most important and useful charitable organizations ever created was made possible.

Ford may have been driven by calculated financial and business considerations, rather than a genuine charitable impulse, to do this; but if ever the phrase "the gift that keeps on giving" applied, it was to the establishment of the Ford Foundation. Education, the arts, and the eradication of poverty are just three areas of American life that have benefited from the foundation in major ways.

As a footnote to his educational activity, Ford in the mid-1920s developed a keen interest in reviving the old-time dancing of his youth, everything from square dancing to the schottische and varsoviana. He organized dances for his employees, offering them instruction, and hired musicians who played old tunes on fiddles and dulcimers. Attendance at these Friday night affairs was all but compulsory for his executives, who were expected to join the dancing Fords in their favorite recreation.

It was yet another way in which the man who had done more than any other individual to drag people into the modern age did everything he could to pretend that age didn't exist. In Ford's opinion, health, work, and fun were all things that drew their sustenance from the worthwhile values and practices of the past. He was effectively denying that he had at last escaped that past himself when he left the farm for Detroit in 1891. In the conduct of all his businesses, he did everything in his power to throw old practices, and the values that sustained them, on the scrapheap as soon as new ideas and systems could take their place. This was the paradox of Henry Ford, who might well have said:

> Appreciate old-time farm life, but come to work in one of my enormous urban factories. Look at the wonderful craftsmanship of old-time machine artifacts in my museums, but work in my factories where craftsmanship is disdained and replaced with relentless mechanical efficiency. Look at old-time consumer items with affection, but make and buy modern ones turned

out by the millions for your benefit. Listen to the clangor of my factories all day long as you work in a time frenzy, but when you go home, don't listen to syncopated, sliding, brassy jazz—No!, listen to sweet old-fashioned melodies and dance to them instead.

Ford saw what was happening around him, but believed that he could bend the private lives and wills of men in the direction he thought best, just as he insisted they do on company time in his factories. It was a battle of wills in which he could never triumph, because the world never reverts, and time never recedes; they proceed in endless, often unexpected, new directions.

Sometimes, however, he was standing on the right beach when the tide of history came rolling in. Ford's view on race relations between whites and blacks in America is one example of this. As bad as Ford's relationship was with Jews, it was the opposite with blacks. In his youth he had worked with a black man, William Perry, at opposite ends of a cross saw in Dearborn. In 1914, he brought Perry to the Highland Park factory and made him his first black employee, admittedly something of a showpiece at first to demonstrate Ford's unorthodox hiring practices. But Perry wasn't just a token, as Ford's distinguished biographer Robert Lacey points out, because by the early 1920s, Ford had more than 5,000 black workers in his employ and by 1926, 10,000, some 10 percent of his total workforce and more than all the other car companies combined.

This last figure did not occur by mere happenstance, but was rather part of a considered response to a civic appeal by the mayor of Detroit, John W. Smith, in early 1926. The previous autumn the city was roiled by one of the most sensational trials of the 1920s, in which Dr. Ossian Sweet and ten other black men were accused of slaying a white man in a predominantly middle-class neighborhood on Detroit's east side. Under police protection, Dr. Sweet and his family had moved into an $18,000 house he had purchased on September 8, 1925. The next night, thousands of whites massed outside the house and began throwing rocks. Tensions escalated until men fired some 30 shots from inside the house; one fired by Sweet's brother killed a neighbor sitting on his porch across the street. After two trials, defense attorney Clarence Darrow, fresh from the Scopes monkey trial in Dayton, Tennessee, obtained an acquittal for all the defendants by putting the matter straight to the jury, after cutting through the rigged testimony of scores of white witnesses: "If eleven white men had shot and killed a black while protecting their home and their lives against a mob of blacks...they would have been given medals."

Racial tensions escalated in Detroit after this trial, and it was obvious that part of the difficulty was that the tens of thousands of blacks who had migrated to the city in the last six years had bad jobs and lived in terrible conditions. In response, Mayor Smith established an interracial committee in 1926, the city's first, which approached all the large employers in the city to see what could be done about getting more jobs and better working conditions for blacks. The committee was frozen out by practically everyone, except Henry Ford.

Ford took the pleas very seriously and immediately set about making more jobs, and better jobs, available to black workers, and at the same rates he paid whites. "Ford never paid a man more, or less, because of his skin," said Lacey. "Henry Ford's black employment policy was genuinely ahead of its time."

There were fights and work stoppages when blacks were given jobs as foremen supervising whites at Ford, so the mayor suggested some segregation to ease tensions. Up until then, most blacks worked at the foundry (where, to be sure, the dirtiest and most dangerous jobs were located). Ford's solution to the mayor's suggestion was to move out the whites and give all jobs at all levels, right up to plant superintendent, to blacks. In recent years, many blacks who worked at the foundry complained about these dangerous jobs, but in 1926, this was a revolutionary employment policy, and the black workers were very proud of this opportunity. So was Ford, for he could boast that the foundry was the most efficient and profitable department of all at the Rouge, suggesting that this result was connected to his policy.

Ford brought equality to his workplace because of an innate sense of fairness about employment and what seems to have been genuine color blindness when it came to questions of race as Nevins and Hill point out. But he didn't do it just out of moral conviction—he did it because he got value from this part of his workforce. Later, when he was deeply mired in labor problems, he took advantage of blacks' feelings for him, using their sense of loyalty to him to fight against union organizers. Still, in 1926, 60 years after the end of the Civil War, when membership in the Ku Klux Klan was at its peak and blacks were often lynched for imagined offenses against white people, Henry Ford was second to none in his treatment of black employees in the workplace.

In addition to his belief in equal treatment for all, Ford was staunchly opposed to capital punishment. He was a believer in criminal reform—give them a chance to make themselves into productive citizens, he felt, instead of locking them up in prisons where they were useless to themselves and everyone else.

His thinking about capital punishment was connected to his opposition to war, behind which were conspiring capitalists whose intent, as David Nye put it, was "to harden the sensibilities of the people, for it serves their ends to have war." During the famous Sacco and Vanzetti trial, a *cause célèbre* of the 1920s, Ford threw his support behind these men, believing as many did that they had been railroaded into a murder conviction because they were self-confessed anarchists. He tried unsuccessfully to get their death sentences, which were carried out in 1927, commuted to life imprisonment, so they would have a chance to present fresh evidence in a new trial. It was part of his commitment to the rights of the working man, the underdog. Probably the last letter Bartolomeo Vanzetti wrote was to thank Henry Ford for his efforts on his behalf.

Ford's stances on so many issues brought him squarely into public life. For a time, in the early 1920s, he was even a serious Republican candidate for the presidency of the United States, though earlier when he was actually running for U.S. senator from Michigan, he ran as a Democrat. How did this come about?

Ford's entry into national politics came in 1916, when Woodrow Wilson, seeking a second term, was on the ropes in his campaign because of a strong challenge from Charles Evans Hughes. It seemed the election would turn on the California vote, as indeed it did. Ford liked Wilson because of his pacifist sympathies, and when he was approached to support him, he agreed, denying a somewhat suspicious grassroots campaign to put his own name in nomination and spending some $35,000 to bolster Wilson's candidacy in California in the waning days of the election. After an all-night cliffhanger, Wilson won the state by 4,000 votes, securing his reelection.

Two years later, just as the war was ending, a grateful Wilson urged Ford to run for senator as a Democrat from Michigan because of his pacifist sympathies. The president knew he would need every vote he could muster to support the League of Nations, and figured that with Ford in this crucial senate seat in this crucial state, he would win.

Ford's opponent for the Senate seat was Truman H. Newberry, scion of the sort of old Detroit elite family that Ford detested in his bones. A very successful businessman (who had joined with Henry B. Joy in bringing Packard to Detroit in 1902) and former secretary of the Navy under Theodore Roosevelt, Newberry was a well-connected, vociferous candidate, very shrewd and capable in his uses of publicity. He had an enormous staff, spent a great deal of money, and made speeches from one end of the state to the other. Knowing that Edsel Ford's lack of military service in the war was a sore spot with many of the electorate, Newberry, who had been a lieutenant commander, had pictures taken of himself and his two sons in uniform and often reminded the public of their service in the conflict.

Ford did exactly the opposite in his campaign. Though he agreed to run, he made no secret of his distaste for ordinary politics and only ran as an outsider, which meant that he had to run on both the Republican and Democratic tickets in the primaries, though in the end it was only the Democrats who nominated him, despite the fact that he was nominally a Republican at the time. "What do you want to do that for?" his good friend Thomas Edison asked him. "You can't speak. You wouldn't say a damn word. You'd be mum."

Ford did run on issues, however. His major campaign promise was to work for the abolition of patent laws as exploitation of the consumer. He also supported both women's suffrage and the League of Nations. During the campaign Ford complained quite a bit that there were too many Wall Street speculators in Congress. It might have been interesting to know how he would have dealt with this issue as the 1920s progressed and financial speculation became an ever-more important aspect of American life.

Ford let the public know early on that he wasn't seeking this Senate seat, but if the public wanted him for it, he would acquiesce. He insisted that he would not spend any money on the campaign or make any speeches. Everybody knew him without his explaining to the public who he was, so if they wanted him, they could just go ahead and vote for him.

What is amazing in retrospect is how well this strategy worked. At this time, Michigan was a solidly Republican state. As an example, in the primaries almost 234,000 votes were split among the Republican candidates Newberry, Ford, and Chase Osborne, whereas the Democratic primary saw only 39,000 votes total, split between Ford and James W. Helme. In fact, Ford's losing Republican total of 71,800 was twice that of his winning Democratic bid.

But laborers and farmers viewed him very favorably, and they were Democrats. Endorsements by such figures as Bernard Baruch and William Jennings Bryan didn't hurt either. Despite the *New York Times* statement that his election would "create a vacancy both in the Senate and in the automobile business" because of his inability to grasp either national or international problems, many Democratic papers praised his abilities and character effusively.

True to his word, in the campaign Ford never gave a speech or spent a nickel, though he gave a few statements to the press about his general views on issues of the day. His friend Harvey Firestone sent lawyers into the field to buck up Democratic leaders, which had some effect, as did a growing scandal about how much Newberry had spent in the primary campaign ($176,000); by mid-September the controversy over this got so bad that Senator Attlee Pomerene of Ohio made a resolution in the Senate for an investigation.

Despite all the obstacles Ford faced, he came very close to being elected, losing by about 7,500 votes. Indeed, he may well have lost due to a shady maneuver by his opponent. On the Sunday before the election, the Republicans placed an ad claiming that Ford's employee Carl Emde, who had a major responsibility for the Liberty Motors Ford had built for airplanes during the war, was a German alien and sympathizer. By the time Ford responded in the press, it was election day, and many voters did not see his defense of Emde, who was in fact a U.S. citizen and true patriot. Though Ford may not have really wanted the Senate seat to begin with, now he was riled up by this shabby tactic, which added to the stinging criticisms he had already endured about his son's patriotism and his own suitability for high office. And Henry Ford was not a man to cross in this way. He vowed to get Newberry for the way he ran his campaign, no matter how much time, money, or manpower it would take.

The investigation into campaign finances came first, and even some in the Republican Party were calling for it. Federal law limited primary expenditures to $10,000 and Michigan law to $3,750, exclusive of advertising. After Newberry's election was certified on December 4, 1918, the forces for the investigation went into overdrive. Ford, convinced that financiers and war profiteers had conspired to defeat him, authorized the expenditure of $40,000 to look into the matter. Forty men combed the state, flushing out rumors of overspending and misappropriation of funds.

Eventually the Department of Justice indicted and tried Newberry, who on March 20, 1920, was convicted of violating the Federal Corrupt Practices Act, as were 16 of the 134 others originally charged. But on May 2, 1921, the Supreme Court ruled that Congress had exceeded its authority in attempting to regulate primary contests, stating that its power to control elections did not extend to nominations.

During this time Ford sent a large number of people into every corner of Michigan to recount the ballots in the election. They found many irregularities, even outright fraud, that reduced Newberry's lead to only 4,200, though still enough for victory. But the debate in Congress over Newberry's campaign finances continued, with many powerful Republicans joining Democrats in calling to unseat him. After a close vote he was seated again in early 1922, but things were about to change.

Ford continued his attack on Newberry by going after his supporters. Michigan's Senator Charles E. Townsend, who had been a vocal Newberry advocate during his campaign, was defeated in his reelection bid in 1922, with substantial help from Henry Ford. After Robert LaFollette Sr., the formerly Republican and now Progressive senator from Wisconsin, announced that he would reopen the Newberry case (the Senate now had a Democratic majority without Townsend), Newberry resigned on November 18, 1922, rather than face certain expulsion. It had taken four years of relentless opposition, but Ford finally had his revenge, which, as Machiavelli tells us, is a dish best served cold. Spencer Ervin's 1935 book *Henry Ford vs. Truman H. Newberry* deals with this episode in scrupulous detail.

And who was Newberry's replacement? It was none other than the tough, uncompromising mayor of Detroit, James Couzens, who had been elected in the same campaign in which Ford was defeated for the Senate.

Ford's presidential ambitions were to surface a few years later, but in the meantime his experience in the public arena left him jealous of his privacy and somewhat ambivalent about the accoutrements of status that he began to acquire.

The impressive stone-trimmed house he had built on Edison Avenue in Detroit had become too accessible to prying eyes and petitioners after the explosion of publicity surrounding the five-dollar day, so he began to construct a huge and rather dismal grey limestone pile of no architectural distinction on the banks of the River Rouge for himself and his family; it was to cost some $2 million. Situated on a large property he had acquired some years before for his bird-watching activities, he named it Fair Lane for an area near Cork in Ireland, whence came his mother's adoptive father, who (like his own father) had instilled in young Henry a love of birds.

Though it was originally supposed to be designed by Frank Lloyd Wright, that didn't work out—a few days after his meeting with Ford, Wright ran off to Europe with the wife of one of his clients—so Ford turned the job over to a Pittsburgh interior designer who was really a building works supervisor, and the final hash of a design resulted. The house was large and comfortable, but it was not very luxurious, reflecting the owner's wishes. The one truly beautiful and immaculately efficient building on the property, the design and construction of which Ford personally supervised, was the powerhouse, to which he repaired frequently. (Prophetically for our age, it contained a power outlet where Mrs. Ford could recharge her electric car, which was her preferred means of transportation.) Despite the modesty of the home's décor, much money and effort were spent on things like a billiards room, bowling alley, and small golf course in the garden, meant to occupy and amuse Edsel. But he was not to stay there for long, for the Fords moved into Fair Lane at the beginning of 1916, and the following November, after Edsel and the beautiful Eleanor Clay married, the couple moved out to an attractive small mansion in the tony Indian Village section of Detroit, where the smart set of young marrieds lived. Edsel spent as much money redecorating it in a spare modern style as he had paid for it.

Then in 1923, the Edsel Fords acquired Haven Hill, a 2,400-acre estate near Pontiac, Michigan. By 1926, they began constructing a beautiful new residence at Gaukler Point on property given to them by Henry at Grosse Pointe, which he had bought before his decision to build Fair Lane. The new estate was quite large, set on 65 acres, with a main building of some 30 rooms designed in the Cotswold style by Albert Kahn. It was as graceful and beautiful as Fair Lane was heavy and oppressive, and one could understand all one needed to know about the differences between Henry and Edsel by simply looking at the type of home that each, at ages 52 and 33 respectively, decided to build.

The private lives of Edsel and Eleanor were indeed very different from those of Henry and Clara. The younger couple socialized frequently, entertained lavishly, drank liquor (in fact, Eleanor had a reputation as a bit of a tippler) and smoked, attended and sponsored cultural events, bought art, and dressed stylishly. Much of this was due to Eleanor's influence, for in her quiet but firm way, she did everything she could to foster an independent life for her shy, gentlemanly, father-dominated husband. Henry didn't like this very much and sometimes complained loudly about various aspects of his son's lifestyle, but he knew he could only go so far, and he learned how to live with that.

In any case, in business Edsel was a Ford man and was crucial in a prestige business acquisition of Henry's in the early 1920s. This was the Lincoln Motor Company, founded by the great engineer Henry M. Leland and his son Wilfred; it was named for the first presidential candidate for whom the elder Leland had voted, Abraham Lincoln. Leland was far and away the most influential force in precision manufacturing in the early history of the automobile, and in 1902, had refashioned Ford's abortive Henry Ford Company car into the first Cadillac. Then, with his son, he built that brand into the most profitable constituent of the newly formed General Motors Company. But with what the actress Mabel Albertson once called "that firm, sure touch on the wrong note," the Lelands introduced their impeccable, ultra-luxurious new Lincoln car in November 1920, in the midst of the most terrible downturn the automobile industry had ever known. A year later, the thousands of small investors the Lelands had induced to invest in their company were on the rocks. There had once been bad blood between Ford and Leland, when Ford had been forced out of his own company by Leland. But all that was seemingly forgotten, as Ford showed great sympathy for the Lelands' plight by bidding a generous $8 million to buy up the firm as the only bidder at the bankruptcy sale on January 4, 1922. Detroit citizens celebrated Ford's magnanimous rescue of the Lelands, even comparing him to the Good Samaritan. But nothing was as it seemed.

Ford could have easily helped out the Lelands months before the bankruptcy, but by waiting he got a well-equipped plant worth at least $16 million for a bargain-basement price (he would have gotten it for $5 million, but the bankruptcy judge rejected that offer). Not 24 hours after the Ford takeover, tough operatives like Sorensen were sent to the Lincoln plant ostensibly to learn quality production techniques to apply to the Model T. But as soon became apparent, these men were actually there to put Ford manufacturing techniques in place at Lincoln. The Lelands became enraged by this strategy and the crude way in which it was being enforced. In a face-to-face meeting with Ford, Wilfred Leland offered to buy back their company at the price Ford had paid, with interest, but Ford declined, saying he wouldn't sell it for $500 million, because it fit in with the business purpose for which he had bought it. He did agree to come to the plant and deal with their grievances, however, and once appeared there saying he was ready to address the problems. But less than two weeks later on June 10, Liebold arrived to cashier Wilfred, and so his father resigned too. Their belongings were escorted out of the building with them.

The stockholders also came away with little to show for the takeover of Lincoln. Ford had made a big show of presenting a check for $363,000 to Henry Leland in front of the workers in his plant on the occasion of the old man's birthday on February 16; this amount represented his investment in the old company, and Ford told him to tell the workers, many of whom were investors, that "they are all going to get the same." Ultimately the investors never got a red cent, despite a succession of lawsuits in which the Lelands tried to get reimbursement for their shareholders. So, in the end, the Good Samaritan of Dearborn had done a good piece of business, gotten a bucketful of terrific publicity for it, and served up another dish of revenge, cold.

After initially glorifying him, the press turned on Ford, who nonetheless redeemed himself the next year by paying off in full some $4 million in Lincoln debts and personal guarantees of seven of its directors. He always kept an eye on the press.

In truth, Ford had bought Lincoln for Edsel. The proliferation of Model T body styles that helped sell so many Ts was due to Edsel's wishes and work, beginning in the mid-1910s. It gave him a chance to exercise his creative bent, and because Ford recognized this while still believing it was the mechanics, rather than the style, that sold the car, it was alright with him. By 1921, given that he was selling every car he could make, he thought it was fine if Edsel amused himself with the Lincoln car, as Ford bought it cheaply and could put it on an efficient basis. Indeed, Edsel got rid of the stodgy, old-fashioned bodies of the original and replaced them with modern, custom-built designs; Lincolns began to sell in much larger quantities that grew into an annual level of 7,000 or so by late in the decade. Lincolns contributed something much more valuable than sales a few years later, when their styling became the basis for the new Model A.

Another wolf-in-Samaritan's-clothing venture of Ford's at this time was the Muscle Shoals project, which became very much involved in his rumored presidential bid for the 1924 election. Muscle Shoals was a huge government project in Alabama, begun during World War I to harness the resources of the Tennessee River to the enormous Wilson Dam. But its main purpose was to produce nitrates to reduce America's dependence on foreign sources of materials for explosives, in addition to its uses as fertilizer. When the war ended, the project was left unfinished despite massive expenditures of $85 million; the government's interest in producing explosives had been abandoned. By 1921, the Harding administration was willing to lease the project to private business, and so it solicited bids.

In July 1921, Ford leapt on the bandwagon with a proposal to lease the power project and buy the rest of it, tailor-made as it seemed to be for his interest in hydroelectric power and productive farming. After criticism of his original proposal as too modest, he altered it in 1922. In so doing, he created a yearlong mania for Muscle Shoals by promoting a vision of it that seemed little short of miraculous. Ford proposed nothing less than a city 75 miles long and 15 miles wide that would connect dams and new hydroelectrically powered industries to be laid out in small towns along the Tennessee River Valley. He would essentially build a new Detroit in an area that was miserably poor and remote. Four million people, mostly farmers, lived there on some 42,000 square miles, and this idea to help them lead better lives, wedded to the self-evident genius of Henry Ford, seemed to herald a great new age of prosperity. All sorts of people, beginning with real estate speculators and city planners, tried to cash in on this extraordinary idea from Ford, who tirelessly sold the public on his unique ability to get gigantic things done through vision and mechanical know-how. To undermine his usual bugbears, Wall Street interests and international bankers, he even proposed a new kind of currency, the previously mentioned "energy dollar" (actually a Thomas Edison idea), whose value would not be based on an inert object like gold, but on what was produced on and out of the land. With his every pronouncement on Muscle Shoals, he was whipping up the public into a heightened frenzy of support.

The problem was that Ford was attempting to secure this property for next to nothing. He proposed a 100-year lease on it (when leases longer than 50 years were forbidden by legislation) for a $5 million investment, with the government agreeing to furnish $68 million to complete the project over time. Thus, he would have gotten a stranglehold on the property into the 2020s for only a minimal outlay. The irony is that if any of the Wall Street bankers or international financiers (in other words, Jews) that the *Dearborn Independent* had besmirched for nearly two years had proposed a deal like this, Ford would have spewed forth paroxysmal tirades against them. He would say that they sought to control this property for their own financial gain, whereas he in contrast wanted it to work for the betterment of society. He probably justified his own rapaciousness in that manner. In reality Ford was taking ambition for power, control, and financial gain and consciously draping it in patriotic bunting to sell it not just to his compatriots, but to all humankind, while simultaneously holding up his well-known scapegoats as dastardly contrasts to his benevolence.

Later on he did indeed construct small manufacturing and farming communities on the banks of bodies of running water that furnished power to them. But that was far in the future, even if the seeds of the idea were planted at this time. Whatever he may have told himself about the possible benefits of Muscle Shoals, the face of his self-aggrandizement was soldered back to back with the face of his greed; simultaneously he showed a face of benevolence to the public, presenting himself as a sort of civic icon before which he expected them to bow low.

And bow they did. One result of the Muscle Shoals campaign was a grassroots movement spreading like wildfire to make Henry Ford the Republican nominee for president of the United States in 1924. Ford-for-President organizations were cropping up spontaneously everywhere. There was no doubt about this because Liebold, who along with Sorensen was a believer in Ford's presidential potential, had each of these organizations fully investigated, and found out that they were the real thing. It wasn't hard to see the reasons people began organizing for Ford. The unbelievably inefficient and corrupt Harding administration, especially after it became bogged down in the Teapot Dome scandal—a real estate boondoggle for presidential cronies—left the public completely disillusioned about Harding. If ever a man looked and sounded presidential, but wasn't, it was Warren G. Harding, the last of many presidents furnished to the nation by the state of Ohio. In such an atmosphere, homespun, clean-living, hardworking, patriotic, xenophobic, peace-loving Henry Ford, who had become the world's first billionaire by bringing prosperity and a measure of ease to the lives of the multitudes, seemed to fill the bill as the man that everyone (except big-city intellectuals, of course) admired most in the United States. He embodied the best qualities that most Americans thought they possessed, writ large. So it was natural that so many were happy to entertain the thought of him as president and to organize on his behalf. A 1923 survey showed that he was far and away the most popular contender for the nation's presidency.

It seems pretty clear that Ford toyed for a while with the idea of running for the presidency, but he didn't really want the job, which would have cramped his style. In the little he said about the matter to his close associates, he indicated that he thought he could run the country the way he ran Ford, leaving a staff in the office to answer correspondence and make low-level decisions, while he ran about from office to office shaking people up and throwing a "monkey wrench" into things. That wouldn't have lasted long. Also, Ford had no desire to run a real campaign. He had learned in the Senate race of 1918 that he couldn't expect a campaign to run itself, and that meant he would have to show himself to the public and, worse, speak to them at gigantic political rallies. Henry Ford was comfortable speaking to a small number of people around a table, but public speaking terrified him and rendered him tongue-tied. In his first public speech, at Sing-Sing prison in Ossining, New York, he started by saying to the convicts, "I'm so glad to see you all here." It gives one pause to think of how history might have been altered if Henry Ford had possessed the ability to speak even reasonably well in public.

The events of August 23, 1923, changed everything. President Harding, who was making a vigorous nationwide speaking tour to try to bolster his reputation, became ill in San Francisco and died suddenly of pneumonia, elevating Calvin Coolidge to the presidency. The support of the Republican Party quickly coalesced around Coolidge, and the presidential ambitions of Ford receded. In any case, Clara Ford, in one of her few, but decisive, outbursts, said that she thought her husband was singularly unsuited for the job, and she threatened to move to England if he were to be elected. So by the time it really counted, the Ford-for-President movement was effectively a dead issue.

Nevertheless, all the hoopla had its uses. The Muscle Shoals situation was dragging on and on in Congress, spearheaded by Senator George W. Norris of Nebraska, chairman of the Senate Agriculture Committee, who thought Ford's proposal was little less than highway robbery (Ford's $5 million bid was worth less than the Muscle Shoals scrap value of $8 million). In December 1923, Ford called on Coolidge at the White House and announced his support for him in the coming campaign; it was rumored that the men had struck a deal in which Ford's support for Coolidge would be reciprocated by Coolidge's support for Ford's Muscle Shoals proposal. No one knows what was actually said, but in March 1924, the House approved Ford's bid, leaving Norris in the Senate still unalterably opposed. Despite the support of others, he tied it up in committee. It was no coincidence that the persecution of Sapiro in the *Independent*, sure to gain the support of many farmers, started almost immediately after the House vote. Ironically, the Sapiro affair long survived the Muscle Shoals situation, for Ford, realizing that he couldn't win against Norris, withdrew his bid in October 1924. Norris, who believed the project should be owned and run by the federal government, tried to effectuate this under both Coolidge and Hoover, to no avail. It would be under Franklin D. Roosevelt that the vast TVA, or Tennessee Valley Authority, would finally be created as a public entity that remains to this day the nation's largest public power company.

To understand how Henry Ford could have gotten so far with so many public issues and even been considered a serious presidential possibility during this period, it is important to understand his celebrity, and the self-consciousness behind it. No other figure of the 1920s, aside from Calvin Coolidge, who was president for six years, received as much newspaper coverage as Henry Ford in the United States. The *New York Times* alone, hardly a source of flashy, unconsidered reprints of public relations handouts, ran an average of 145 stories a year on Ford during those ten years. Even in a comparatively mild year for him such as 1922, the *Detroit Free Press* featured him in an average of 34 stories a month. *Detroit Saturday Night* said the American people were suffering from "Ford-osis": "They gobble the Ford stuff, and never stop to reason whether they like it, or whether it has any real merit in it." A wag at another Detroit paper occasionally ran a two-page index on the front page called "What the World Is Doing to FORD Today." The press in the rest of the world was the same. Only leaders of the great powers and India got as much publicity as Ford, and not even such worldwide figures as Thomas Edison, Charlie Chaplin, and the Prince of Wales got as much press as he did.

And then there were the books, starting with a biographical sketch by Elbert Hubbard, the author of *A Message to Garcia*, in 1913, and *Henry Ford's Own Story*, a collection of not very accurate articles by Rose Wilder Lane four years later. In 1922 and 1923 alone, there were four books, some encomiums and one a forceful attack by E. G. Pipp, first editor of the *Independent*, who feared Ford's possible success in the political arena. Another book that was less than flattering in all its particulars was by the Reverend Samuel S. Marquis, who had headed the Ford Motor Company's Sociological Department, first greatly admired Ford, and then became disillusioned with him as his darker side became apparent. His book, *Henry Ford: an Interpretation*, was the most balanced and profound study of Ford's character ever written. Marquis's disillusionment with a man who seemed to be a truly caring and enlightened industrialist was tinged with great sorrow, still moving even today. Ford did all he could to suppress Pipp's and Marquis' books, buying up as many copies as possible to keep them from the market. However, the other books were widely circulated and did much to enhance Ford's reputation.

But by far the most influential of all was Ford's "autobiography," *My Life and Work*, ghost-written for him by Samuel Crowther, a journalist with a background in economics.

Crowther stitched the book together from parts of "Mr. Ford's Own Page" from the *Independent* and from interviews with the man himself. In a masterly fashion, he wrote a book that was intimate, informative, and philosophical in a conversational style that made it seem as though the reader was having a chat with a man sitting across from him. It was a huge hit all over the world, translated into 12 languages and Braille. The men collaborated on two very popular sequels that dealt with Ford's economic theories, *Today and Tomorrow* (1926) and *Moving Forward* (1930). (Another non-Crowther collaboration, *Things I've Been Thinking About*, which appeared a few years later, was an *American Magazine* article reprinted into a book.) In 1926, a justifiably famous article on mass production appeared in *The Encyclopedia Britannica* under Henry Ford's name. Every bit of it was ghost-written.

Many people insisted that all the publicity about Ford was primarily due to the clever public relations men he had around him. And much was made of the fact that in statements or interviews, people like William Cameron and others would "interpret" Ford's often cryptic remarks, which contributed to the notion that others did the intellectual heavy lifting for him. But Fred L. Black, a colleague of Cameron's at the *Independent* who was certainly in a position to know, said otherwise: "Nobody made Henry Ford from a publicity standpoint except himself; Cameron or any of the rest of us merely *helped*. Any Ford legend would start with the boss himself, and it was nursed along by the newspapermen, rather than engineered by any staff at Ford's. This idea that Henry Ford was an ignoramus, and had his smartness due to his public relations men who engineered all his stuff, is absolutely untrue."

A 71-year-old man who could create a stir by saying an ankle bandage he sported was due to a football injury (rather than the truth, which was that it was covering a blister) knew instinctively what publicity was all about. Ford would make all sorts of shocking statements, saying, for instance, that heavyweight boxing champion Gene Tunney should become a preacher, or that "the world would be better off without meat. It's 75 percent ashes anyway." And if these pronouncements took hold among reporters, he'd repeat them for wider audiences.

In the end, by design, through audacity, and with careful help from a devoted staff and a mesmerized press, the World's Richest and Most Successful Businessman was transformed into the Sage of Dearborn, an icon of one of the most materialistic ages in American history. Though he came to be enamored of the image that he had created of himself, there seems to have been a wee, small voice inside at certain crucial moments reminding him of his limitations, in ability, reach, and desire. The presidential campaign of 1924 seems to have been one of those moments. If only that voice had been louder and more frequent.

Ten

―――――――

Everything Old Is New Again

W<small>HEN 1920 DAWNED, HENRY FORD WAS 56 YEARS OLD, AN AGE AT</small> which most important men of that period would be thinking of winding down and most likely resting on the laurels proffered to them for past activities. That didn't suit him, or the times. The 1920s would prove to be modern, comfortable, untraditional, prosperous, materialistic, and more peaceful than any other decade in the 20th century. The war years were past, people were looking forward to better times, and so was Henry Ford. He wasn't straining to catch up to the new age, but rather never thought of himself as anything but in the thick of it. He was healthy, vigorous, and with the ever-expanding Rouge facility and annual production of 2 million Model Ts on the horizon, he would ascend to the peak of his business achievement by the middle of the decade. Then, at a stroke, Ford would completely reinvent his business, leaving old ways and products discarded behind him. He often said that the best place from which to start anything new was from wherever you happened to be, and in the 1920s he continued to follow his own advice.

While the Rouge was expanding, Muscle Shoals was being hotly debated, the *Dearborn Independent* was spewing its bilious opinions, and considerable numbers of citizens were clamoring for him to enter the presidential race, Henry Ford entered yet another new arena of personal creation: he had a baby, and not with his wife.

Ford had a roving eye, which seemed to fit in with his general theory of the robust physical functioning of the body: "Women don't do you any harm," he said to engineer Harold Hicks. "You can screw any woman on earth, excepting for one thing; never let your wife find out." Once Clara did, in the case of a servant in their home, and there was hell to pay. But in the case of the mother of his new child, even though she knew he had cheated on her, it was different.

Evangeline Cote went to work at Ford in 1909 as a stenographer, soon rising to be the head of the department. She became acquainted with Ford a few years later when she became Harold Wills's secretary. She was petite, curvaceous, intelligent, flirtatious, amusing, and outspoken. She was the sporty type too, boating, horseback-riding, and even flying, and was in fact the first woman in Michigan to get a pilot's license. In many ways she was tailor-made to attract Ford's interest. A relationship began between them; soon he began visiting Cote at her little farmhouse, and their intimacy increased. By 1917, he decided she needed the shield of a husband, and he supplied her with one in the person of Ray Dahlinger, Ford's chauffeur and devoted employee. Though it was hard for Dahlinger in many ways, he was a compliant beard for their liaison, in no small part because he enjoyed the many material benefits Ford bestowed upon them both. Eventually, Evangeline became pregnant with Ford's child, and on April 9, 1923, gave birth to a son, John. Ford was barely four months shy of 60. By this time, Dahlinger was the manager of Ford's farm properties, and an estate near to Fair Lane was being constructed for the couple.

Though Ford's parentage was never admitted, it was obvious to all. He was a constant visitor to the Dahlinger home, lavishing attention and gifts on the child, who also played with Henry's grandchildren. Later on, he spent a great deal of private time with John, trying to instill in him his personal values.

At first, and for many years thereafter, Clara disliked the situation, though she accepted it, for she recognized that this was something much different from a casual flirtation with a housemaid. And Ford never embarrassed her with this relationship. Later on she and Cote formed a close and genuine friendship, which meant a great deal to both of them. When Ford passed on many years later, Cote was called immediately to his bedside, where she stood by Clara.

Simultaneously with the changes in his personal life, Ford was also continuing to introduce modern innovations into his business. We have already noted his entry into the iron, coal, and lumber industries, and his attempts to run them more efficiently by buying up and modernizing railroads and lake shipping lines. But Ford also made another venture into the transportation industry, one that required both courage and foresight on his part.

Almost since the beginnings of aviation, Ford maintained a curiosity about it, especially after he began to build aircraft engines for the Army in World War I. Railroads and shipping were mature industries when Ford got involved in them, but his entry into commercial aviation was really on the ground floor.

Having investigated and decided against an involvement with dirigibles, he and Edsel became among 127 Michigan investors in the Stout Metal Airplane Company, at $1,000 apiece, in 1922. The company was named for William B. Stout, an aviation engineer and promoter of considerable ability who had built an aluminum-bodied monoplane that had commercial possibilities. But Stout complained about bad Detroit-area airport facilities, so in 1924, Ford built one of the finest, and eventually busiest, airports in the world.

He also built a factory for Stout and, in early 1925, bought out Stout's company by paying the investors double their original outlay. This widely publicized event meant that a commercially viable airplane industry had "arrived" in the eyes of the public, which was treated to cartoons showing the skies filled with "flying flivvers." On April 13, 1925, Ford started the first U.S. commercial airline, inaugurating an air freight service between Detroit and Chicago, with Detroit-Cleveland service coming two and a half months later. In early 1926, the company had government contracts to carry mail on these routes.

But the big publicity coup came about with the National Air Reliability Tours, begun in 1925 under the auspices of the Detroit Aviation Society. These were annual 1,900-mile contests that began and ended at the Ford airport, with Ford himself greeting each incoming flyer. For the first event, 35,000 people jammed the airport, and the contest was front-page news nationwide for six days. This prompted the John Wanamaker Company to become the first commercial buyer of a Ford plane, which it promptly displayed in its shop window at a price of $25,000.

By 1929, the event attracted 150,000 people to the airport and prompted 30,000 newspaper articles. Many of them featured Edsel too, allowing him to be nationally known for the first time to millions of Americans (save for the opprobrium heaped on him for not serving in World War I, but that was long before this).

One Ford ad of a series intended to sell commercial aviation to the general public in 1927 caused a national impact. It was called "Lift Up Your Eyes," and it pictured a farm family doing just that, pointing skyward as the shadow of an airplane glided over their lawn. In 1949, it was named one of the "100 Greatest Advertisements" in a book of that name by a top advertising man.

As of the spring of 1926, the company decided to build only multi-engine planes, these being the famous Ford Tri-Motors, which had a 70-foot wingspan, carried eight passengers plus freight, and could, if necessary, operate on only one engine. Top customers, from the Army and the Navy to Standard Oil and Pan-American Airways, signed on for these planes. Ford sold 36 in 1928 and more than double that, 86, in 1929, an enormous number for the time, probably making the company the world's largest manufacturer of commercial planes.

There were flops of course. The 350-pound "flivver plane," built in 1926 with a 22-foot wingspan and a 15-foot length, was an endurance world-record holder at 986 miles for awhile, but when a company pilot, Harry Brooks, was killed in one, Ford shelved it after just two years. A huge 58-passenger plane, or six-ton freight plane, the 14-AT, never got off the ground in 1932 because of the impractical water-cooled motors installed in it.

But despite all the activity, the Depression killed off this burgeoning business. And there were competitors like Douglass that were offering stronger new models with greater range and load capacity. Sales fell dramatically to 26 in 1930, 21 in 1931, and only 3 in 1932. A cumulative operating loss of $5.6 million and total expenditures of $10.4 million by 1932 caused Ford to exit commercial aviation in this most terrible year of the Depression, when the parent company was having its worst year in history. But Ford's contributions here were both pioneering and of lasting value.

Perhaps the strongest challenge of Ford's career came during the late 1920s, and his response to it was the greatest comeback in industrial history up until that time. For the Model T, the most successful and influential industrial product ever devised and made, finally outlived its usefulness after 19 years. By 1927, its sales were collapsing, despite attempts to modernize and beautify it. For its successor, Henry Ford, the Model T's staunchest and most intransigent defender until the very end of its life, did a complete about-face, replacing it literally from scratch in a half year's time with a vehicle as modern, fresh, and stylish as the Model T had been stodgy, stale, and utilitarian. Once he convinced himself of the necessity of bowing to the new age of motordom, Ford threw himself into the creation of his new product with unswerving energy and conviction, overseeing all aspects of the design of the Model A and driving everyone crazy with his personal methods and standards until he was convinced the product was right. Furthermore, he did this when he was in his mid-60s, when even many of his fiercest supporters were convinced he didn't have it in him.

Even at the height of its sales power from 1923 to 1925, the Model T was becoming outmoded. Cheapness, durability, and utility were its hallmarks; but by the mid-1920s, those features were becoming less important to the consumer. He, and increasingly she, wanted color and style in the car's body and appointments; men in particular wanted more power and the latest technical innovations. Everyone had more money to spend on motor transportation, and increasingly they took their money to dealers for more advanced and attractive Chevrolet, Dodge, Buick, and Willys cars, the prices of which had been drastically cut in recent years. Charles Wilson of GM famously stated that what America wanted in a car was "a blonde who could cook."

The Model T had precious little in the way of newfangled attractions to offer, and besides, who cared anymore if it could pull you out of a muddy ditch when most of the nation's roads were now paved? Even a 1925 facelift that added larger fenders, nickel-plated radiators, and five new color choices didn't help. Sales declined 20 percent from 1925 to 1926, and neither the resumption of large-scale advertising (Ford had done none for six years) nor price cuts helped; it was the first time that such strategies had failed to succeed. Sales declines in 1927 became catastrophic, and finally, with rumors rife, Ford announced on May 25, 1927, that he would discontinue the T. The next day the 15 millionth Model T was built, and Henry and Edsel drove it to join the first one and the original 1896 quadricycle at the Detroit Engineering Laboratory. The last Model Ts were officially produced on May 31, but in fact hundreds of thousands more of them were still manufactured in the United States, Canada, and Mexico for months to come.

The T was beloved by millions, both the humble and the exalted; Sinclair Lewis and E. B. White held theirs in great affection, and Gertrude Stein's garage owner coined the phrase "a lost generation" to describe a young French mechanic who couldn't fix her stalwart T in World War I. But now it was chugging its way to the end of the line. The big question of the day was what would replace it? The rumor mill was teeming with fanciful ideas of what Henry had up his sleeve, but the truth was, he didn't have much. However, he knew he had to come up with something, and quick.

The idea of a new model, as a supplement to the T, had been on Ford's mind for some time. From 1920 on, he had experimented with an X-shaped eight-cylinder engine that worked spectacularly everywhere but on the road, where the spark plugs clogged up with dirt. As usual, he was a diehard about the success of this product, abandoning it only in 1926. He had a prejudice against six-cylinder engines that went all the way back to problems with the Model K and flatly refused to consider the prospect of building one, even though rivals were cleaning up with their own fast and efficient sixes. When the time came, he knew the new car would have a four-cylinder engine.

But he didn't know much else. Everyone was working with him on a crash course to produce the new car, which had been thought about in earnest since the summer of 1926 and was finally begun in January 1927. First, he and Edsel decided on the length and wheelbase, and everything else proceeded from that. Henry and Laurence Sheldrick, who had worked at Lincoln, were in charge of engineering the Model A, and Edsel was in charge of the styling.

Edsel created a design derived from a Lincoln prototype that he was working on. He was so successful adapting the styling to the Model A that the car was informally known as a Baby Lincoln, quite a coup in an era when style and prestige had come to mean so very much to the car-buying public. To our eye today, there might not seem to be that much of a difference between the T and the A, but looked at closely, especially from the viewpoint of 1927, there was as much difference between the two as between a tin can and a Tiffany jewel box. Seventeen different body styles could be had in attractive color combinations, with beautifully upholstered interiors featuring informative, well-designed, and illuminated dashboards.

Ford was on top of every mechanical part that went into the new Model A. Models of all sorts were cobbled together and sent out on the road for testing. The process by which they were assembled was both chaotic and imperialistic. Henry would see a part he disliked and exhort the engineers to do better, sometimes giving them a paper sketch of what he had in mind before walking out. When it was finished the next day, if he still didn't like it, he'd growl some more and walk out again. A man from the N. W. Ayer advertising agency that Ford had hired, who had heard about the famous Ford efficiency, couldn't believe what he saw on the design floor.

In the end, scores of different prototypes were built and tested in an unscientific, seat-of- the-pants process that Henry loved but which left the engineering staff scratching their heads. Ray Dahlinger, who had started as a Model T tester, would drive out a new model and return saying either "It's no damn good" or "It's God-damn good." What could anyone make of that? But some good would come out of it. One day Ford shocked everybody by breezing in and taking a prototype out for a spin over a rocky, rutted field, and he returned saying, "Rides too hard. Put on hydraulic shock absorbers," and thus added one of the best new features to the car. When one of his test drivers, a friend, was thrown through a windshield in a crash and got a badly mangled arm, Ford insisted on a new development for the Model A, safety glass, which was first used in the prestigious 1926 Stutz and provided great added value.

Henry and Edsel disagreed over the transmission, but in the end Edsel's desire for a sliding gear stick shift won out over Henry's desire to keep the old gear pedal-operated transmission. That was predictable, for when the T's sales began to fall, Henry was told that one of the big problems was the old transmission. Edsel also got equal pressure four-wheel brakes, balloon tires, and electric ignition, though he lost out on coil springs for the suspension system, a big frustration. In the end, Edsel had an enormous impact on the A, but he would have liked to have done more. Nonetheless, Henry uncharacteristically praised his son for his contributions: "We've got a pretty good man in my son," he said. "He knows style—how a car ought to look. And he has mechanical horse sense too." For Henry Ford, who usually wanted all the praise, whether he deserved it or not, that was practically an encomium.

Aside from its looks, what seemed to impress people most about the Model A was its performance. It had a top speed of 65 miles per hour, as opposed to the 43 of the model T, and when you stepped on the accelerator, it went like a bat out of hell.

Well, maybe that wasn't what impressed people *most*. That would have to be the price, which averaged out at $495, pound for pound cheaper than the lighter T and over $100 less than a comparable Chevrolet. One could even get a stripped-down roadster for $385.

Engineer Laurence S. Sheldrick said that the time in which the Model A was being put together was "the most terrific pressure period that anyone ever spent in their lives." No wonder.

From the late May announcement of the new car to the delivery of the final design prototype on August 10, 1927, only 76 days had elapsed—this is mind-boggling when one considers the years it takes to bring a completely new model to the production stage today.

But finishing the car was only one part of the Model A introduction. The next problem was producing it. Model T production wound down in the summer, and more than 60,000 people were thrown out of work in Detroit. Despite rosy predictions by Henry Ford that only 25,000 men would be out of work at one time, as their departments tooled up for the new model, in fact everybody was out of work until October, except for pattern makers, tool and die makers, and others who were making new machines or modifying old ones. The Model A contained 5,580 new parts. Thirty-two thousand of the 43,000 machine tools the company owned were for the Model T, developed over two decades to produce that product and only that product. Three-quarters of them now needed to be rebuilt or scrapped, and 4,500 new ones were purchased. All new plant layouts had to be devised, a million square feet of factory space added, and tens of thousands of workers had to be retrained. Nothing like it, in comparable speed and size, had ever been done before.

It was much more complicated than Ford had realized and was therefore much delayed. The first car wasn't produced until October 21. By the end of the year, a top production of only 125 per day was achieved. Considering the demand for the vehicle, that was a disaster. Auto sales were down by a million units in 1927, despite gains from other manufacturers; this was mostly due to the end of the Model T and the fact that most buyers would not purchase a new vehicle until they saw the new car

Henry Ford was going to offer to the public. Not being able to supply it in a timely fashion was quite a strain on the company.

Ford realized early on that curiosity about the Model A was intense, and he dealt with it the way Mama Rose advised her daughter Gypsy Rose Lee to deal with the same kind of curiosity in *Gypsy*: "Find out what they want, and then don't give it to them." Not one word came from Ford's (or the company's) lips from May 25 to August 10, when Edsel announced to the world that the new Ford car was a reality. In the meantime, millions of dollars of free publicity was generated by thousands of newspaper columns, many of which included speculative sketches, photos, and descriptions, mostly inaccurate, of the new car. By the time the first Model A rolled off the line in late October, orders for 125,000 of them had been taken at dealerships, sight unseen. The publicity built to a crescendo that climaxed on the day of its official unveiling, December 2, 1927.

From Monday, November 28, to Friday, December 2, ads at last appeared, in a campaign the breadth of which had never existed before. Full-page ads were placed in every one of America's 2,000 daily newspapers, at a cost of $1.3 million. This was in addition to some $400,000 spent by individual dealers and dealer groups. The first ad discussed the car in general terms and was signed by Henry Ford. Mechanical features and a promise of a low price were in the second and third ads, and the fourth ad at last had a picture and price list. The fifth ad summarized the rest. As one commentator said, "Everyone who can read is reading them."

There was a press preview in Detroit on November 30, and a special showing to 7,000 of New York's upper crust the following day at the Waldorf Astoria. At last, the next day, the public was let in.

In Detroit, 115,000 people saw the car at Convention Hall. In New York, the crush was so great that the showing had to be hastily moved from the Ford Showroom to Madison Square Garden, where one and a quarter million people saw the new car in the first five days. In such cities as Denver, Cleveland, Kansas City, Dallas, and New Orleans, mounted police often had to be called in as crowds pushed forward in a frenzy to see the new car. Some ten million people in the United States saw it in the first 36 hours it was on display, and more than 25 million, almost 20 percent of the nation's entire population, viewed it in the first week. Overseas, police were called in to fight the crowds in Berlin, and 150,000 saw the Model A in Madrid.

Never before, or since, has there been such a mania for a new automobile. It got about as much publicity as any other event in the 1920s, including the Scopes monkey trial and the Sacco and Vanzetti trial and execution, and almost as much as Lindbergh's pioneering flight to Paris earlier that year. There had not been such a countrywide outpouring into public spaces since the announcement of the armistice in 1918.

Sales exploded. Four hundred thousand orders were written up in a fortnight, and by January 10, 1928, 727,000 cars were sold. But production was a big hassle. Dealers didn't have one example of most models until February, and some didn't even have a single car until July. Though celebrities like Douglas Fairbanks, Mary Pickford, and Franklin Roosevelt got deliveries, the ordinary man was unlikely to be able to put one in his garage, as only 100,000 were on the road by mid-1928. By the end of August though, 275,000 were delivered and production was ratcheted up so that 788,000 were assembled by year's end. That still wasn't enough to unseat Chevrolet as the sales leader, but it made a large dent in that lead. At Edsel's relentless urging, the establishment of installment buying of Ford's products for the first time contributed to the ever-escalating demand for the new product. (It is interesting to note here that Chevrolet, which introduced a new Six in early 1929, got it up to full production in just 90 days; flexible mass production, which responded to desired and necessary changes in products quickly under the scientific management of William S. Knudsen and Alfred P. Sloan at GM, made all the difference, putting the chaotic changeover process at Ford in the shade.)

But money wasn't being made. Slow delivery of new machines was part of the problem, as was the difficult introduction of electric welding and the large number of deficient parts that were turned out at first. There was also the new starter, which Ford first tried to produce himself with no success, at last consenting to buy it from Bendix. Then there was Sorensen's purge of the rest of "the old Model T sons-of-bitches" from Highland Park, which he instigated at that time. He considered them stubborn and obsolete, but in firing them, he robbed the company of some of its most valuable engineers and created a warlike atmosphere just when it was needed least. Ford's insistence on bizarre specifications for some parts didn't help either, nor did the fact that he initially refused to be convinced that some parts could be better and more cheaply made from castings and stampings than from forgings. Factory figures from March 1928 showed that Ford was losing between $246 and $335 on every Model A he made. It was figures like this that at last got Ford to insist on saving money on production, as he always had in the past, by using the best production methods available. He might not like certain ideas, but if they saved money, he used them. By 1929, he was going full blast, producing 1.85 million Model As, and capturing 34 percent of the market, leaving Chevrolet far behind with only 20 percent. And with the new economies he had instituted and the sheer volume of sales, Ford made $91 million, though this did not make up for what he had lost in the previous two years getting the A into full-volume production. Difficulties continued (there were some 200 major changes and 19,000 minor ones in every area during the Model A's lifetime), but everything seemed to be on a good path, and Henry Ford believed he had a new product that would last as long as the Model T had.

But it was not to be. For in 1929, the bottom fell out of an overheated economy, beginning with the stock market crash in October. There had already been signs of difficulties in the summer, as auto inventories were building up and sales leveling off throughout the industry, though Ford was doing better than others because he was still catching up with unmet demand for the Model A.

People began to panic and severely restricted their purchases in 1930, but even though production was off 20 percent at Ford, things were still reasonably good. In concert with President Hoover and most business leaders just after the crash, Ford issued optimistic statements about the soundness of the economy and a quick return to prosperity. But unlike the rest, he did something startling, announcing on December 1, 1929, that the six-dollar day, which had been standard at Ford for a decade, would now become the seven-dollar day. This was so amazing to the public that the uproar it caused almost rivaled the announcement of the original five-dollar day 15 years before. No one believed Ford could do this. Edsel said that in time-honored fashion, Ford was just sharing the economic benefits he had obtained with his workers, as he had just done with his customers when the Model A was introduced.

Once again, however, the wage story had a back story. In 1926, Ford had announced a five-day week, supplanting the standard six-day week, supposedly to give more family time to his workers, with no less compensation. In actuality this came just as Model T sales were slumping badly, and much less production was required. Furthermore, as Keith Sward points out, compensation was actually reduced at first, a new speed-up was introduced, skilled workers' pay was substantially lowered, and older workers were let go in favor of boys whose apprentice wage was $3.20 per day, often less than half of what regular workers were earning. The shortfall in five-day compensation wasn't made up until February 1928, just as Model A production really ramped up, and long after Ford had paid for it with his attendant conditions. But few outside the factories realized this, and the Ford reputation was burnished anew.

The seven-dollar wage was also much different than it seemed as time went on. Ford still reduced the wages of skilled workers and put in an even more stringent speed-up than before, so workers got new quotas that were far greater than their attendant raises justified. Then too, the company quietly laid off workers at higher pay scales, only to rehire them at lower ones. As sales continued to slump in the Depression, Ford stopped producing more and more of his components himself, farming them out instead to low-wage employers. He used 2,200 such businesses in 1929, but by 1931 that number had ballooned to 5,500. The notorious Briggs Body Works, the worst sweatshop in the industry, which had leased the Highland Park plant from him, was one of them. By 1932, the seven-dollar-a-day wage at Ford itself was out the window. And because of inflation, even at its inception, the wage itself was worth far less than the five-dollar-a-day wage was worth in 1914. (However, we note that some of those outside suppliers were used to produce Model A parts the company had never produced, and Ford said they farmed out other production to keep many supplier companies in dire straits from going under.) Ultimately, despite disguised or hidden problems, Ford came out of the 1920s riding a wave of public acclaim, as he had done so many times before.

Today, many people don't realize that the crash wasn't the beginning of a sudden, complete slide into economic and social disaster for America. True, some shaky businesses closed quickly, and many stock market investors who had bought heavily on margin were wiped out. But the market itself rebounded considerably from those October lows. For awhile it even seemed that this downturn might be like the steep, but short, inventory depression of 1920–1921. In the auto industry, many thought that manufacturers had gotten ahead of a market that had reached a long-predicted "saturation point," which could be corrected by more closely matching output with demand. Things in the stock market improved so much that William C. Durant, the founder of GM and the highest flying of stock market speculators, who had correctly predicted the crash and cashed out before it, got back into the market in 1930. It was a disastrous call, but in the first part of 1930, few people would have realized it.

By the end of 1930, the big slide was unmistakably on, however, and it worsened steadily throughout 1931. A redesigned Model A with a price reduction had bolstered sales at the beginning of the previous year, but that momentum had long since dissipated. A long list of venerable automobile firms, like Chandler, Moon, and Locomobile, were gone now, and others, like Marmon, Franklin, Reo, Pierce-Arrow, and Auburn, would follow in a few years. Ford's sales were almost cut in half from 1930 to 1931, and his $40 million profit turned into a loss of over $37 million. Even the much heralded seven-dollar day was becoming a source of criticism, as by now people had come to realize what was going on behind the scenes at Ford with layoffs, wage savings, and finally a reduction in the workweek to only three days, in concert with the rest of the industry. Increasing the number of dealers and cutting the dealer discount from 20 percent to 17.5 percent, allowing another price reduction in an effort to raise sales, was a disaster. Shortly, the company had to raise the discount to 22 percent and sweeten its ways in general to keep its dealers. Then too, competition was ramping up. Not only was Chevrolet producing ever smarter Sixes, but Walter Chrysler's low-priced Plymouth was making considerable inroads into Ford's market. The new Plymouth introduced for 1931 was a dandy, stylish car that featured "Floating Power" rubber engine mounts that gave the car a remarkably smooth ride. Though Plymouth sold less than 100,000 copies that year, the number of sales it made had risen steadily since the marque was introduced in 1928, and it was an increasingly serious competitor in the low-price field, just as that field was gro   count for almost all sales in the marketpl

of the Model T, with over 15
                    el A saw only a four-year run
o   e it finished production in
Au   reinvent his main product,
but   times. And the transfor-
matio   eavier, and more stylish

Model B, still a four-cylinder, wasn't going to do the trick. So, when that model was announced on February 11, 1932, it was as the opening act for something that was truly groundbreaking: Ford would now build its first V-8.

Ford first considered this in late 1929, after Chevrolet had gone from a Four to a Six. Since he wouldn't build a Six, and he characteristically wanted to be a jump ahead, he went for the Eight. When his engineering aides had collected nine Eights for his inspection, and he saw they were constructed in a segmented fashion, he decreed that his V-8 should have a one-piece cylinder block, to make it cheap enough for the Ford market. His staff worked like yeomen to make this happen, laying out the first V-8 in May 1930 and the second in November, followed quickly by almost 30 more, all to make the new engine both better and, most important, cheaper.

Ford, however, was unimpressed. His dissatisfaction mounted through the fall of 1931, until on December 7 of that year, after conferring with Edsel, he took the whole project into his own hands and pushed it through, designing and ordering new machines the company didn't make from outsiders, throwing out the old ones, and getting the new ones installed in record time. The plant reorganization turned out to be much cheaper and less extensive by far than what had occurred in 1927 with the introduction of the Model A. On March 31, 1932, the V-8 was introduced in 14 models in showrooms throughout a nation preoccupied with all the problems of the Depression. Despite this, it got a very warm reception from six million people who crowded in to see it. Curvy, roomy, and comfortable, the car featured a powerful 65-horsepower V-8 engine that left competing cars in the dust (even if it was a terrible oil burner.) Two years later, both John Dillinger and Clyde Barrow of Bonnie and Clyde fame wrote letters of praise to Henry Ford extolling the virtues of the V-8 as a getaway car. ("I have drove Fords exclusively when I could get away with one," enthused Barrow, who, with Bonnie, met his end in a tan Fordor riddled with 107 bullets; after the barrage was over, it started up on the first try.) At $460 to $650, the V-8 was a terrific buy, but despite all this, 1932 sales fell another 30 percent from the terrible levels of 1931 to the dismal level of only 395,000. But in that worst year of the Great Depression, total sales for the industry were only 1.1 million, down from 4.5 million just three years before in 1929. The Ford seven-dollar day had already reverted to the six-dollar day, and employment was little more than half what it had been in 1929. In another year, the six-dollar day would become the four-dollar day. It was said that a man who bought a Ford car could get a job at Ford's, and thus the greatest capitalist in the world was reduced to barter, as Lacey points out. William Cameron said at the time that the Depression was "so terrible that I believe he doesn't dare let himself think about it." He certainly didn't talk about it; the man who was always ready to give America a pep talk about how it could improve its lot had almost nothing to say in these dark times. Even the Inkster, Michigan, project (about which, more to come later) was a silent admission that he couldn't help people with the kind of regular employment he had provided for 30 years. Anne O'Hare McCormick, in a *New York Times* series of articles about the effects of the Depression in Detroit and Dearborn said, "Something has happened to Ford, and perhaps through him to the America he represents."

The year 1933 was better, but only a little, and in total Ford lost $125 million from 1931 to 1933. It must have been an extremely disheartening experience for Ford at 70 years of age to have put everything he had into reinventing his company to produce the amazing V-8, only to see it unable to turn things around. Things got better by 1934, and the company was once again on the road to making profits, but it is never quite the same thing when one has looked over the edge into the abyss, and seen it stare back.

However, there was one first-rate and irrefutable success for Ford at this time that built on a longtime knowledge of agriculture and concern for the farmer. Many of his achievements came about through contemplation of the work of the farmer, which he himself had done and detested as a young man. Originally, his decision to get into motor transportation stemmed from his desire to build tractors to make the farmers' wearisome work easier by replacing the horse with a machine that could do the work faster and much more cheaply.

Ford got into the car business first only because it was easier to sell cars to the public than tractors, which in any case were much more difficult to perfect for the market. Though he constantly experimented with different tractor models early on, it was World War I that finally got him into the business of manufacturing them, as we saw. By that time he had developed a lightweight model that was near to production anyway. Others had been in the tractor business before and had done well, but their models were large, heavy, and hard to manipulate, in addition to being expensive. Ford wanted to build a cheap, lightweight tractor that Every Farmer could afford, and that Every Farmer would want. He incorporated Henry Ford and Son to go into the tractor business on July 17, 1917, and turned out 254 machines by the end of that year. As noted earlier, his first customer was the British government, which was facing a severe food crisis during the war. Originally the tractors were to have been built in Britain, but when German air raids became a danger, all available factory space was put into service building aircraft engines, and so Ford built the tractors for Britain in Dearborn instead. He delivered 7,000 of them by April 1918, and by the year's end had produced 34,000 in total, mostly for American farmers, who were eager to snap them up. Tractor production doubled by 1920 and reached peaks of over 100,000 in 1923 and 1925 because of evolving models and significant price cuts begun in the recession of 1921. In time, however, other companies produced models that were as good or better than the Fordson, and even though sales were strong, Ford decided to switch all production to his factory in Cork, Ireland, as he needed all the room he had to supply the explosive demand for the Model A. Besides, labor costs were lower in Ireland, and it was much closer to the lucrative European market (in a six-year period ending in 1926, the Soviets alone had ordered 24,600 tractors).

In addition to his work in producing and refining tractors, Ford made other contributions to agriculture that were sometimes startling in their prescience and, in at least one instance, both long lasting and invaluable. Most contributions stemmed from his abhorrence of waste. He looked around at nature and saw an abundance that could be limitless, if only people could understand that the infinite could be reached by using and valuing even the smallest and most common items found in nature.

Take motor fuel, for example. Reynold M. Wik points out that in the mid-1910s, Ford grasped that gasoline supplies were not boundless and indeed saw them as a diminishing resource. Instead he proposed that alcohol be considered as fuel for internal combustion engines because it exists in potens in all vegetation, and proper distillation techniques could create a renewable supply of it. His first foray was in extracting it from Danish potatoes, but he realized that it could also be obtained from all sorts of diverse sources, from sugarcane and grains to swamp vegetation and garbage. He also noted that, since half of a tree was left behind as sawdust from lumber production, that could be used for fuel as well.

This idea came at a good time, in the run up to Prohibition, when alcohol production and sales would be banned throughout the United States. Farmers were delighted with the notion that their products could be used to fuel cars and trucks, as this could be an enormous new source of income for them. Many offered suggestions on how this idea could be brought to fruition by using items as different as corn and Russian thistles.

Ford continued experimenting with alcohol extraction from 1915 to 1918, but then he cooled on it. The problem was twofold. First, only 16 percent alcohol can be distilled from fermenting vegetation, leaving behind the rest as impurities and water. Even more importantly, high temperatures are needed to distill alcohol from vegetation; this requires fuel, defeating the entire purpose of the process, for in the end it is neither cost- nor energy-efficient. The same problem persists today with corn-based ethanol, despite much ballyhoo about it. (Sugarcane-based ethanol produced in South America is much more successful.) He may not have figured out a way to make his idea practical, but almost 100 years later, his notion of finding new solutions for propelling vehicles is more relevant than ever.

Ford also proposed that rubber could be made from farmland debris like sunflowers and sow thistle, and in 1924, he began conducting experiments in this line on 29,000 acres in Florida;

in 1929, Edison began testing plants for this use in Wayside, Georgia. At the beginning of 1930 after testing some 10,000 goldenrod plants in 70 varieties, Edison chose one of them, *Solidago leavenworthii*, to cultivate in his rubber experiments. But though testing continued for several years after Edison's death, the results were weak, and Firestone, an important backer, left the project in 1936 and it folded. A few years later synthetic rubber was invented, obviating the need for such research, but for a few years, it gave farmers hope for new markets, as the alcohol experiments once had done.

Having reversed the ratio of horses to motor vehicles in the 20 years from 1900 to 1920, Ford began a publicity-grabbing campaign in 1921 to replace the cow on the farm with the manufacture of synthetic artificial milk. Again, he felt the amount of money and time spent maintaining cows was a huge waste of farmers' resources. Surely, he reasoned, one could figure out a way to duplicate the cow's process of turning vegetation into milk. Although some thought this idea could be a boon to humanity, it mostly produced a lot of ribbing in the daily press about knocking down tin cows for shipment and cranking them up each day to produce phony milk. In reality Ford had no idea what this milk would be made of or how it would be produced until the Depression had already begun. The item he turned to would involve much more than milk, and it would have a Fordian impact on the world second only to his work in the automobile business.

After a good deal of research and experimentation, Ford chose the soybean as the raw vegetable material with the most possibilities. It could be grown anywhere in the United States, was resistant to a severe lack of water, and its cultivation enriched the soil with nitrogen. It had been grown in East

Asia for thousands of years, where its nutritional value made it second in importance only to rice. Though introduced to the United States in 1904, it was used only as cattle fodder and in World War I as a cheap fertilizer, until Ford experimented with it and publicized its possibilities in the 1930s. Ford spent over $3 million on soybean research from 1930 to 1933, planting 300 varieties on 8,000 acres, and processed the beans in huge machines that simultaneously turned out both soybean oil and soybean meal. He used the oil for high-grade auto enamel and shock-absorber fluid. The meal was molded into all sorts of auto products, from horn buttons to distributor cases. At the Century of Progress World's Fair exhibition in Chicago in 1933, visitors watched soybeans transformed into everything from soap, margarine, and glycerin to table tops, varnish, glue, and linoleum.

By 1937, Ford scientists developed a process to turn soybean protein into textile filament, the first time this had been done from a vegetable source. It could be turned into cloth for upholstery, blankets, and clothing. Once Ford turned up at a press conference in an outfit made entirely of this material (except for his shoes of course); he couldn't cross his legs when he sat, however, or it would crack. With refinements, he tried to sell it to the government for use in World War II soldiers' uniforms, but it was not economically competitive with items made from conventional materials or with new synthetics like rayon and nylon. Ford sold the company he used to produce the textile filament to another firm, which could never make a go of it either.

Ford himself thought late in life that his most important contribution to society could be soybean plastics. Plastics, fabricated from cotton cellulose and wood pulp, were used extensively in cars by the mid-1910s, and later on other vegetable products like soybeans were included in these processes too. A famous 1940 publicity shot showed Ford taking a sledgehammer to a plastic car trunk without causing damage, thus showing the strength of the material in a demonstration he had been repeating for years. But though plastics were indeed the coming thing in so many aspects of American life, by the early 1940s, it was clear that vegetable-based plastics could not compete against plastic materials made from coal, natural gas, and petroleum. These worked much better in terms of tolerances and heat. So eventually Ford gave up touting his version of plastics, although soy is used today in many aspects of plastic production.

Nevertheless, Ford did find success with foods based on the soybean. He hired his boyhood friend Edsel Ruddiman to experiment on vegetable alcohol production in 1916, and in the early 1930s directed him to examine the possibilities of the soybean as human food. Many disparaging comments were made about inedible soy vitamin biscuits, pies, burgers, and such that Ford served at company lunches. But despite these problematic, forced taste tests, the benefits of soy food began to spread, especially when he offered elaborate samples of much improved recipes at the World's Fair. Nutritional value, digestibility, and economy gave incentives to scientists to create more and better soy food products. Ruddiman, who combined water with rubbed soybeans and other substances, considered himself to be one of the prime creators of soybean milk, which turned out to be one of the most valuable of all foods derived from the plant. According to Ruddiman, Ford kept close tabs on all the soybean research. Things went so well that by the early 1940s, with the acceptance of improved soybean milk, Ford was again trotting out his old "The Cow Must Go" slogan and creating a stir.

In large part due to his efforts, the acreage of soybeans under cultivation in the United States jumped from 1 million in 1934 to 12 million in 1944. By 1959, production expanded from just 1 million bushels in 1920 to 534 million, making it the country's fifth largest crop. By 1985, it was second only to corn, as more and more products were created from it. It was the great success of Ford's later life, proving in the most graphic fashion that untold social benefits can be derived from the soil with true vision and untrammeled imagination and support.

As was true of many of Ford's accomplishments, he wasn't the pioneer in recognizing the value of the soybean, but he was its popularizer and the extender of its possibilities. An admirer of men like Luther Burbank and George Washington Carver, who discovered over 300 uses for the peanut, he found common cause with people who wished to expand the potential of everyday items in nature for the benefit of all humanity.

It is also true that Ford was able to attract wide interest in his experiments and results because of the plight of the farmer, that iconic American figure who both watered the roots of our national identity and provided daily nourishment for our ever-expanding population. In large part due to the abundance of the land and constantly improving techniques, farmers were growing much more food than the nation consumed, and their products became cheaper and cheaper. Adjusted for inflation, some farm products like wheat were selling at a 300-year low in the 1920s and 1930s. Farmers were ironically being paid to plow 25 percent of their crops under in 1933, just as many starving Americans couldn't afford to buy them. Ford was one of many people trying to find new markets for agricultural products in an attempt to fix the current and largest problem of the farmers—no market.

His ideas were in perfect harmony with the chemurgy movement, a scientific enterprise that promoted the chemical and industrial use of organic raw materials, especially farm products. Ford had been urging this for at least a decade and a half, but it did not become truly noticed and organized as a movement until farmers became desperate and bewildered in the late 1920s. By the mid-1930s, there was more than a groundswell for it, and Ford hosted the first National Chemurgical Conference in Dearborn in 1935, when his soybean research was in full swing. Out of this meeting came the organization of the Farm Chemurgic Council, which eventually induced the government to set up four large crop-utilization laboratories in different parts of the country. More than 8,000 new processes and scores of new industries came out of their work during the next 35 years.

In a certain sense, all of this had to do with Ford's roots in puritanical, Protestant America. "Waste not, want not," one read in a *McGuffey Reader*, and it was one of his lifelong guiding principles. In fact it was a mania. Everything at the Ford works was saved and utilized to cut costs and make money. Wood shavings were turned into charcoal briquettes, formaldehyde, creosote, and ethyl acetate; and derivatives of coal supplied coke, ammonium sulfate, and benzol, the latter of which was sold in 88 gas stations in the Detroit area at prices competitive with gasoline. Even Dearborn garbage was turned into alcohol, heating gas, and refined oil, while Detroit sewage became soap. By 1928, he was selling $20 million in byproducts per year. In all, his drive to use or transform every item he found or made in his factories or elsewhere was responsible for the creation of some 53 industries in his lifetime.

The abhorrence of waste encompassed much more than material things for Ford. His objection to war was that it caused waste, of civilization and lives. Beneath his enlightened labor policies offering employment for all was something similar. "That is our business," he told Henry L. Stidger in 1923, "We salvage everything, even men."

In another sense, this was a reflection of American optimism. The frontier may have been closed, but possibilities were not; they surrounded you, in places and ways you may not even have dreamed about. Rather than saving to hoard what one had, Ford believed in saving to use and make new things from what you had put by. This creative energy led to extended or new life for many products. In a certain way this was a contradiction to old-line Protestant frugality. It was something much more modern, evangelical in fact, like many religious movements that were so popular at the time. He was preaching a new sort of gospel for the 20th century. Its text could be summed up by the title of an article he "wrote" in 1927: "The Machine Is the New Messiah." It was the machine that would bring people into the paradise of material comfort in the new age, and every bit of raw material and energy should be given to it, like sacrifices to the gods of old, so that all could benefit.

Ford wasn't a deep thinker, but he was a visionary, and his purview was broad. As do all visionaries, he peered into the future. He was able to actualize some extremely important ideas in agriculture, as he was also able to do in industry and society. He could often be naïve, reactionary, simplistic, and simply wrong. But when he was right, Ford was able to effect substantive change with lasting results. In speaking of his agricultural enterprises, Reynold Wik said it best: "His views on technology, conservation, ecology, and the mechanization of rural America were generally prophetic, enlightened, progressive, and often far ahead of his times." Had he never achieved his overarching reputation for the mass production of automobiles, this alone would have allowed him to leave a considerable mark on American history.

ELEVEN

EFFLORESCENCE AND HARD ENDINGS

Henry Ford was catapulted into worldwide fame as the "friend of the working man" with the introduction of the five-dollar day in 1914. He set up part of this new wage program as profit sharing for the working man and presented it as such at its unveiling. Indeed it was shocking to capitalists to hear a businessman they recognized as one of their own promote such an idea. That kind of talk was supposed to be the preserve of fire-breathing socialist or communist radicals, even if Ford had solid business reasons for doing it. In a single stroke it made him what Carol Gelderman called a "wayward capitalist," by proposing that a worker had a *right* to participate in the profits of his employer at the same time that the employer had an *obligation* to share those profits with him. According to Ford, business was supposed to be conducted in the service of providing a better life for everyone, not just the owner of capital and his customers.

This thinking came from a man who was on his way to owning 100 percent of his vast company in a few years, far more than titans like Rockefeller, Carnegie, or Morgan ever owned of theirs. Under these circumstances, it was both predictable and truly startling that he could say during the Dodge Brothers lawsuit five years later that he was in business mainly to achieve his true goal of giving service to his fellow man and only incidentally to make money. Instead of class war over the division of capital between owners and laborers, as Marx had predicted, Ford was proposing class cooperation between the two groups over the same issue, remaking the proletariat into prosperous consumers. The Ford worker walked into the same plant the day after the announcement of the five-dollar day that he had left the day before, but his attitude toward it and toward Ford himself was completely different. The afterglow lasted a long time for both the workers and the public in general.

The world caught up with the five-dollar day by 1919, by which time wartime inflation had eroded its buying power. Ford had to institute the six-dollar day, which in fact was not worth as much as its predecessor, though that evened out in the Depression of 1920–1921. Still, the bright, clean, and airy workplace that Ford provided and improved; his egalitarian hiring practices that extended employment to any member of society who wanted it; the relatively high wages; the Sociological Department that attempted to make life better for employees and their families; all these and other beneficent policies created six years of goodwill at Ford that were unequaled in their time.

But there was a dark angel hovering over Ford in this period. There was the Antisemitism, the Newberry affair, the callousness with which he tried to treat his fellow investors in Ford, and more, as we saw. In the beginning of the 1920s though, a more pervasive darkness began to take hold that he could not, or would not, shake.

Even in the earliest happy days, Oliver Barthel noticed that Ford liked to be around men who were tough and mean. Those were the kinds of guys who succeeded with him. That proclivity never left him and in fact grew as time went on. It was as if some evolutionary throwback were living among the finer angels of his being, staring wild-eyed at them and baring its fangs. And it was a pervasive creature. Douglas Brinkley, author of *Wheels for the World*, says, "Demonization of the strong, and destruction of the weak, except for Clara, was the inevitable end of any close relationship with Henry Ford."

In 1915, Harry Bennett went to work in the Ford motion picture department. A prize-winning ex-pugilist and Navy man, he was noticed after awhile; through John Dahlinger, Henry Ford hired him to do various kinds of personal work. Bennett was tough, combative, fiercely loyal, and willing to carry out any orders Ford gave him. With contacts from the highest levels of law enforcement to the lowest levels of the underworld, he was able to accomplish quite a lot, and as time went by, his influence grew even more substantial. Bennett was in charge of security, and as the workforce ballooned at Ford and fears of militant unionism increased, he ran a large security force whose spying and rough tactics with the workers seemed to have taken many cues from gangster squads and fascist military and paramilitary groups in Europe. And also from the federal government, which looked at plant workers very closely to make sure there was no sabotage during the war; after it ended, the government was gone, but the system of spying it used remained. Many thought Bennett ran security in his own way without consultation with his boss; but those who got an inside glimpse of what was really going on knew that when Ford said " jump," his job was to say "how high?" As Bennett himself said, "I am Mr. Ford's man." What Liebold was as a secretary, and Cameron as a spokesperson, Bennett was as an enforcer.

Charles Sorensen was another tough guy, as good a production man as Ford could possibly find to head that aspect of his company. A charming, handsome man with an explosive temper, he was a hard man to work for, though without him Ford would never have been able to live up to the demand for the Model T.

The growth in the number of Ford employees proceeded at a torrid pace throughout the early 1920s, and it was Sorensen who dealt with them as much as he dealt with machines, factory layouts, and the pace of shipments. If it hadn't been for the need to exercise firm control over the labor force, Bennett's influence might not have become so powerful so quickly, but tabs had to be kept, and all sorts of work, including dirty work, needed to be done to keep personnel in line. Bennett was happy to do it, in his own belligerent way. Between the two men, the atmosphere at the Rouge became much tighter and more ominous.

Ford himself, in the crisis of 1920–1921, showed just how tough and belligerent he could be when it came to saving his enterprise. He forced cars down the throats of his dealers, laid off his workforce, demoted executives to watchmen, consolidated or eliminated whole departments, sold off every scrap that was unnecessary, and even managed to lower prices, spearheading a movement among his flummoxed competitors to do the same. It was truly remarkable that he came through this crisis with flying colors and managed to do so without resort to financial help from the dreaded Wall Street bankers and financiers that he so loathed.

The trouble was that he did some of these things with a sort of evil glee. Salaried men would go home one day and come back the next to find their telephones and desks gone and their entire departments eliminated. Important executives were fired or "allowed to depart" to use a business euphemism, even those as important as Knudsen. Tellingly, the Reverend Marquis, after a humiliating round with Sorensen and Ford over the termination of an employee, came to the realization that the idealist he had once worked for had disappeared, and so he left as head of the Sociological Department, which had been concerned with overseeing the welfare of Ford employees. In fact, Ford had lost all enthusiasm for this department and let it continue for a while only as a shadow of its former self.

Then there was the speed-up on the assembly line. Everyone noticed it when they came back to work in early 1921. Ford (and Sorensen) took the opportunity provided by the plant shutdown to replace and rearrange the machinery to make the assembly process move faster, often by eliminating jobs to make it necessary for a man to turn out more work in a given period of time. Everything was a bit tighter, quicker, and more in earnest, and the workers felt more and more pinched. With production doubling in a two-year period, it didn't get any easier in the plant. "Hurry up, hurry up" became the phrase most heard at the Rouge, and foremen learned to say it in many languages. The humanity Ford had shown his workers was gradually calcifying in the fires of overheated production. Eventually it would be clear that even he knew his enterprise had grown too large for it to continue on its former, more considerate, basis. It was part of the Emersonian "price" he paid for the vast production he wanted.

To be sure, health and safety were still important concerns at Ford, and at every hour some part of the plant was being cleaned, polished, or painted. The air was constantly filtered in every part of the building, even those least accessible, and 2,900 drinking fountains were installed, with salt tablets available in summer. Even the slightest injury or indisposition was to be reported and dealt with immediately at a first aid station, and there was a gleaming, fully equipped, and noise-free infirmary right in the middle of the plant, from which workers with serious conditions could be dispatched in ambulances if necessary to the Henry Ford Hospital in Detroit.

But workers stood all day on the line and had a mere 15 minutes for lunch, including washing up beforehand. They couldn't speak, whistle, or sing, for fear of distracting themselves or others. Workers constantly had to fight the ill effects from the monotony of their repetitive tasks and the somnolence produced by constant, repetitive noise (though it was true that they could request transfers to other departments if they wished).

There was something else about work in these plants that was onerous. Workers were completely at the mercy of an arbitrary employment system. Management could hire and fire employees at will and determine their wages and benefits however they saw fit. Company supervisors and spies were always on the lookout for infractions of the rules. No one ever felt secure, no matter how well or long they had worked for Ford (this was true at all auto companies). It was this last fact, more than any other, that would eventually contribute to the rise of unionism in the auto industry. Ford was probably better than any other automobile company in matters of the health and welfare of his employees, but even the best was none too good.

The toughest of the "driver" periods at Ford came between 1921 and 1923, the time of greatest expansion, when workers were pushed to the limits to churn out work at a constantly increasing pace. After that, and up to the changeover to the Model A, things leveled out a bit. The number of employees came within shouting distance of tripling, new machinery made it possible to work more efficiently, and attention was paid to finding a normal work rhythm on the line. After all, it was much to the advantage of the company to find the proper pace of work to avoid disruptions in the production schedule. (They had found that it was mostly the abnormally slow workers or the excessively quick ones who had a hard time adjusting to the regularized pace and momentum.) In this way, the work came out faster, and while there was still the sense of "driving," most of the improvements did not come out of the hides of the workers as they had previously.

The changeover to the Model A created another problem in the workforce, as there was confusion and difficulty at the Rouge in every department as they adjusted. The problem was caused in large measure by the shutdown of the final assembly line at Highland Park, a break that occurred naturally at the conclusion of Model T production. Everything "T" was over, and everything "A" was beginning at the Rouge. Sorensen, who had the enormous responsibility of supervising this, and who also wanted to consolidate his own power, attempted to achieve both aims by getting rid of as many Highland Park workers as possible, in what could later be referred to as a Stalinist manner: "no man, no problem."

P. E. Martin, who had once been Sorensen's boss of production at Highland Park, now deferred to him, sticking to production details at the Rouge. Another important production man, Mead L. Bricker, went to supervise Highland Park and began getting rid of men there as their activities were transferred to the newer plant. Those who went to the Rouge often found inferior jobs or no jobs there, and quit. Much of the dirty work of firing people was given to William C. Klann, yet another experienced production man. In this period, many important executives and their best assistants left the company at the very time their expertise was sorely needed. But Sorensen was intransigent and did things his way, which was often arbitrary and cruel. The appointment of Bennett as personnel supervisor at this time shook up many people, as they knew what this would mean for Sorensen's plan. Eventually when the lines were up and running in 1928, Klann himself was let go, and when he was offered the chance to return, he declined, not wanting to be thrown out rather than asked to leave next time.

The uncertainty of the executives and skilled workers filtered down to the rank and file too. Loyalty and longtime service didn't seem to matter much on this new Model A job. Supervisors wanted to hire physically strong and able men under 35 when filling jobs on the line, so older men took to using hair dye and shoe polish to look younger when applying for a job at Ford. Once you got a job, the pressures of the "hurry up" were relentless. It was only natural that everyone felt unsettled.

Though Ford himself remained aloof from all this, anyone who knew him realized that he had to have a major hand in these policies. Times had changed, and Ford had changed with them. The idealist of the five-dollar day and the Sociological Department was long gone. By 1930, the friend of the working man could openly state that "A great business is really too big to be human."

Nevertheless, Ford jobs were seen as good jobs in the 1920s, and people were generally happy to get and keep them. And as we have seen, Ford became a hero when he instituted the seven-dollar day on December 1, 1929, when the nation was in the grip of panic over the Crash. But by 1932, the Depression had cut that goodwill to ribbons as the few workers with jobs were lucky to make even four dollars a day three days a week. An entirely new atmosphere reigned at the Rouge. Ford was now in an adversarial relationship with his employees, which was not entirely his fault, but it led to one of the saddest labor incidents of the Great Depression, the Ford Hunger March of March 7, 1932. This was a communist-organized demonstration in which 3,000 desperately poor men carrying red banners marched on the Rouge demanding redress for a long list of labor grievances, ranging from hours and medical care to hiring practices. Because Ford owned three-fifths of the taxable property in Dearborn, the police chief, a former Ford serviceman, was at the company's disposal. The demonstrators hadn't applied for a permit, and the police were determined to break things up, which they did in violent ways, aided by Service Department men using fire hoses on the demonstrators in sub-freezing weather. Eventually a personal confrontation between Bennett and Joseph York, the 19-year-old head of the Young Communist League, turned into a mêlée that led to the death of the latter and three others in a hail of bullets from the guns of the Service Department and the police; 20 others were injured. The press was manhandled and complained loudly about it, as they made clear that the demonstrators were unarmed.

Four days later, 15,000 mourners showed up at the three-mile funeral procession for the four men, waving red banners and singing "The Internationale." It was a terribly sad and stirring sight. As for Ford, the words of Robert Cruden said it all: "The legend of high wages, good conditions and contented workers was riddled by the bullets that killed four unemployed workers." At the funeral, Ford servicemen took pictures of the many employees that showed up; as they were recognized in the developed photos, they were gradually dismissed. This didn't seem at all unusual at a time when Ford espionage agents both in the plant and outside regularly filed reports on employees attempting to organize workers, with the goal of rooting them out of the labor force. Many other infractions of factory rules were treated in the same way. And there was absolutely no redress, especially in this terrible time when jobs were at a premium. Ford's reputation among workingmen had slid to an all-time low.

True to form though, Ford almost simultaneously rescued a whole town of idled workingmen in Inkster, Michigan. Their lives had fallen into desuetude and their homes and community had collapsed into a state of decrepitude. Inkster was a pitiful town west of Dearborn, with unemployed inhabitants who were mostly black and had worked in the Ford foundry, which suffered along with all other departments as production sank. The town was so destitute that its electricity had been cut off and it had no police force. Ford arrived in November 1931 and cleaned up the town by helping its inhabitants get back on their feet. He reopened the school, provided seeds for gardens, gave sewing machines and dressmaking classes to women, and opened one of his supermarket-style commissaries to sell food, clothing, and other items at cut-rate prices. Then he provided jobs at the

Rouge facility and for cleanup in the town itself at four dollars per day; one dollar went to the worker, and three dollars went to the revival of community services and to repay inhabitants' documented debts. Within a few short months the town was revived, and Ford took out ads extolling the self-help success of Inkster as a model for economic restoration, along with his suggestion that village industries and family gardens grow food: "One foot on the land and another foot on industry...America is Safe," he proclaimed. In fact, America was yet to hit bottom, but the salvation of Inkster was a heartening story of encouragement for working men, and blacks in particular never forgot that he did it for them. Years later, longtime resident Leo Meyer said that, without Ford, Inkster would have disappeared.

Keith Sward, in *The Legend of Henry Ford*, points out that in the larger scheme of things in the Depression, the Fords were less munificent than the Inkster project would indicate. In 1931, the Fords took some $8.5 million in cash dividends from the company for their own personal use, but Edsel, with a $140,000 check, was the only one of the three who contributed to the Community Fund that took care of the desperate and unemployed in Detroit, many of whom were former Ford workers. Harry Bennett boasted that the revived Sociological Department at Ford gave out some $75,000 the same year, but this was only three ten-thousandths of the $248 million in cash and marketable securities it had on hand at the close of the fiscal year.

In the winter of 1933, the ever-worsening economic condition of the United States came to a sickening climax, and a recalcitrant Henry Ford became for a brief time the central figure in this affair, known as the Banking Crisis of 1933. It could be seen as the longest awaited, coldest banquet of revenge in his entire life.

It ruined Detroit and its elites, and threatened to ruin the United States before it was over. In a most personal vein, it also deeply humiliated his son.

Detroit in the early 20th century was the biggest boomtown America had ever known, having ballooned from a population of 285,000 in 1900 to almost 1.57 million in 1930, and caused echo booms in other Michigan cities like Lansing and Flint. It was not a mature city, however, being completely dependent on the rest of the country for just about everything else not related to its one product, the automobile. In banking Detroit was a quarter century behind the times, dependent on New York and Chicago for most of its financing and other monetary needs. By the mid-1920s, that began to change, as local groups saw an opportunity to make considerable money by establishing important local banks.

One of those groups was the brainchild of Ernest Kanzler, the suave and elegant brother-in-law of Edsel Ford, who had injudiciously suggested to Henry Ford in a long memorandum in 1926 that it was time to replace the aging Model T, and been fired from the company as a result. He and a few others had an investment group that managed to draw in Edsel Ford and, in June 1927, obtained a state charter for a holding company called the Guardian Detroit Bank, a complex that consisted of a bank, an investment company, and a trust company. It quickly became known as—what else?—an automobile bank and, in 1928, when Ford finally consented to finance sales for his new Model A, an entity to accomplish that purpose, the Universal Credit Company, was formed as a partnership between Ford and Guardian; 400,000 contracts were written in that year alone. The bank expanded quickly in the way things were done at that time, by opening or acquiring other banks, rather than by opening branches; it was widely known that Edsel Ford, with 50,000 shares, was the largest stockholder, and this helped attract capital. By December 1929, having doubled its capital earlier that year by 50 percent, Guardian merged with another holding company, the Union Commerce Company of Detroit, to form the Guardian Detroit Union Group, which controlled all the stock (except directors' shares) of 23 banks and trust companies, and then took over eight more institutions through exchanges of stock. The idea was to make the standards, practices, and resources of the best banks available to all in the group who could not afford these things on their own. The very next month, in an analogous manner, the Detroit Bankers Company, a much larger holding company, was formed in the same way.

Ford's company maintained large deposits in both institutions and, on the surface of it, seemed to have a contented relationship with both, especially the Guardian, which he dominated. This fact was hardly bruited about, because of his well-known opinions of both banks and bankers.

Underneath, however, there were strong currents of resentment toward this whole situation in the soul of Henry Ford. The Guardian Bank was begun and invested in by the sort of Detroit elites whom he despised; even the son of the much-loathed Truman Newberry was one of the prominent investors. Ford was willing to invest with them for the sake of expediency, though he never paid too much attention to the activities of the bank. Chief among them was the financing of large numbers of commercial and residential buildings that were sprouting up all over Detroit. As these investments went sour in the spreading Depression from 1930 on, and the companies resorted to increasingly desperate measures to save themselves, Ford, when he was finally forced to focus on the situation, was little inclined to salvage it.

Directors of the company had been borrowing from it to buy stocks during the mania of the 1920s, some even pledging their Guardian shares as collateral, which was technically illegal, but could be wriggled out of, just barely. As the stock drifted down from $350 to nothing, those loans had no backing at all. As workers lost jobs, they couldn't repay their mortgages or, by 1933, even the interest on their mortgages. As there was no market for the houses, the bank loans on them and commercial properties in similar situations were impaired. By February 1933, 72 percent of the Union Guardian Trust Company's holdings were frozen.

Added to this was the incredible fact that the various bank constituents continued to pay dividends in this period, no matter what, in order to maintain public confidence in the underlying company; one unit paid out 24.75 percent of its capital in dividends in 1931; another had $700,000 more in questionable loans than it had capital. To keep one jump ahead of the bank examiners, Guardian moved funds from one constituent to another in maneuvers that were nothing short of outright deception. The Detroit Bankers Company was even worse, so much so that the chief national bank examiner said in 1932 that one of its members, the First National Bank of Detroit "was not rotten—it's putrid."

The thinking was that if the situation was supported long enough, eventually conditions would change, and the banks would be rescued. But what no one knew was that nothing would improve until the total collapse of the banking system was at hand.

Guardian had already borrowed $15 million in 1932 from the Reconstruction Finance Corporation (RFC), which Herbert Hoover had started to help banks out of temporary difficulties.

By January 1933, the Guardian Detroit Union Group (part of the Union Guardian Trust Co.), pressed by an insurance company for loans it had made, asked for $50 million more, $37 million of which was agreed to, if Ford and Kanzler could come up with the other $13 million.

Everything seemed to be going through, but then an enormous problem cropped up out of nowhere. Senator James Couzens, now head of a Senate Banking and Currency subcommittee, objected fiercely to the RFC loan, saying it was not proper for taxpayers' money to prop up private banks (he was piqued that the president of the RFC had just made such a loan to his own Chicago bank!). If this loan was made to a Ford-backed bank, he would "shout against it from the rooftops."

Henry Ford, nearing 70, had only a dim sense of the Guardian's affairs until then. He was preoccupied with such things as his museum and Greenfield Village, his new V-8, and his failing airplane business. But Couzens's linking of him to the troubles of the Guardian Bank got his attention in a big way. A mortified and tearful Edsel approached Liebold about the desperation of his own personal circumstances (he had lost up to $20 million of his own money) and those of his bank. He knew that his father's reaction was likely to be completely unsympathetic, and was despairing of his fate. Liebold, who never remonstrated with Ford, went so far as to tell him that, as far as this matter was concerned, "you do not take good care of your son." No one knows what went on between father and son in their meetings then, or how much humble pie the latter had to ingest, but Henry replenished Edsel's accounts with millions in short order. He certainly had the cash to do it, never having participated in the stock market mania in any way, or in its subsequent losses.

The Guardian Group was another matter. It was absolutely essential to the RFC rescue for Henry Ford to subordinate his $7.5 million deposits in Guardian so that others would do so also, making up the rest of the money the RFC required to permit the loan. Both Ford and Couzens agreed that taxpayers should not have to rescue the bank, but Ford thought the government should do it, and Couzens thought Ford should do it.

Arthur A. Ballantine and Roy D. Chapin, late of the Hudson Motor Car Company and now secretary of commerce and a member of the Guardian board, went to see Ford to try to persuade him to cooperate. Ford would have none of it. Even when Ballantine painted a grim picture of the suffering of millions and paralysis of the state's business if the plan did not go through, Ford told them the state should be fully responsible for it all; a few millions from the government shouldn't prevent the rescue from happening. He also spoke darkly of a "conspiracy," meaning a conspiracy of the Treasury, his competitors, and the "people back of them" (meaning Wall Street) trying to take control of the nation's banking system by destroying his business. He became even more incensed, stating that if the RFC didn't make the loan promptly, he would withdraw his funds from both the Guardian and Detroit Bankers companies. As he had done something similar during the panic of 1914, everyone had good reason to believe him.

When Chapin pleaded that such an action "would almost certainly bring down the whole banking structure of the country and lead...very likely to the failure of very many manufacturers and business institutions as well," Ford memorably replied, "All right, let the crash come. Everything will go down the chute. But I feel young. I can build again."

Not even a last-ditch offer from Couzens to put up half the money could change his mind. And so, the crash came. Accordingly, after a couple of hectic days of futile negotiations to solve the problem, Governor Comstock was forced to declare a bank holiday throughout Michigan, closing down 550 state and national banks with $1.5 billion on deposit from 900,000 customers. Money swiftly dried up, and soon the state had to resort to issuing scrip so that Detroit could function. For a while, large companies with deposits in other states trucked in money to pay their employees, but starting with Maryland on February 23, 1933, other states swiftly closed down their banks too, and by March 4, very few banks in only 14 states were still open. Franklin D. Roosevelt, inaugurated on that day, immediately declared a national bank holiday lasting until March 12, when after examination and reorganization, sound banks were gradually allowed to reopen.

The Fords came out of this rather well, for they offered to take over the whole of Michigan's banking system by putting up $8,225 million; they looked like saviors, as the public put up banners and shouted, "Bank with Hank!" But as with Muscle Shoals ten years before, this was quickly seen as a devious way to gain control of all of the state's banking at a bargain-basement price.

For Couzens, the reaction was harsh: The citizens of Michigan never forgave him for not standing up for his constituents' interests at a time when they needed his help most. He was reviled throughout the state.

The elites of the city were ruined, for not only did the banking board members lose their investments, but they were also liable for making good on their depositors' losses. (It should be said that none of the other Detroit moguls came forward to aid in alleviating this crisis either, agreeing with Ford that the government should take full responsibility for solving it.)

Detroit never recovered, because it was now revealed as nothing but a one-industry town completely dependent on the rest of the country for its needs, a city that was far away from being able to sustain a banking industry that could be thought of as the powerhouse of the Midwest. Construction cranes rusted at abandoned building sites for decades. Although it had periods of prosperity from the 1940s to the mid-1960s, Detroit gradually became shabby and insecure, especially after the race riots of 1967 caused much of its white population to flee. Sadly it continues its decline today, because it never did diversify beyond autos, and car manufacturing has steadily departed from Detroit for decades. Once the fourth largest city in the United States, parts of it today look like ghost towns.

Edsel was saved, because his father needed him too much, but any thought of him taking over the business from his father was out of the question after this.

The irony of the Detroit banking crisis is that all the depositors of these banks were ultimately paid off; in retrospect, it also appears that none of the banks was actually insolvent when declared to be so. If Couzens had not been so adamant, and Ford had risen above his intransigence and paranoia and shown himself to be the friend of the working man he had once been, none of this need have happened. But the altruistic, civic-minded Henry Ford of 1915 had long ago disappeared.

Ford was right about one thing though; he did feel young again. He had created the new V-8 in the same hands-on way he involved himself in the creation of the Models T and A. And after it was done, he continued to play an active role in the engineering department on a constant basis.

True, he had his prejudices (*only* mechanical brakes, *only* transverse springs), and they hampered development of his products, as did such things as the lack of a wind tunnel, a test track, and university-trained engineers. There was no organizational chart either, and the impressive engineering building he opened in 1924 was in fact a hodgepodge of mixed uses. To make matters worse, Ford's frequent intervention in various engineering projects, often before they were started, created a great deal of frustration in the area of engineering design. Edsel and Sorensen solved this in time for the 1937 models by separating experimental engineering from the rest, leaving it in Dearborn while everything else moved to the Rouge, where Henry was far less likely to come around and interfere. Body design was left to Edsel, because of a lack of interest on his own part and a realization of his son's real talent in this area.

But unlike the early days of the Model T, and very much like the early days of the Model A, Henry Ford lost money in buckets in the early days of the V-8. Of course, it was launched in the very depths of the Depression, but once again there were big problems getting it into production, which happened so slowly that Ford lost $70 million on it in 1933 alone. By 1934, things had righted themselves again, and the next year the expanding popularity of the V-8 landed Ford back in second place in the industry, ahead of Chrysler (which regained the number-two position the next year and held it until 1950).

Ford had no medium-priced car in those years, no Buick, De Soto, or Pontiac, just the low-priced Ford and the luxury Lincoln, which undoubtedly hurt sales as the economy recovered. Edsel did get the company into the upper middle-low end luxury market, created when LaSalle halved its price with a new model in 1934, and especially when Packard quadrupled its sales with the striking 120 in 1935. Edsel and designer John Tjaarda brought out the beautifully streamlined Lincoln Zephyr in 1936, which competed squarely in this market. By 1938, Ford finally had a medium-priced car with the new Mercury, originally a sort of large and luxo Ford that was a big success in the marketplace from the beginning. Under Edsel's supervision, all the car lines became more handsome, and eventually in 1939, he created what many thought was the most beautiful production car ever, the Lincoln Continental.

Still, the company lost $26 million on its operations between 1926 and 1936, despite the most successful new car introduction ever with the Model A and the later V-8. By contrast, GM never had a single losing year, even when scraping the bottom of the barrel in 1932. Intermittently, Ford did well, millions were satisfied with its products, and tens of thousands had good jobs. But the question remains: Would the Ford Motor Company have done much better financially without the quirky, eccentric management style of its founder? True, it was fiscally sound in the Depression, and never even close to financial trouble due to Henry Ford's prudent management of his finances. It was also true that Edsel showed himself to be less than sound in his financial judgment during the banking crisis. But he would almost certainly have managed the company in a more efficient, moneymaking manner over the years, and he would have avoided the debilitating and damaging struggle with labor that did much to undermine Henry Ford's reputation for a number of years.

Things had not gone well for the labor union movement in the 1920s and 1930s. There were unfavorable court decisions; huge strike battles that had been lost in the steel, railway, and coal-mining industries; solid support among manufacturers for the open shop; and the sometimes sickening exploitation of workers (child labor, decrepit, dirty workplaces, and abysmal wages for long hours) in shaky businesses like Southern textile mills.

Unionism had never really taken hold in the auto industry. It was a relatively new, booming business with little history of big labor disputes. Furthermore, the biggest force in labor then, the American Federation of Labor, was at heart a craft-based union, offering little to unskilled or semiskilled workers. Factionalism among its various constituents, which precluded a single-purpose effort, and employer intransigence combined to prevent any meaningful organization for the vast numbers of autoworkers in the plants. And while they were disparaging of some auto manufacturers, unions usually gave Henry Ford a pass because of his long-established history of high wages and liberal employment policies.

Communists inevitably seized opportunities in this and other industries as conditions deteriorated during the Depression, just as they had in the textile industry in the 1920s. Indeed, the Ford Hunger March in March 1932 was one of many such organized by Communists during the period when increasing numbers of desperate, unemployed people were searching for relief from their problems.

Despite the increasingly severe economic situation as the Depression rolled on, unions had still not penetrated the auto industry. Adamantly opposed manufacturers were having none of it, and with jobs in such short supply (in 1932, employment in their factories was off 60.8 percent from the year before), workers fearfully put up with any conditions just to keep working, because they knew how easily and arbitrarily they could be dismissed. Management espionage agents reported any workplace infraction, and attempts to organize, attend union meetings, or even read union literature were sure tickets to unemployment.

The turning point came in January 1933, when 9,000 workers at the awful Briggs Body Factory put down their tools in protest against their terrible working conditions, which included pay as low as ten cents an hour. Workers at other companies like Hudson joined them, and their actions caused the idling of 60,000 people. It didn't last long, but Briggs was forced to guarantee a wage of 25¢ an hour along with other concessions, and for the first time, the wider public recognized the necessity and fairness of better conditions for auto laborers.

By May of that year, after his inauguration, Roosevelt put the National Industrial Recovery Act (NIRA, later the NRA) into effect, which was charged with creating labor codes for each industry, guaranteeing minimum wages, maximum hours, and the right to collective bargaining, the latter in the notorious Section 7A. All the manufacturers hated this provision, but they agreed to it, circumventing it whenever possible, often with their own "company unions" and rehires of nonunion workers after layoffs. The automobile code was promulgated in July 1933 and approved by the president in August. Everyone signed, with one exception: Henry Ford. He refused and didn't care about anybody's opinion of his decision. Ford was not about to let anyone give him codes for running his business. He referred to the Blue Eagle, the symbol of compliance with the code, as

"Roosevelt's Buzzard." There were strikes at Ford factories, notably at Chester, Pennsylvania, and Edgewater, New Jersey, but they went nowhere. When Ford restored the five-dollar day in 1934, he undermined unionizing efforts in his plants.

The year 1935 brought events that put the unions in a much stronger position. The unloved, weak NRA was declared unconstitutional in the Schecter Poultry case in May, and was then succeeded by the much tougher Wagner-Connery Act in July, which not only guaranteed the right to collective bargaining, but put teeth in it as well. Then, at the AFL convention in October in Atlantic City, John L. Lewis walked out, characterizing the AFL record as one of 25 years of unbroken failure. Many other unions went with his 500,000-strong United Mine Workers Union, and from this act came the birth of the CIO, which finally represented ordinary workers from a position of great strength. The next year the United Automobile Workers joined the CIO, and it was clear that gains for autoworkers were imminent. They didn't come as quickly as they did in the steel and textile industries, both mature businesses with enlightened management. But come they did. In 1936, significant advances were made in strikes at Bendix, Midland Steel, and Kelsey-Hayes Wheel Works, and only a last-minute capitulation by management avoided a strike at Dodge.

The dominoes really started to fall with strikes at Fisher Body in Cleveland and then in Flint at the end of 1936 and in early 1937. These were tough confrontations, employing a new method imported from Britain that would soon spread like wildfire: the sit-down strike, in which workers simply dropped their tools and refused to leave the plants. By early February, GM had struck an agreement that recognized the UAW as the sole bargaining agent for its workers on such issues as wages, seniority, layoffs, and plant speed-ups. It was a tremendous victory, and shortly thereafter, it was followed by another on April 8, 1937, when Walter Chrysler reached a similar agreement after a sit-down strike in his plants. The only major difference was that Chrysler did not grant the UAW exclusive bargaining rights.

When the union set its sights on Ford, it met something else entirely: complete intransigence. Ford was entirely opposed to unionization, and through his chief lieutenant Harry Bennett, he had built up a powerful and effective way of opposing it. Bennett, playing on Ford's fears of kidnapping threats to his family, had explored and set up relationships with leading underworld figures in Detroit, a city filled with them, due to the running of illegal liquor into the United States from Canada during Prohibition. He began hiring a collection of thugs and former jailbirds to work in his Service Department; they joined the ex-boxers and football stars he already had on the payroll, in addition to the men of all work who formed a large part of his force that enabled him to do any type of service that Mr. Ford required. When it became obvious that Ford would become the next target of the union in the spring of 1937, Bennett was ready. The confrontation, one of the most famous in labor history, took place on May 26, 1937, and would be known as "the Battle of the Overpass."

The overpass in question connected a parking lot to the main Rouge factory, where Walter P. Reuther, Richard Frankensteen, and two other UAW officials intended to distribute pamphlets, a perfectly legal activity enshrined in the Wagner Act; the Dearborn City Council approved of this action, having no choice in the matter. On the overpass, however, the four men were ruthlessly set upon and beaten up by several goons from Bennett's Service

Department. All were severely injured (one had his back broken), and their bleeding bodies were dumped over the parking lot edge of the overpass, where they bounced down 39 steel steps. The incident became a nationwide sensation, because a news photographer took pictures that were published in every newspaper in the country, to the shock of millions.

It was no secret that this was done with Ford's approval, for he had told both Edsel and Sorensen that he would meet with no union official, and that anything to do with the unions was to be handled not by them, but by "a strong, aggressive man who can handle himself in any situation." This of course was Harry Bennett.

Many don't realize it today, but this was just the beginning of a protracted campaign against unionism at Ford. In the end, everyone, perhaps even Ford himself, realized that this fight against unionism was a losing proposition, for the law of the land had permanently changed, and public support was solidly behind it. But a combination of thuggery, masterful political maneuvering by Bennett, and dissension in the union itself staved off Ford's capitulation for almost four years.

Bennett organized "outside squads" of toughs who often administered terrible beatings and broke up any sort of union-oriented meetings anywhere it was thought trouble was brewing. In Dallas in the summer of 1937, one attorney was so brutalized that he left the city as soon as he was able. Thugs busted up the showing of a pro-union film on another occasion, first beating up and then tarring and feathering the projectionist. Ford may not have been aware of the details of these actions in advance, but they certainly didn't fit well with his avowed ideas about nonviolence.

Force was not always resorted to. In Kansas City, Ford simply announced he would close his plant and move its operations to Omaha when the plant voted for the UAW; civic leaders compromised immediately to save 2,500 jobs. An outside squad that was arrested and then set free by a compliant district attorney was in place there. They were armed to the teeth.

Bennett, who was a personally charming, compact, little (5'6") dynamo of a man, entertained lavishly on his estate, and freely dispensed jobs, favors, and even a steady supply of free cars to make alliances and win allegiances from all sorts of people, from petty crooks and big-time gangsters, to promising young college athletes, all the way up to top politicians and judges. You never knew whom you would need and when, so he had them all at the ready. J. Edgar Hoover originally distrusted Bennett in 1935, when he provided evidence of corruption in the Michigan governor's office, but over the next several years he changed his mind when Bennett was able to come up with all sorts of useful and accurate information relating to crime activities in Detroit and elsewhere in Michigan. He was also able to supply information on the activities of Communists in the labor movement; some of the names he supplied came from Gerald L. K. Smith, local head of the Fascists, who sold them for one dollar a head. Robert Lacey points out that FBI papers from the late 1930s and early 1940s make it clear that, because of his close cooperation with the FBI, Bennett had license to operate outside the law for a very long time.

Bennett also used his powers of persuasion on Homer Martin, the susceptible head of the UAW, courting favor with him by means of questionable gifts and credit to obtain his complacency with regard to the relationship between the Ford Motor Company and the union. This came at a time when other hard-line men like Frankensteen were vying for the leadership of the union, causing divisions among its ranks, a situation that lasted well into 1940.

Then too, there was widespread unemployment in Detroit during the deep recession of 1937–1938, caused in part by over-production in the former year. With only 11,000 of the 87,000 Ford workers employed at that time, there was little stomach for a strike against the company.

Those who *were* employed in 1938 were affected by the worst speed-up yet in the Ford plants. The men were given new, much higher quotas in every department, and if they met them, they were raised again. The Service Department was more watchful than ever over all the other employees, reporting even the slight-est infraction of work rules. Workers weren't allowed to talk to each other on the job, for fear of conversations about organiz-ing. If they were spotted doing so, they were fired, usually on trumped-up charges of starting a fight (in which they would be badly beaten).

In 1937, the National Labor Relations Board (NLRB) stated that "[t]he River Rouge plant has taken on many aspects of a community in which martial law has been declared, and in which a huge military organization...has been imposed on the regular civil authorities." The next year respected labor leader Benjamin Stolberg called the Service Department "The Storm Troops, keeping order in the plant community through terror...because of this highly organized terror and spy system the fear in the plant is something indescribable." A new illness, "Forditis," was coined by Logan Miller, assistant superintendent of the Rouge plant, to describe the nervous tension often coupled with physical exhaus-tion that resulted from employment at Ford in this period.

Astonishingly, despite all of this, Ford retained a good reputation among the general public for its treatment of labor. A May 1937 survey by the Curtis Publishing Company showed that 59.1 percent of Americans believed that Ford Motor Company treated its labor better than any other; next in line was Bell Telephone at 14.1 percent. This was in the very month of the Battle of the Overpass; GM, which had capitulated to the UAW three months before, got only a 6.3 percent rating.

There were in fact reasons for this public perception. The spotless plants, good health care, enlightened employment policies toward the handicapped, convicts, and blacks were well known and admired (10 percent of all Ford employees in 1935 were black). At the height of the Depression in 1933, any man who was a member of the Wayne County American Legion (up to 5,000) could get a job at Ford. Then there was the trade school, with diplomas that had national recognition. These things gave many employees reasons for gratitude and hope for a better future. The problem, as Theodore A. Mallon stated, was that "things were really okay except the men really couldn't call their souls their own."

But the forward lurch of history finally caught up with Ford in April 1941. Since recent Supreme Court decisions had reinforced the positions of the UAW and the NLRB, the unions were much more open and bold at Ford. A walkout of 1,500 men in the rolling mill quickly spread, and Bennett's scab squads who replaced them fell apart in a drunken frenzy when liquor was smuggled into the plant. Bennett was having nothing to do with the negotiations, but the sudden reappearance of Edsel from a Florida vacation changed all that when he finally stood up to his father and insisted that he negotiate with the UAW-CIO. Workers returned to their jobs when it was determined that a contract would be negotiated after elections to determine which union would represent the workers.

On May 21, 1941, 69.9 percent of the workforce voted for the CIO, and 27.4 percent for the AFL. Henry Ford was fully confident that his workforce would vote overwhelmingly for the nonunion shop option, but only 1,958, or 2.7 percent, did. It stunned the old man. Charles Sorensen called it "perhaps the greatest disappointment he had in all his business experience. He was never the same after that."

When it was prepared, the contract presented to Henry Ford on June 18, 1941 (he did not take part in the negotiations) was the most generous ever agreed to by a major industrial enterprise. Ford would allow an almost totally closed union shop, the highest wage rate in the industry, a grievance procedure for seniority and speed-ups that was very close to what the union had proposed, and back wages for those discharged in the union struggles of the last few years. The company even agreed to be the union's agent, deducting monthly fees and dues from workers' paychecks. Thus, in one fell swoop, the most recalcitrant automobile company in America became by far the most labor-friendly of all.

At first Ford balked at this, but when he went home, Clara confronted him and said that if he didn't sign it, she was leaving him. There had been too much violence over this issue, one that could never be won by Ford. He caved in. "What could I do?" he said later. "Don't ever discredit the power of a woman."

In actuality, there was more to it than that. Clearly, big defense contracts were coming up, and the government would never do business with a company that had such regressive labor policies.

And of course there was the surprise factor. Agreeing to these terms recalled Ford's apology to Jews in 1927. He was going further than anyone could ever have expected, to the admiration of all (except his competitors and the heads of other businesses, who were horrified).

Indeed, the influence of those big defense contracts was looming large in the spring of 1941. Henry Ford had been adamantly opposed to the start of another war since its first rumblings became apparent in the mid-1930s. The Munich Accord of September 1938 actually pleased him, for he stated right afterward, "I'll bet anyone even money there will never be another war." Even on August 28, 1939, four days before hostilities started when Nazi tanks rolled into Poland, he declared, "They don't dare have a war and they know it." In general, he agreed with his good friend Colonel Lindbergh who, though favoring military preparedness more than Ford, counseled Americans in a speech on September 15, 1939, not to get involved in European wars. "We must keep foreign propaganda from pushing our country blindly into another war," he warned.

Though many Americans sympathized with what the allies were going through, most did not want to go to war then; with Russia the only great power actively involved outside of Britain, there was some reason for Americans to think it wasn't their concern. But after the Blitzkrieg that flattened the Netherlands, Belgium, and France began in May 1940, people's sympathies began to change. Congress appropriated one and a half billion dollars for defense preparedness, the Office for Emergency Management was created to coordinate this effort, and William S. Knudsen, the president of General Motors, was named Commissioner for Industrial Production.

Lindbergh, though still opposed to war, was feeling stronger about American preparedness and conferred with Henry Ford. Ford himself made a public statement in favor of preparedness, mentioning that he could begin producing 1,000 planes a day, a statement that amazed the nation. In short order, he was asked to manufacture 9,000 Rolls Royce aircraft engines for the United States. He agreed only to reverse himself when he found out that these engines were then to be sold to the British, who were of course belligerents in the war. Nothing would convince him to manufacture under these conditions, fearing as he did that the United States would be drawn into the conflict. Packard ultimately fulfilled the contract.

But by August 1940, Edsel and Sorensen convinced Ford to start manufacturing an 18- cylinder air-cooled engine for a new Douglas Aircraft bomber, an all-American product to which Ford could readily contribute improvements. By September, a 1.3-million square foot building started to go up at the Rouge plant, and production of the complete engine was begun on August 23, 1941.

At the same time Ford created a design for a new jeep that was chosen by the government and began work on a "swamp buggy," a type of jeep that could function in wet terrain. But still he inveighed against American entry into the war, echoing the sentiments of Lindbergh. But events were causing public sentiment to turn, and more and more, both Ford and Lindbergh were taken to task for their isolationist stances.

For the 25th anniversary of the Peace Ship in December 1940, Ford was asked to comment. He said that in history untold numbers of ships had been made for war, but only one was devoted to peace.

The very next month, over Ford's initial objection, Edsel and Sorensen went to the Douglas and Consolidated aircraft factories in California to investigate the possibility of Ford building B-24 Liberator bombers. Sorensen was in despair at the ability of the facilities he saw to build the bombers in sufficient quantities, but overnight, in a burst of engineering and architectural genius, he figured out a way to break down the construction and assembly of the planes and also devised a factory floor plan that would make it all work. Nothing this daring had ever been attempted in the aircraft industry before. When Consolidated President Reuben H. Fleet proposed that Ford manufacture parts for Consolidated to assemble, Sorensen countered, "We'll make the complete plane or nothing," a sentiment echoed by Henry Ford, who loved the plan's bold scope. Sorensen believed he could make one plane an hour in this factory, or 540 a month, as opposed to the 520 a year that the others could manage.

The Army at first agreed to Ford manufacturing parts for Consolidated and Douglas to assemble, rather than the entire plane. Though it dragged its heels a bit on Sorensen's proposal, eventually the Army agreed.

The plant Ford was to build to assemble his own bombers based on the Sorensen plan was a gigantic operation at Willow Run, a stream that emptied into Lake Huron. Once again, Albert Kahn was the architect for the ground floor and factory elevations. The building Kahn designed was L-shaped, some 3,200 feet long, and 1,279 feet at the transverse, with a factory area of 3.5-million square feet and hangars of 4.7-million square feet. The adjacent landing field had seven runways, one of which was 6,250 feet long.

Before Ford could get the other companies to build components according to its specifications, it had to settle with them on production methods. Ford had a mostly unskilled workforce and therefore required precise blueprints for every component in the plane (there were 700,000 rivets and 1,550,000 other parts). The others had highly skilled, adaptable workers, and therefore saw the Ford methods as overly detailed to the point of madness. Consolidated, for instance, thought the fuselage should be in two parts, whereas Ford broke it down into 33 sections. And Ford would need easy access for its workers, for it intended to build its planes on a moving assembly line, planning to attach all the needed fixtures in the fuselage when it was split in two sections before final riveting. Consolidated was dragging everything in through the door after it assembled the fuselage, which drove Sorensen nuts. Eventually, the two factions worked everything out.

It was a great challenge to get the giant Willow Run facility built, not to mention the task of finding the thousands of workers the plant required. There was also a terrible shortage of machine tools to contend with, as they had to be created for the specifications of the new job. On top of this, the Army had asked Ford to help with the design and manufacture of a new, improved M-4 tank at the same time that he was trying to perfect a liquid-cooled plane engine, which turned out to be completely impractical. Eventually, much modified, this engine was adapted for use in the tank. The manufacture of the wildly complicated M-7 anti-aircraft gun detector (1,820 parts and 11,130 pieces) also fell to Ford. But come hell or high water, the planes were finally turned out at Willow Run, which became *the* iconic plant of World War II production (Chrysler actually had a plant that was larger, but it was Willow Run that captured the public's imagination).

Hell was doused and high water quelled by such measures as bringing the manufacture of some parts to Detroit and nearby areas where workers already lived; developing ingenious new time- saving methods for the manufacture of heavily revised (and sometimes totally new) items; and insisting on completely detailed blueprints for every item and every part. "Mass production without thorough preparation is and forever will be impossible," *Mill and Factory* magazine stated at the time, and the company that created mass production chalked up many successes by paying close attention to this dictum. Even the enormous and growing struggle between Sorensen and Bennett for hegemony in the company was not allowed to stand in the way of its patriotic duty.

In the end, Ford ranked eighth in the United States in producing wartime goods, including jeeps, Liberator bombers, gliders of superior quality, and gun mounts. Considering that the company was headed by a near octogenarian (albeit still one of remarkable vision and determination) and was nearly torn apart by internal strife at the highest levels, Nevins and Hill are quite correct in describing its performance as "a sudden new efflorescence."

But there was no admiring what went on at Ford-Werke in Germany during the war. Started in 1925 as Ford A.G., its centerpiece was a large plant built in 1929 in Cologne that employed many German workers. Never paying a dividend until 1938, it was forced into a complete German identity by Nazi policy on foreign-owned businesses in 1939, when its name was changed. It built cars, trucks, and other vehicles for use by the regime from this time forward, in addition to exporting vehicles to South America and Japan. The Ford Motor Company in the United States held the majority interest in it, which was cut back to 52 percent after America entered the war. The U.S. government forbade Dearborn contact with the German branch after this, although some took place surreptitiously. So Ford was producing for both sides in the war, though it hardly had a choice. Tragically, when Cologne was liberated in 1945, starving slave and forced laborers, mostly from Eastern Europe, were discovered behind barbed wire at Ford-Werke, where they had worked 12-hour days on 200 grams of food and a little water. There remain many controversies today about the relationship between Ford and the Nazi regime. Neil Baldwin points out that "[u]nlike other American-owned property in Nazi Germany, the Ford plant was never confiscated by the German government." But Ford had no control over it either.

Henry Ford was remarkably fit and robust until he was considerably past 75 years of age, racing up stairs, ice skating, and challenging much younger men to footraces he usually won, even into his 70s. He suffered a minor stroke in 1938, but recovered quickly and seemed to show no ill effects from it. For this reason he was still an important and vital part of the Ford Motor Company's response to calls for preparedness in the coming world war during the period up to Pearl Harbor. But a second stroke in late 1941 was much more serious, and it had permanently debilitating effects on his mind, noticed by many at the beginning of December of that year. At first, his walking and other physical movements became slower, he constantly complained of chills, and certain mental lapses began to appear; sometimes he did not seem to recognize longtime associates with whom he had interacted daily for many years. His previous scunners against bankers, Wall Street, Roosevelt, competitors, and even his son's misguided (in his view) lifestyle became much worse, sometimes going far beyond the pale of rationality. As Nevins and Hill state, "The years of the Mad Hatter were beginning; anything could happen."

The ever-watchful lieutenant Harry Bennett made things worse. He could clearly see what was coming and strove at every juncture to consolidate more and more power into his own hands, whether it was good for the company or not. Thus, little by little some of the most important executives were let go or quit in disgust, as Bennett poured poisons into his master's ear. This left only a confused and timid bunch of mid-level executives between the head of the company and the technical people whose job was to do Ford's bidding, which was becoming more and more obscure. Even Edsel, by now in frail health, as well as overworked and disheartened, was ground down by Bennett's depredations.

But sometime before this period, Henry Ford created even more trouble than Bennett. When his grandsons Henry II and Benson went to work on the line at Ford toward the end of 1940 to gain some knowledge of the business, Ford was so hostile to the idea that he tried to throw them out, after displaying both indifference and antipathy toward them. He did not want to be reminded that there would be a future after his own. It took a confrontation with Edsel and a Sorensen so outraged by Ford's behavior that he threatened to quit, to get the old man to back off. A bit later, the highly respected and thoroughly honest head of purchasing, A. M. Wibel (who had been with Henry since 1912), was fired in a dispute with Bennett. This bothered Edsel so much that he began to make plans to leave the company. Sorensen might have gone with him, but Edsel persuaded him not to, because the company would have been thrown into the disastrous de facto control of Harry Bennett, who knew a great deal about how to run a fascist police state, but precious little about how to run a car company.

Edsel's physical decline, which began with stomach ulcers that became so bad they eventually required surgery, became precipitous in late 1942. The ulcers turned into stomach cancer. His condition was complicated by undulant fever (brucellosis), caused directly by his father, who had insisted on his drinking unpasteurized milk (which contained *Brucella* bacteria) from the Ford farms. Ford preached that if only Edsel would switch to a healthier regime of exercise and proper diet, give up drinking, and associate with the sort of people his father approved of, he would surely recover his strength. Edsel's mother Clara and his wife Eleanor were increasingly concerned about the rapid deterioration of his health in early 1943; when it became clear that the situation was irreversible, they despaired.

Ford refused to acknowledge this state of affairs to the last. In the wee hours of May 26, Edsel died. Deep sorrow was pervasive throughout Dearborn and the Motor City, for Edsel had been loved and admired by all who knew him. Clara especially was inconsolable in her grief, and clearly blamed her husband for this calamity. As for Henry, it was simply the worst thing that had ever happened to him. He wandered about in a daze, unable to comprehend how such a misery could have befallen him. Clara froze him out for quite some time thereafter, until one day months later when she asked him to join her in picking peonies in her garden; he was her husband of 55 years again.

For a superstitious man like Henry Ford, May 26 must certainly have seemed like an inauspicious day: the end of the Model T in 1927, the Battle of the Overpass in 1937, and the death of his only son Edsel in 1943.

A few days after Edsel's death, in a reorganization of the board, Ford resumed the presidency of his company, replacing his son. He was then just two months shy of his 80th birthday and far from his prime. Without Edsel's support, Sorensen was now exposed to the factional infighting at Ford. As a result, Harry Bennett was in the ascendancy at the company. Shortly thereafter, Sorensen was seriously undermined as production chief when Bennett appointed himself as his assistant for administrative problems; in actuality, this confined Sorensen's authority to Willow Run. By November 1943, as important leaders left the company one by one, Sorensen saw the handwriting on the wall and told a shocked Henry Ford that he wished to leave the company himself as of January 1, 1944. All Ford could say was, "I guess there's something in life besides work." Sorensen left for Florida during the winter, finally tendering his resignation officially in March 1944, after being told by Ford's secretary, Frank Campsall, that the old man wanted him to resign because he was angling for the company's presidency.

The quagmire that was the Ford Motor Company in those days now thickened as Bennett continued to consolidate his control. The publicity department, which should have had hundreds of personnel, consisted of only five (albeit very competent) men when John Gunther visited in 1945. Fortunately for the company, the J. Walter Thompson Advertising Agency, which had been hired in 1943, was highly skilled in the management of its new account. (It's crowning achievement was the creation of the most effective and long lasting of all postwar automobile slogans: "There's a Ford in Your Future.") There was so little clear authority anywhere in management that people were willing to listen to anyone who even *seemed* authoritative in manner. Because of the vast wartime profits that accrued to the company, it was awash in cash, but absolutely no one had any idea of costs, or where, when, or how much money was flowing out of the coffers. After all, the increasingly detached and often mentally absent Henry Ford figured that the money was his, so what did it matter if it was spent at the foundry or on square dances? Henry Ford II later insisted that, in one department, costs were determined by weighing invoices. Profits were determined by the amount of cash on deposit.

But there was considerable hope for the future of the Ford Motor Company in Ford's grandson and namesake, Henry Ford II. He had been recalled from the Navy in August 1943 to rejoin the company after the death of his father. Old Henry had the presence of mind to give him free rein to wander about the firm and learn whatever he could about its workings; in this manner he was immune from the internecine warfare between Bennett and Sorensen, though he was well aware of it. Young Henry was tall, roundly handsome, egalitarian, and immensely affable in his attitude to all, from department heads to ordinary workers on the line. He gave the place something it had not had in quite some time: a breath of fresh air. By late 1943, he was elected a vice-president of the company and found a good niche for his abilities in sales and advertising. By the following April, he became executive vice-president, the post next to the presidency in rank. By the middle of that year, he had begun to retreat from his involvements in sales and advertising to concentrate on general management, the black hole at the center of the firm. In this position young Henry strove to untangle the pervasive administrative confusion that plagued Ford and replace it with sound, clear policies; at the same time he sought to surround himself with capable, honest men to aid him in bringing the Ford Motor Company into the looming postwar world.

As young Henry rose in the company, his public recognition rose too. Virtually unknown at the time he joined Ford in August 1943, he was correctly identified by 9.5 percent of the population less than a year later. By the spring of 1945, William Cameron was writing speeches for him, as he was swamped with speaking engagements, which he took on as part of a low-key publicity buildup that was being organized by the company in his behalf. In June, he put Mead L. Bricker in place as production head of the company, replacing Ray R. Rausch, Bennett's man. The way forward was becoming clearer all the time, especially as young Henry had the firm support of Clara and Eleanor, who both held large blocks of Ford stock, and his brothers Benson and William Clay.

This is not to say that he didn't feel opposed, perhaps even threatened, by Bennett and his fiercely loyal henchmen. Things at the company were so contentious that, for a time, young Henry took to carrying a gun for self-protection. More menacing still was that, by the middle of 1944, he learned of a threat to his future from Bennett that could have been far more deadly than any physical harm from that quarter. He discovered that Harry Bennett had made a secret alteration to his father's will, which, though Henry didn't yet know it, was in the form of a codicil that would place power in the hands of a Bennett-friendly board, of which Bennett himself would be a prominent part, for ten years after the death of the founder. All of Ford's grandchildren would be explicitly excluded from the board, thus in effect delivering the company into Bennett's control. Young Henry was so outraged at this alteration that he went to John R. Bugas, a former FBI man who had joined Ford in late 1938 and recently allied himself firmly with young Henry. He threatened to quit the company and write a letter to all its dealers telling them what they were soon going to be up against, and urging them to sever their associations with it. Bugas calmed Henry down and went to Bennett's office to confront him about the changes to Ford's will. Bennett was flabbergasted that anyone knew about the codicil, and he offered to settle the matter the following day, which he did by pulling it out of his drawer, burning it in Bugas's presence, and sweeping it into an envelope, with instructions to deliver it to his boss. That ended that.

Clara, who nourished a deep antipathy to both Sorensen, now gone, and Bennett, whom she saw as instrumental in the death of Edsel, became more and more confident in the ability of her grandson to head the company. She tried very hard to convince her husband to turn over the reins of Ford to her grandson to no avail. Ford would not give up control of the eponymous firm he had founded 43 years previously and dominated completely (and without opposition for the past quarter of a century). Finally, Eleanor forced the situation by allying herself with her mother-in-law, obliging Ford to give way in the same way Clara alone had forced him to give in to the UAW four years earlier. She threatened to sell her considerable block of stock in Ford if he would not agree. Threatened in this way, he finally gave in.

Accordingly, young Henry was summoned to Fair Lane by old Henry to discuss the transfer of power. The young man insisted that he would accede to this only if he could have a completely free hand to make any changes he wished within the company. He did not want to be a powerless figurehead; he had seen a vivid example of that in his father's life and did not wish to have history repeat itself. A lively discussion ensued, and eventually the old man conceded.

On September 21, 1945, a special meeting of the board of directors was convened to receive Ford's resignation and ratify young Henry as the new president of the company. The minute the formal part of the meeting began, Bennett stood up and hurled a word of congratulations at Henry as if it were an imprecation, and went to the door to storm out; but he was prevailed upon to remain until the final vote was taken. Before the meeting was completely finished, young Henry marched into Bennett's office, closed the door, and fired him (though he was offered a temporary transitional directorship to save face). The young man approached his grandfather to tell him of the firing with some trepidation, but the old man received the news in silence, finally saying, "Well, now Harry is back where he started from."

So also were most of his cronies, because for the next two years, young Henry fired, transferred, or demoted some 1,000 of them. He gave the company "a shaking that rattled its teeth."

When Henry Ford I was wheeled out of the boardroom, he was also wheeled into the shadows of history. A few years before, he was one of the grandest titans of American industry, but now he was frail, mentally vague, and emotionally fragile. Even as late as 1943, Ford could leap over his yacht's railing, and in 1944, he could walk briskly enough to tire out Harry Bennett. But a debilitating stroke in the spring of 1945 changed all that. By late 1945, no one knew from day to day, or sometimes even from hour to hour, whether they would encounter a man in full possession of his faculties, or a sort of pathetic, rusted-out mental hulk. The public, which was fed pleasant, though entirely fictitious, tales of his vigor and industrious bustling around the plants, was kept in the dark about his true state; much the same thing was done seven years before when Walter P. Chrysler suffered a debilitating stroke. It was generally considered better for business if the masses thought a benevolent founder was keeping a watchful eye on the affairs of the company that bore his name.

Increasingly, Ford was given to following Clara about like a lost child, and she made sure that everyone around him kept a watchful eye, lest he wander off in bewilderment or inattention. His rounds at the office and the Dearborn engineering laboratory became less and less frequent. Photographs from public appearances at the time show him as alert and fully present at some occasions and vague and absent at others. Once he could not recognize Mrs. Henry B. Joy, an old friend, at a party, but when prompted by Ray Dahlinger, his confusion lifted, and he was shortly seen chatting away amiably with her.

But in this uncertain mental state, Ford was kept away from the press, to avoid public gaffes. Once, when he was confined to his bed in a fit of depression toward the end of his life, a friendly physician arranged for a reporter to interview him to lift his spirits. When asked if he could see his company eventually going public, the old man lifted himself from his torpor to declaim loudly, "I'll take my factory down brick by brick before I'll let any of those Jew speculators get stock in the company!" Interview closed, on doctor's orders. It was much better indeed to let the Ford public relations office deal with any official statements from Mr. Ford. But he was trotted out from time to time for publicity purposes. In a very late photo of him and Clara in the original quadricycle, Ford looked decrepit, puffy, and old.

Young Henry saw his grandfather from time to time, keeping him up to date on the company and sometimes even seeking his advice. At the end of the war, Ford advised his grandson to hang on to the Willow Run bomber factory "because you'll need it." He sold it though, to nascent auto manufacturer Henry Kaiser, and came to regret his decision, as his grandfather had predicted.

Ford was much removed from the company by this point. It fell to Henry Ford II to deal with steel and other material shortages that hampered production, government restrictions on the prices he could charge for his cars (Washington was fearful of postwar inflation), and planning for an all-new model that he knew the public would demand after the immediate postwar sellers' market subsided. (The new model was the sensational 1949 Ford, an early model of which old Henry had seen and liked.)

In the winter of 1947, Ford and Clara went to Richmond Hill, their estate near Ways, Georgia, that he had built on the advice of his naturalist friend John Burroughs, who told him there was very good bird-watching in those parts. It was also near Berry College in Rome, the charity that was perhaps nearest to his heart, with its combination of academic and agricultural training to help the rural poor lead better, more fulfilled lives for both themselves and their communities. It was there on March 31, 1947, that he made his last public appearance, at a tree- planting ceremony he helped supervise.

On April 6, Easter Sunday, the Fords returned to Fair Lane in Dearborn, where the early spring weather was particularly foul. Days of relentless rain had caused the Rouge River to flood, though Fair Lane was not affected, built as it was on higher ground. The immaculate power plant that ran it, downstream from the house, was put out of commission, however. The turbines were switched off on the morning of April 7, and the house had to be heated by fireplaces and lit by candles and oil lamps. Ford arose feeling quite chipper and ate an unusually hearty breakfast, proclaiming his oatmeal the best he had ever tasted.

Then he called for his chauffeur and went about to inspect the flood damage, finding a good deal of it. At Greenfield Village, his Suwanee Riverboat was underwater, and he was prevented from going to the Rouge plant to see young Henry because the roads were impassable. Instead he visited a small Catholic cemetery where he pointed out the graves of many old friends and distant relatives, before stopping at another small cemetery on Joy Road, where he told his chauffeur, "This is where I'm going to be buried when I die. In among the rest of my folks here."

On returning home, he and Clara enjoyed a turkey dinner by candlelight, after which she read to him by firelight for a while. Then he retired early with a glass of milk to get a good night's sleep. After undressing, he had a coughing fit before he went to bed.

A couple of hours later, he awoke coughing again and breathing heavily, and complaining of a bad headache and a dry throat. As his condition got worse, men were dispatched from the house to find working telephones to summon his doctor and young Henry. Clara comforted him by giving him sips of water as he rested his head on her shoulder. In this manner, Ford passed away, about 20 minutes before the doctor arrived around midnight. Mrs. Ford stood in shock with Eve Dahlinger, who had been summoned too, by her side. The doctor surmised that a blood vessel in Ford's brain had burst when he untied his shoes, causing first the coughing fit and then his death. Ironically, he left the world by candlelight and a wood fire, the same way he came into it 83 years before.

In his pockets were found a Jew's harp, a pocket knife, and a comb. He had $26.5 million in cash in a personal bank account and was owed $20 for a sale of hay from a Ford farm. He also left a personal library of 2,246 books, many annotated in his own writing, mostly on scientific and engineering subjects. Though some speculated his estate was worth $700 million, the government valued it at $80 million, plus a $466 million valuation for the company. Of course, this did not take into account the Ford Foundation, which was to be worth the hundreds of millions that Henry and Edsel had given it in their stock transfer plan.

Plans had been made for Ford's funeral some time before, and now they were carried out. He was laid out in state in Greenfield Village on April 9, where a mile-long line of at least 100,000 people filed past his open casket. Most who came to pay their respects were the ordinary workers, farmers, clerks, shopgirls, and housewives whose day-to-day lives he had touched so profoundly. The next day hundreds of invited dignitaries and other guests crowded into St. Paul's Cathedral in Detroit, while outside a crowd of some 30,000 assembled. All offices in Detroit were closed, and when the funeral began at 2:30, church bells throughout the city began to toll. A parade of Lincoln sedans ferried hundreds to the cemetery on Joy Road; thousands of somber black-clad mourners lined the route, the sole exception being the nurses assembled outside the Henry Ford Hospital, who were all dressed in crisp and gleaming white uniforms in tribute to him. Twenty thousand people attended at the graveside.

Ironically, Ford's body rode in a Packard hearse, though the fact that he never manufactured such grand, occasional vehicles makes it understandable. Although the day was gloomy, a brilliant ray of sunshine broke through just as the bronze casket was lowered into the ground.

Business leaders and politicians from President Truman on down had high words of praise for Ford; Alfred P. Sloan called his influence "incalculable." Newspapers throughout the country and abroad published huge obituaries, and editorials came in fast and furiously. Most were highly favorable, recalling Ford's achievements as both an industrialist and social thinker and organizer who had permanently altered the course of modern life. Even B'nai B'rith expressed "deep admiration" for Ford's "great contribution to the American economy and to social relations." *The Journal of Negro History* said he was "a great benefactor of the Negro race, probably the greatest that ever lived." Of course there were some who dissented. *PM* in New York called his mind "a jungle of fear, ignorance and prejudice in social affairs," while the *Detroit Jewish News* said he was "on the top of the list of the world's Antisemites." The worst cut came from abroad, when Russian newspapers merely reported the bare, unembellished facts of his death. Considering that during the war in September 1944, Stalin himself had called Ford "the world's greatest industrialist. God preserve him!" this was quite a comedown.

But such reports were minor in comparison to the flood tide of praise. Very few public figures had ever been so lavishly eulogized, which was in sharp contrast to what was said about other business figures of the time like John D. Rockefeller Sr., who was referred to as "old skull and bones." Maybe it was because those figures always seemed removed and aloof from the common folk, whereas Henry Ford, with his modest, homespun life, simple tastes, and recognizably all-American values centered on family and work, seemed in a very deep and obvious way to be "one of us." Maybe too it was because Ford's success was based on a product that everyone could use and afford, something that made people's lives better and more enjoyable, rather than something abstract, or something that could be hoarded or cornered.

Clara lived on for three more years after her husband's death, dying of a heart ailment on September 27, 1950. In her last years she devoted herself to her charities and gardens, and visited old friends and relatives. She was very lonely though without her life-time companion. Nothing could replace him in her heart. Ford businesses worldwide observed three minutes of silence at her death, and flags in Detroit flew at half mast, the first time such a tribute had been paid to a woman.

Henry Ford II proved to be an able steward of the Ford Motor Company over the next several decades, overseeing the creation of all sorts of new cars, from Mustangs and Falcons to elegant Continentals, as well as the world's top-selling trucks. He was a tough, hard-drinking, and very colorful auto man, in the tra-ditional mode never exemplified by Henry I. He was unlike his grandfather in two other important ways too. In 1956, he finally oversaw taking the company public in order to raise funds for the increasing competition he knew it would face (though he still managed to keep virtual control within the family). And when he retired, he shredded most of the documents related to his term of office; he was as closed to historical scrutiny as his grandfather had been open and unafraid.

Today Bill Ford, Henry Ford I's genial and respected great-grandson, maintains an active part in the leadership of the Ford Motor Company, 110 years after its founding. No other automobile company, and few companies in other fields, can make such a claim to durability and continuity from the beginning to the present. After all this time, Ford products still contribute to the economic and social well-being of the world in a vital and even progressive way. And it still makes money. Through several years of wrenching economic upheaval in the present day, its prudent management can make a unique boast: It is the only one of the three major American car companies that never went bankrupt to survive.

Many people, from strangers and outsiders to his closest intimates, from casual observers to journalists and scholars, have tried to figure out Henry Ford, to find the secret that made his character function in so many spectacularly good and terrible ways. But no matter how hard they have tried, no one seems to have found the schematic for the inner workings of his soul. Instead they discovered an enigma machine, some of its parts recognizable, others a puzzlement, as it emerged from the mist from time to time, only to disappear again into some unknown and unseeable private world. Despite the fact that Henry Ford had one of the most completely well-documented lives in history—and was indeed the progenitor of the modern publicity-driven public life—everyone, from the most prejudicial to the least biased, wound up shaking their heads when attempting to define him. James Couzens simply chalked up the mystery to the man's genius, which is something he thought could never be analyzed. But for many of us, that assessment doesn't suffice, and so the search to understand the fundamental Henry Ford continues.

As with any man who affected the course of history so greatly, we strive to know where he came from and where he landed us, so we can perhaps better understand where we may be going. We hope we will get to know a heroic figure, a guide for life. But every man is much like an unfinished quarry stone, still rough and filled with flaws, never to be really completed into a polished monument for unabashed civic admiration. We have great expectations of great men, but to claim greatness for all, or even most, of a man's life is false and misleading. By exposing the faulty seams that need to be brought to light, one might find things that are, with luck, of beauty and value.

Henry Ford proved to be the right man at the right time to lead the effort to turn mass production into a reality. In doing so, Ford replaced a society built on an economy of scarcity with one built on an economy of plenty. The meaning of work and leisure changed, as did the type, value, and amounts of industrial goods produced. The material changes led to changes in mores and social relations. It was a true revolution in the lives of humans, and amazingly, it was accomplished without bullets, barricades, or assassinations. To the great masses of people, Ford was "one of us," an ordinary sort of man, who nevertheless said Ford was going to change people's daily lives and did just that. As a Georgia farmwife said, "Henry, you pulled us out of the mud."

The late 1910s of the 20th century were Ford's golden age, but as with any golden age, it did not last. This does not mean that many of the things he did weren't of great value. There are quite a lot of major accomplishments to place at Henry Ford's doorstep in this period, from the Model A to the modern soybean industry.

But how did he manage to do these things, when his ideas came from a mind perennially clotted with ignorance and prejudice, and tangled up with an unkind, often brutal and unforgiving, spirit? There is no denying that something happened when Ford was around, and men worked on his behalf as if he, and not the Machine, were the new Messiah. Men like Sorensen, Couzens, and C. Harold Wills may have been giants in their own right, but without Ford their efforts might never have been made at all or might have had no lasting meaning. As a Chevy worker who had been fired from Ford said when he was asked why he still liked the man, "That guy has a bird in his head."

Would that the bird had always been a nightingale; sometimes, alas, it was a crow.

Many men and women wrote about Henry Ford, but the Reverend Samuel S. Marquis is probably the one who best took his measure, most likely because he understood the difficulty of trying to comprehend the whole man. "There are in him lights so high and shadows so deep that I cannot get the whole of him in proper focus at the same time," he said.

> A cross section of the mind of Henry Ford would reveal some striking contrasts.... A complex mind of strength and weakness, of wisdom and foolishness, in which the shallows are more pronounced because of the profound depths which lie between...there is no middle ground in his makeup...no unifying spirit in the warring elements of his nature.
>
> The true explanation of him seems to be this: his mind has never been organized...and his moral qualities and impulses, among which are to be found some of the highest and noblest I have ever known grouped in any one man, have never been compounded and blended into a stable, unified character...he has failed to appreciate the supreme importance of the proper assembly, adjustment and balance of the parts of the mental and moral machine within himself.

Did Henry Ford himself leave any clues about his inner self? Yes, one can deduce some by observation. One was that he kept his own counsel, never letting anyone too close to him or privy to his innermost thoughts; from the time of his mother's death, when he walled himself off from everyone, that was how he conducted himself. Another was, as Sorensen said, that he created an atmosphere of "constant ferment" about him: "Keep things stirred up and other people guessing was the elder Ford's working formula for progress." A third clue was that even in the worst of times, his attitude was "Get out and get me an optimist!" After all, at 69 years old, his response to the possible collapse of the whole country's financial system in 1933 was to say that he "felt young again" and was ready to start over.

But maybe what is most revealing is something he said just before his 73rd birthday in 1936. It perhaps explains both the vision that led him to unparalleled social and industrial accomplishment for the betterment of humanity, and the moral blindness by which he could excuse himself for the terrible results of his tremendous moral failings. "There is nothing evil," he said. "Everything has its purpose, its reason for being. Something may look evil, but if it arouses people to bringing about a better state of affairs, then it has been a good influence, hasn't it? No, there's no such thing as evil. Everything that happens is working toward good or it wouldn't happen." Perhaps it wasn't just an education that was lacking in Henry Ford, as Marquis believed, but also an ability to look into what Norman Mailer called the "beast in the human heart." The death of Edsel in 1943 and the concentration camp films he viewed in 1945 forced him to see that beast in his own heart at the end of his life. He was complicit in both these terrible events, and he could no longer escape the guilt that went with them.

Around the time of his death, Niven Busch Jr. thought that if one man from each age of history could be preserved for the future, and not necessarily the brightest or the best, but the most representative, the man for our age should be Henry Ford. And Charles Kettering said that "a thousand years from now, when the Churchills and the Roosevelts are but a footnote in history, Henry Ford will loom as the most significant figure of our age." These are large claims.

But who can predict what the uses of history will be for the events and people of Henry Ford's time, or ours? Will the titanic political struggles of the 20th century continue to remain galvanizing chapters in history, or will they become as obscure as the battles of the Guelphs and the Ghibellines are to us today? Will Ford's discovery of how to bring material prosperity to all be considered in the same breath as Guttenberg's discovery of how to bring words and ideas to all 500 years ago, or will some new political, economic, and environmental structure make his work appear barbaric, primitive, and wrongheaded? Will the man be considered a hero as Columbus was in 1892, or virtually a pariah as he was in 1992? Chou En Lai, when asked almost 200 years after the French Revolution what its effects were on western civilization, said, "It's too soon to tell."

All we can do now is consider what Ford's importance was to our own time, and let history sort out the rest. As Will Rogers said of him, "It will take a hundred years to tell if he helped us or hurt us, but he certainly didn't leave us where he found us."

Acknowledgments

John davis was very generous to me in giving me his collection of Henry Ford books, some of which are quite rare and difficult to find. Steven Englund made an important contribution to this book by providing materials and guidance that considerably deepened my understanding of the context of Henry Ford's complex relationship to the Jews. I would like to thank my agent, Georges Borchardt, for placing this book with Oxford University Press, and also Elda Rotor, the acquiring editor. Herbert J. Addison, my previous editor at Oxford, was also helpful in the acquisition process. I am extremely grateful to Timothy Bent, the editor of this book, for his patience, insight, and wisdom in helping me to shape this into a better book. Glenn C. Altshuler of Cornell University cast a very helpful criticial eye on it late in the editing process. As always, the librarians, facilities, and collections of the New York Public Library were of great assistance to me in my research.

A Note on Sources

IN A CERTAIN SENSE, RESEARCHING THIS BOOK ON HENRY FORD WAS like observing a multifaceted conversation, the participants of which were the many and diverse authors of books about Ford and his times and influences. Each one was valuable for what he or she wrote about, in terms of perspective and intention. Some offered immediacy, others analysis or distillation. All were worthy of attention on their own terms and led me to my eventual conclusions about this unusual man, seemingly simple in some ways, and yet complex and almost incomprehensible in others.

Works that were very useful in conveying the facts included the comprehensive three-volume Ford study from the 1950s and 1960s by Allan Nevins and Frank Ernest Hill, *Ford: the Man, the Times and the Company* (New York: Charles Scribner's Sons, 1954); *Ford: Expansion and Challenge, 1915–1933* (New York: Charles Scribner's Sons, 1957); and *Ford: Decline and Rebirth, 1933–1962* (New York: Charles Scribner's Sons, 1962); Steven Watts, *The People's Tycoon: Henry Ford and the American Century* (New York: Alfred A. Knopf, 2005); Douglas Brinkley, *Wheels For The World* (New York: Penguin, 2004); Roger Burlingame, *Henry Ford: A Great Life in Brief* (New York: Alfred A. Knopf, 1955); Peter Collier and David Horowitz, *The Fords: An American Epic* (New York: Summit Books, 1987); and Robert Lacey, *Ford: The Men and the Machine* (New York: Little, Brown and Company, 1986). All had their special virtues. Lacey, for instance, was especially good in his analysis of topics like the influence of Emerson and Orlando J. Smith on Ford's spiritual development, and the Muscle Shoals episode.

David Hounshell's *From the American System to Mass Production, 1800–1932* (Baltimore: The Johns Hopkins University Press, 1984) gave an indispensible overview of how Ford's mass production was achieved, and William Cameron's "Henry Ford" article on that subject in the 1926 *Encyclopedia Britannica* (13th edition, Suppl. Vol. 2; pp. 821–823) was a brilliant condensation. Horace Lucien Arnold and Faye Leone Faurote's *Ford Methods and the Ford Shops* (New York: The Engineering Magazine Company, 1915) gave an on-the-ground view of the birth of the system.

Carol Gelderman's *Henry Ford: The Wayward Capitalist* (New York: Dial Press, 1981) dealt in part with the ways in which Ford's thinking upended received notions of capitalism. Susan Estabrook Kennedy's *The Banking Crisis of 1933* (Lexington, KY: The University Press of Kentucky, 1973) gave a chilling picture of Ford's role in that situation. David E. Nye's *Henry Ford: Ignorant Idealist* (Port Washington, NY: Kennikat Press, 1979) addressed the many contradictions in Ford's nature when it came to the material existence of his fellow man.

Edward D. Kennedy's *The Automobile Industry: The Coming of Age of Capitalism's Favorite Child* (New York: Reynal & Hitchcock, 1941) and Donald Finlay Davis's *Conspicuous Production: Automobiles and Elites in Detroit, 1899–1933* (Philadelphia: Temple University Press, 1988) gave good analyses of the economic conditions under which Ford's business grew and thrived.

Henry Ford and Grass Roots America by Reynold M. Wik (Ann Arbor, MI: University of Michigan Press, 1972) provided a fine view into Ford's practical, philosophical, and political connections to mainstream America.

The Public Image of Henry Ford by David L. Lewis (Detroit, MI: Wayne State University Press, 1976) covered the creation and implementation of what is perhaps America's first major publicity-driven life, in all its self-consciousness. Keith Sward's *The Legend of Henry Ford* (New York: Rinehart and Company, 1949) also considered the man and the image, often harshly.

When it came to understanding Ford's Antisemitism, two books provided important considerations of the subject: *Henry Ford and the Jews* by Albert Lee (New York: Stein and Day, 1980), and *Henry Ford and the Jews: The Mass Production of Hate* by Neil Baldwin (New York: Public Affairs, 2001). *Warrant for Genocide: the Myth of the Jewish World Conspiracy and the Protocols of the Elders of Zion* by Norman Cohn (New York: Harper & Row, 1967) was an exhaustive study of the absurd and counterfactual underpinnings of this subject. Further insights came from David Nirenberg's *Anti-Judaism: the Western Tradition* (New York: W. W. Norton, 2013), and Steven Englund's forthcoming *The Origins of Political Antisemitism: Germany, Austria -Hungary and France, 1870–1920. History, Religion and Anti-Semitism* by Gavin Langmuir (Berkeley, CA: University of California Press, 1993) brought great intelligence to the reading of this subject, and *The Jew and American Ideals* by John Spargo (New York: Harper & Brothers, 1921) gave a sense of the indignation surrounding Ford's contemporary attacks on Jews. Reading *The Protocols* themselves and *The International Jew* (*The Dearborn Independent*, 1920–1922, 4 vols.) provided the frightening background to Ford's Antisemitism. The latest book on the subject is Victoria Saker

Woeste's *Henry Ford's War on the Jews and the Legal Battle Against Hate Speech* (Stanford University Press, 2012).

Books about Henry Ford written by people who knew and worked with him, or who had conducted personal interviews with him, have an immediacy that is revealing in a way that can't be duplicated or discounted, despite their individual biases. Rose Wilder Lane's *Henry Ford's Own Story* (New York: Ellis O. Jones, 1917) remains touching despite her naïvety and overly sympathetic view of the man; something similar can be said about Sarah Bushnell's *The Truth about Henry Ford* (Chicago: The Reilly and Lee Company, 1922). *Henry Ford: The Man and His Motives* by William L. Stidger (New York: George H. Doran Company, 1923) gave a sense of a man encountered and considered firsthand. Allan L. Benson's *The New Henry Ford* (New York: Funk & Wagnalls, 1923) was another helpful contemporary view. Charles E. Sorensen, in *My Forty Years with Ford* (New York: W. W. Norton, 1956; written with Samuel T. Williamson) brought a crackling intelligence to unvarnished truth-telling about his subject. In addition to his criticisms, one knew that whatever words of praise he gave Ford were earned, and not casually given. In "The Real Henry Ford" (*Pipp's Weekly*, 1922) and "Henry Ford: Both Sides of Him" (*Pipp's Magazine*, 1926), Edward G. Pipp's disillusionment and sense of alarm were very real to the reader, without discounting Ford's achievements. Reverend Samuel S. Marquis's *Henry Ford: An Interpretation* (New York: Little, Brown and Company, 1923) had a novelist's insight and a poet's sense of grace in his analysis of the man's character.

J. G. de Roulhac Hamilton's admiring *Henry Ford: the Man, the Worker, the Citizen* (New York: Henry Holt & Company) had a significant positive impact when it was published in 1927, but Spencer Ervin's *Henry Ford vs. Truman H. Newberry* (New York: Richard R. Smith, 1935) was as devastating a portrait of Ford's paranoia and lust for revenge as one could find. There was much hagiography about Ford early on, but despite his best efforts to produce and control such things, there were a fair number of devil's advocates roaming the landscape too.

Those books "by" Henry Ford (actually written by others) contained ideas and locutions that rang very true, especially after reading newspaper and magazine articles in which reporters quoted him directly. *My Life and Work* (New York: Doubleday, Page and Company, 1923); *Today and Tomorrow* (London: William Heineman, Ltd., 1926); *Moving Forward* (New York: Doubleday, Doran and Company, 1930), Ford's collaborations with Samuel Crowther, all told things as he saw them, no matter how much interpreting and cleaning up may have been done by his interlocutor. They were part pep talks, part history, and part instruction manuals for their readers, but Ford shines through in each of them, whatever the motivations behind the statements. Articles that were turned into books, like *My Philosophy of Industry* (New York: Coward-McCann, 1929) and *Things I've Been Thinking About* (Grand Rapids, MI: Fleming H. Revell Company, 1936), are much the same.

Humorous anecdotes about Henry Ford do not abound. But in sorting out the histories, mysteries, myths, and legends that swirl about and through his life, it is good to remember this one.

Theodore McManus, the most effective and important publicist in the early years of the automobile industry, was once made to wait for a very long time in the outer office of William C. "Billy" Durant, the charismatic founder of General Motors, a man who had no sense of the value of other people's time. To relieve the boredom before he was summoned to the great man's office, McManus composed this little verse:

> I'm glad I'm not a vacuum,
> I'm glad I'm not a myth,
> I'm glad I'm not the sort of stuff
> They fill pincushions with,
> But most of all I'm glad, O Lord,
> You did not make me Henry Ford.

When he shoved the paper with the verse over to Durant, the other man howled with laughter and screeched, "Oh, you villain!" McManus and Durant weren't the only ones who relished that sentiment, then or now. It helps to keep Henry Ford in a certain perspective.

Index

collaborators with Ford
  devotion of, 33–34
  in early experimental models, 26–29
  Ford's ability to keep together, 33
  Ford's unwillingness to share credit
    with, 19, 31
collective bargaining rights, New Deal
    guarantees of, 243–44
Columbia Electric, 24
Colvin, Fred, 68, 70
commissary shops at Ford, 80
Communists
  Bennet's surveillance of, 247
  exploitation of Depression-era
    suffering, 242
  and Ford Hunger March, 230–31, 242
Comstock, William, 238
Congress of Industrial Organizations
    (CIO), 244
conservation, Ford's views on, as ahead
    of his time, 221
Consolidated Aircraft Corporation,
    253, 254
Conspicuous Production (Davis), 54
Coolidge, Calvin, 187
Cooper, Tom, 37–38
Cornaro, Luigi, 114
Cosmopolitan magazine, 34
Cote, Evangeline. *See* Dahlinger,
    Evangeline "Eve" Cote
Coudert, Frederic, 52
Court of International Arbitration
    (Hague), 86
Couzens, James
  and Banking Crisis of 1933, 236–38
  character and personality of, 39
  on character of Ford, 270
  and dealer network, development
    of, 48, 49
  departure from Ford, 94–96
  financial management by, 43–44, 64
  first meeting with Ford, 39
  first production runs and, 44–45
  and five-dollar day, 76, 77
  Ford's influence on, 271
  and funding of manufacturing, 41,
    42, 43

influence on Ford organization,
    64, 94
Liebold and, 140
and Malcomson, power struggle
    with, 53, 55
and marketing strategies, 64
political career after Ford, 96, 179
relations with Ford, 94–95, 96
Couzens, Rosetta, 43
criminal record, Ford's employment
    policies and, xii, 74, 160
criminals, reform of, Ford's views on,
    173–74
Crowther, Samuel S., 147, 189–90
Cruden, Robert, 231
Crystal Palace. *See* Highland Park
    factory
Cugnot, Nicolas-Joseph, 23
Curie, Marie, 166

Dagenham works (England), 117
Dahlinger, Evangeline "Eve" Cote,
    193–94, 266
Dahlinger, John, 194, 224
Dahlinger, Ray, 193–94, 200, 264
Daimler, Gottlieb, 18, 25, 26
Daniels, Josephus, 100
Darrow, Clarence, 146, 172
Davis, Donald Finlay, 54
dealerships
  demand for, 64
  design of, 64
  network, early development of, 48,
    49
Dearborn, Michigan
  in 1830s, 1
  Ford family migration to, 1–2
  Ford's departures for Detroit, 9,
    18, 20
  Ford's returns to, 12–13, 16–18
Dearborn Independent newspaper. *See
    also The International Jew*
    series
  cost of operating, 154
  factions at, 133
  and farm cooperatives, efforts to
    organize, 150

and Ford's Peace Ship mission, 90
on Ford's Senate campaign, 175
Greenfield Village museum and,
165, 167
synthetic rubber research, 215
Edison Illuminating Company, 20–21,
27, 28, 29, 30, 31
Edison Institute, 166
education
of Ford, 5, 13, 16
Ford on, 162, 163
Ford's charitable projects in, 162–64
efficiency and cost effectiveness, Ford's
focus on, 63, 68, 123, 228
Einstein, Albert, 166
electric car(s), Mrs. Ford's use of,
179–80
electric engines, advantages and
disadvantages of, 23
electric power in Ford plants, DC, as
Ford misstep, 127–28
elitism, Ford on, 163–64
Emde, Carl, 50, 177
Emerson, Ralph W., 47, 75–76
E-M-F Co., 62
employees. *See also* pay; staff of Ford
Motor Co.; unionization at
Ford; working conditions at
Ford plants
anger with Depression era cutbacks,
230
anger with Ford's anti-unionization
efforts, 231
development into modern urban
beings, 112, 129–30
Ford's concern with improving lives
of, 77, 81–84, 127, 130
Ford's efforts to provide moral
guidance to, 112–13, 130, 170–71
Ford's views on, 129
improved economic status of under
Ford, 83
living conditions of, 81–82
views on Ford as employer, 223, 249
employers, Ford's belief in
responsibilities of, 84, 105,
222–23

employment policies
cavalier hiring and firing policies,
226, 227, 228–29
criminal record and, xii, 74, 160
and employee good will, 223
and Ford legacy, 271
on handicapped, xii, 74, 77, 159–60
ideology underlying, 220
on minorities, xii, 74, 160, 171–73
on non-English speakers,
82–83, 160
public perception of, xi, 79–80, 85,
207, 222, 223, 249
tubercular employees, 160
on veterans, 249
on women, xii, 74, 160
Encyclopedia Britannica, Ford article
on mass production in, 84, 190
energy dollars, Ford's promotion of,
147, 184
engine(s)
airplane, *See* aircraft construction
by Ford
design of as group effort, 51–52
electric, advantages and
disadvantages of, 23
for Ford passenger car, 38
Ford's early research on, 13, 17, 18,
27, 28–29
gasoline
advantages of, 23, 24
Ford's early experiments with,
27, 28–29
19th-century developments in, 18
superiority, Ford's recognition
of, 19, 22
superiority, general acceptance
of, 34
internal combustion
history of, 18, 24–25
and Selden patent dispute, 50–53
of Model T, innovations in, 60
19th century advances in, 18
six-cylinder, Ford's dislike of, 199
steam
advantages and disadvantages
of, 23

on Ford's race driving, 36
Ford's sexual liaisons and, 195
life after Henry's death, 269
and Peace Ship mission, 88, 90
support for Ford, 15, 20, 27, 29, 32
support for Henry II's management,
	261, 262
and unionization, 250
Ford, Edsel (son)
and Banking Crisis of 1933, 233–34,
	236, 239
Bennett's power grab and, 257
birth of, 21
and buyout of minority
	shareholders, 106
charitable giving by, 168, 232
design role of, 183, 199–200, 201,
	210, 240
financial management of Ford and,
	241
and Ford engineering, restructuring
	of, 240
and Ford Foundation, 169
Ford on lifestyle of, 180–81
Ford's antisemitism and, 147
and Ford's commercial aviation
	venture, 195, 196
Ford's difficult behavior of later
	years and, 257
Ford's praise of, 201
and Henry Ford Hospital, 160
and Henry Ford Museum, 165
illness and death of, 257, 258, 273
and installment buying,
	introduction of, 205
and Lincoln Motor Co. acquisition,
	181, 183
marriage, 104
and mid-priced models,
	introduction of, 241
and Model A (2nd version), design
	of, 199–200, 201
Model T body styles and, 183
popularity of, 258
postwar cutbacks and, 121, 123
private life of, 180–81
relations with father, 102–3

residences, 180
rise in Ford organization, 102
son, birth of, 101
21st-birthday gift from father, 102
and unionization efforts, 246, 249
and V-8 engine design, 210
wealth of, willingness to enjoy, 102
will of, 261–62
World War I conscription, Ford's
	quashing of, 101–2, 132, 175
and World War II defense contracts,
	252, 253
Ford, Eleanor Lothian Clay (daughter-
	in-law), 104, 180, 258, 261, 262
Ford, George (grand-uncle), 1
Ford, Henry. *See also* character and
	personality of Ford; *other
	specific topics*
accomplishments of, xiii, 19, 159
appearance of, 14
birth of, 4
complex, jumbled speech
	characteristic of, 134, 190
financial acumen of, 123
hard work of, 44
management style of, 186
relations with son, 102–3
as representative man of his age,
	273–74
siblings, 4
whirlwind of activity, in 1920s and
	30s, 113
Ford, Henry (grand-uncle), 1
Ford, Henry II (grandson)
and Bennett, firing of, 263
Bennett's efforts to undermine,
	261–62, 263
birth of, 101
character and personality of, 269
emergence as public figure, 261
Ford's transfer of control to,
	262–63
as president of Ford
	consultations with Henry I,
		264–65
	IPO, 269
	postwar issues faced by, 265

and five-dollar day, Ford's
  introduction of, 73–77
Ford's formation of plan for, 12, 17,
  19–20
as Ford's goal, 48, 53–54
Ford's system
  Ford's willingness to share, x,
    67–68
  movement as key principle in,
    x–xi
  output increases, 126
  savings from, put toward price
    reductions, 68, 69
  standardization of parts and, 56,
    61, 65
  Taylorism and, 72–73
materialism of modern age, Ford's
  dismay at, 130
Maxim, Hiram Percy, 24
Maxwell, Jonathan Dixon, 26
Maxwell-Chalmers Co., 119–20
Maybury, William C., 30–31, 33
Mayo, William B., 117
McCormick, Anne O'Hare, 211
McCormick, Robert, 107, 108
McGill Jewelry Store, 11
McGuffey, William Holmes, 5
McGuffey's Eclectic Readers, xii, 5–6,
  86–87, 138, 219
media. *See* press
medicine
  Henry Ford Hospital, Ford's
    construction and operation of,
    160–61
  surgical practice, Ford's impact on,
    161–62
Mein Kampf (Hitler), 144
Mellon, Andrew, 100
Mercury, introduction of, 241
Metzger, William A., 62
Meyer, Eugene, 150
Meyer, Leo, 232
Michigan Car Company, 10
mid-priced models, introduction of,
  240–41
milk, synthetic, Ford's research on,
  215–16, 217

Mill and Factory magazine, 255
Miller, Logan, 248
minorities, Ford's employment policies
  and, xii, 74, 160
Model A (1903–1904), 42–43, 44–45, 48
Model A (1927–1931)
  body design, 183
  celebrity owners of, 204
  changeover to, impact on workers,
    205, 228–29
  design of, 157, 197, 199–202
  end of production, 209
  and installment buying, introduction
    of, 205, 233
  marketing campaign for, 203–4
  price of, 201, 208, 209
  production
    problems with, 202–3, 204, 205–6
    retooling required for, 202
  public reaction to, 201, 203–4
  sales, 204, 206, 208, 209
Model B (1904–1906), 48
Model B (1932–1934), 210
Model C, 48
Model F, 48
Model K, 53, 56, 199
Model N, 56, 59, 60
Model R, 56
Model S, 56
Model T
  body styles, variety in, 183
  celebrity owners of, 198–199
  competition from other
    manufacturers, 198
  concept for, 58–59
  cultural impact of, 78
  design of, 58–60
  end of production, 197–199
  15-millionth (final) vehicle,
    preservation of, 198
  Ford's happiness with, 61
  improvements in over time, 59–60,
    115–16, 197
  materials for, 59–60
  price of, 65, 68, 69
  price reductions in, 68, 103, 126, 198
  production run for, 61

Olds, Ransom E., 26, 31, 40, 54
Oldsmobile
    early assembly methods, 42
    early history of, 31, 40–41, 48
On Compensation (Emerson), 75–76
Order of the Grand Cross of the
        German Eagle, 156
ore-bearing lands, Ford's purchase of,
        124, 125
Osborne, Chase, 176
Oscar II (ship), 89
Otto, Nikolaus, 18, 25
Otto engine, 18, 19
outsourcing of parts, Great Depression
        and, 207–8

pacifism of Ford, 86–88
    and Couzens, alienation of, 95
    Ford Times editorials on, 95
    public reactions to, 87–88, 90–91
    roots of, 6, 86–87
    support for U.S. war effort and, 96–97
Packard Motor Car Co.
    early history of, 31
    five-dollar day and, 79
    as maker of hearse at Ford's funeral,
        267
    plant design, 66
    sales, 241
    World War I airplane engine
        production, 99
    World War II airplane engine
        production, 252
Palma, Joseph A., 153
Panhard et Levassor, 25, 35
panic of 1907, Ford marketing
        strategies and, 64
Parker, Ralzemond A., 50–51
parts
    outsourcing of, in Great Depression,
        207–8
    standardization of, as goal of Ford
        manufacturing process, 56,
        61, 65
patents
    Ford's dislike of, 50–51, 175–76
    Selden patent dispute, 50–53

paternalism
    criticism of Ford for, 77, 81
    Fordlandia plantation and, 127
    Ford Sociological Department and,
        81–83
    planned communities for workers
        and, 127, 130
    postwar end of, 127
pay
    five-dollar day
        conditions for receipt of, 80,
            81–83
        debate on origin of, 76
        and fame of Ford, 85
        Ford's introduction of, 73–77
        impact of, 76
        local economy and, 80
        reactions to, xi, 79–80, 222, 223
        reasons for adopting, 77, 80, 222,
            244
    Great Depression and, 206–7, 211,
        230
    increases in after World War I, 116
    postwar tightening of, 127
    seven-dollar day
        critics of, 209
        introduction of, 206–7
        reactions to, 230
        rescinding of, 207–8, 211
    six-dollar day, introduction of, 116,
        223
Payton's rooming house, 11
Peace Ship mission, 88–93
    Declaration of Principles of, 90–91
    Ford on, 91–92, 92–93, 252
    Ford's departure after arrival of, 91
    impact on Ford, 139
    poor preparation for, 89–90
    press response to, 89, 90
    and publicity, 88–89, 93
    and public perception of Ford, xi, 132
    results of, 91–92
The Perils of Racial Prejudice
        (Spargo), 146
Perlman, Nathan D., 153
Perry, Percival, 98, 117
Perry, William, 171